ASCENT®
CENTER FOR TECHNICAL KNOWLEDGE

Autodesk® Vehicle Tracking 2022 Fundamentals

Learning Guide

Imperial Units - 1st Edition

AUTODESK.
Authorized Publisher

ASCENT - Center for Technical Knowledge®
Autodesk® Vehicle Tracking 2022
Fundamentals

Imperial Units - 1st Edition

Prepared and produced by:

ASCENT Center for Technical Knowledge
630 Peter Jefferson Parkway, Suite 175
Charlottesville, VA 22911

866-527-2368
www.ASCENTed.com

Lead Contributors: Jeff Morris and Heather Adams

ASCENT - Center for Technical Knowledge (a division of Rand Worldwide Inc.) is a leading developer of professional learning materials and knowledge products for engineering software applications. ASCENT specializes in designing targeted content that facilitates application-based learning with hands-on software experience. For over 25 years, ASCENT has helped users become more productive through tailored custom learning solutions.

We welcome any comments you may have regarding this guide, or any of our products. To contact us please email: feedback@ASCENTed.com.

AS-AVT2201-FND1IM-SG // IS-AVT2201-FND1IM-SG

Contents

Preface

This guide will provide an introduction to the Autodesk® Vehicle Tracking module that can be added to Autodesk® Civil 3D®, as well as to the AutoCAD® and AutoCAD® Architecture software. The Vehicle Tracking module is an extensive transportation analysis and design solution for vehicles of all sorts. This software also features specialized tools for parking lot layout and roundabout design.

Topics Covered

- Navigate through the Vehicle Tracking user interface.
- Use the Vehicle Library.
- Create and edit paths using options such as Arc mode, Bearing mode, or Guided Paths.
- Run Vertical Clearance to check for clash locations.
- Use Design Checks to further analyze the design.
- Create animations of navigating through a chosen path.
- Create and edit parking lots using various row options.
- Create and edit roundabouts with and without corridor functionality.

Prerequisites

- Access to the 2022.0 version of the software, to ensure compatibility with this guide. Future software updates that are released by Autodesk may include changes that are not reflected in this guide. The practices and files included with this guide might not be compatible with prior versions (e.g., 2021).

Note on Software Setup

This guide assumes a standard installation of the software using the default preferences during installation. Lectures and practices use the standard software templates and default options for the Content Libraries.

Students and Educators Can Access Free Autodesk Software and Resources

Autodesk challenges you to get started with free educational licenses for professional software and creativity apps used by millions of architects, engineers, designers, and hobbyists today. Bring Autodesk software into your classroom, studio, or workshop to learn, teach, and explore real-world design challenges the way professionals do.

Get started today - register at the Autodesk Education Community and download one of the many Autodesk software applications available.

Visit www.autodesk.com/education/home/

Note: Free products are subject to the terms and conditions of the end-user license and services agreement that accompanies the software. The software is for personal use for education purposes and is not intended for classroom or lab use.

Lead Contributor: Jeff Morris

Specializing in the civil engineering industry, Jeff authors training guides and provides instruction, support, and implementation on all Autodesk infrastructure solutions.

Jeff brings to bear over 20 years of diverse work experience in the civil engineering industry. He has played multiple roles, including Sales, Trainer, Application Specialist, Implementation and Customization Consultant, CAD Coordinator, and CAD/BIM Manager, in civil engineering and architecture firms, and Autodesk reseller organizations. He has worked for government organizations and private firms, small companies and large multinational corporations and in multiple geographies across the globe. Through his extensive experience in Building and Infrastructure design, Jeff has acquired a thorough understanding of CAD Standards and Procedures and an in-depth knowledge of CAD and BIM.

Jeff studied Architecture and a diploma in Systems Analysis and Programming. He is an Autodesk Certified Instructor (ACI) and holds the Autodesk Certified Professional certification for Civil 3D and Revit.

Jeff Morris has been a Lead Contributor for *Autodesk Vehicle Tracking: Fundamentals* since 2020.

Lead Contributor: Heather Adams

Heather is an Education Specialist Manager with more than 15 years of technical experience in software installation, customization, training, and template development. As part of her role, she helps to enhance training content and class delivery, in addition to training students in the Infrastructure division.

Heather is an Authorized Certified Instructor (ACI) and has achieved the Autodesk Certified Professional certification for both Civil 3D and AutoCAD. Before entering the Autodesk business, she worked for consulting firms.

Heather received her Bachelor of Science in Civil Engineering from the University of Tennessee. She later earned her PE in Water Resources.

Heather Adams has been a Lead Contributor for *Autodesk Vehicle Tracking: Fundamentals* since 2020.

In This Guide

The following highlights the key features of this guide.

Feature	Description
Practice Files	The Practice Files page includes a link to the practice files and instructions on how to download and install them. The practice files are required to complete the practices in this guide.
Chapters	A chapter consists of the following - Learning Objectives, Instructional Content, Practices, Chapter Review Questions, and Command Summary. • **Learning Objectives** define the skills you can acquire by learning the content provided in the chapter. • **Instructional Content**, which begins right after Learning Objectives, refers to the descriptive and procedural information related to various topics. Each main topic introduces a product feature, discusses various aspects of that feature, and provides step-by-step procedures on how to use that feature. Where relevant, examples, figures, helpful hints, and notes are provided. • **Practice** for a topic follows the instructional content. Practices enable you to use the software to perform a hands-on review of a topic. It is required that you download the practice files (using the link found on the Practice Files page) prior to starting the first practice. • **Chapter Review Questions**, located close to the end of a chapter, enable you to test your knowledge of the key concepts discussed in the chapter.

Practice Files

To download the practice files for this guide, use the following steps:

1. Type the URL ***exactly as shown below*** into the address bar of your Internet browser, to access the Course File Download page.

   Note: If you are using the ebook, you do not have to type the URL. Instead, you can access the page simply by clicking the URL below.

   https://www.ascented.com/getfile/id/prochilodusPF

2. On the Course File Download page, click the **DOWNLOAD NOW** button, as shown below, to download the .ZIP file that contains the practice files.

3. Once the download is complete, unzip the file and extract its contents.

   The recommended practice files folder location is:
   C:\Autodesk Vehicle Tracking

   Note: It is recommended that you do not change the location of the practice files folder. Doing so may cause errors when completing the practices.

Stay Informed!

To receive information about upcoming events, promotional offers, and complimentary webcasts, visit:

www.ASCENTed.com/updates

Chapter 1

Getting Started

In this chapter, you will learn what Autodesk® Vehicle Tracking is and its software compatibility. This chapter will also cover the Vehicle Tracking user interface and settings.

Learning Objectives in This Chapter

- Comprehend the use and purpose of Vehicle Tracking.
- Navigate through the Vehicle Tracking user interface.
- Set appropriate settings for design use.

1.1 Introduction to Vehicle Tracking

Autodesk® Vehicle Tracking software is an extensive transportation analysis and design solution for vehicle swept path analysis, parking lot layouts, and roundabout design. The software enables engineers, designers, and planners to:

- accurately predict the movements of steered vehicles, including cars, trucks, service vehicles, streetcars, and airplanes, throughout the design process;
- optimize road layout and quickly evaluate design alternatives;
- perform real-time analysis to efficiently get information or feedback; and
- monitor adherence to design standards.

Vehicle Tracking Software Compatibility

Vehicle Tracking can be used directly within your CAD system and is compatible with the following software:

- Autodesk® AutoCAD®
- Autodesk® Civil 3D®
- Autodesk® AutoCAD® Architecture
- Autodesk® AutoCAD® Plant 3D
- Autodesk® AutoCAD® Map 3D

Why Use Vehicle Tracking?

There are over 500 types of vehicles in the standard Vehicle Library included in the software, crossing multiple industries and national and international standards. For example, you can use Vehicle Tracking to check if a garbage truck or utility truck can safely navigate through the proposed parking lots in a newly developed subdivision, or if there is sufficient room for fire trucks or emergency vehicles to access a building in a cul-de-sac.

The table below lists many of the vehicle types included in the software.

Transportation	Architecture	Plant and MFG
• Cars • Trucks • Articulated Vehicles • Buses • Refuse Trucks • Oversize and Overweight • Lowboys and Low Loaders • Heavy Haulers • Emergency Vehicles • Construction Equipment • Trams, LRT, and Street Cars • Airplanes and Helicopters • Airside Support Vehicles • Autonomous Guided Vehicles	• Private and Public Cars • Disabled Vehicle Access • Delivery Trucks • Wheelchairs • Mobility Scooters • School Buses • Hospital Beds • Electric Carts • Construction Equipment • Refuse Trucks • Fire Appliances	• Forklifts • Trolleys • Carts • Cart Trains • Multiple Trailers • Autonomous Guided Vehicles • Abnormal Loads • Large Loads • Delivery Trucks

1.2 User Interface

The Vehicle Tracking software is loaded into the Autodesk application you are using. A new ribbon tab will appear once the install is complete, as shown in Figure 1–1.

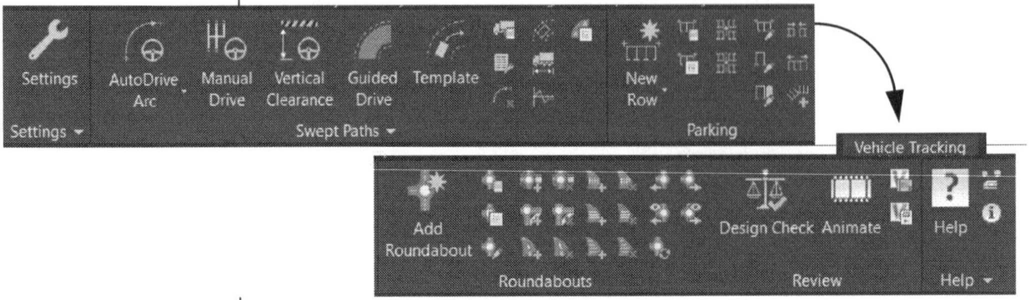

Figure 1–1

The Settings panel, shown in Figure 1–2, includes:

- System and drawing settings
- Import and export options
- Purge and repair data commands

Figure 1–2

The Swept Paths panel, shown in Figure 1–3, includes:

- Access to the Vehicle Library
- Various commands to create paths
- Analysis and report options

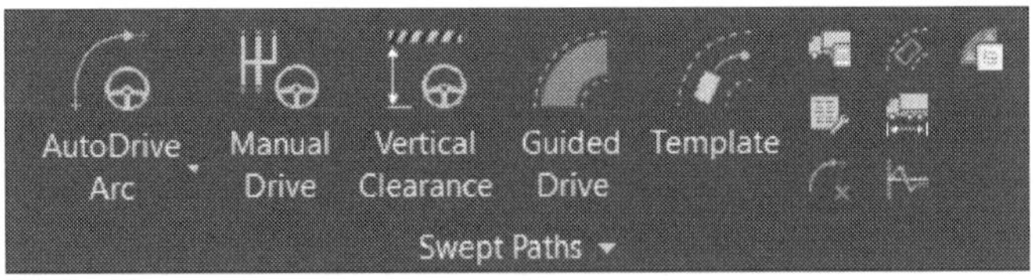

Figure 1–3

The Parking panel, shown in Figure 1–4, includes:

- Access to parking lot settings
- Commands to create and edit parking lots
- Report options

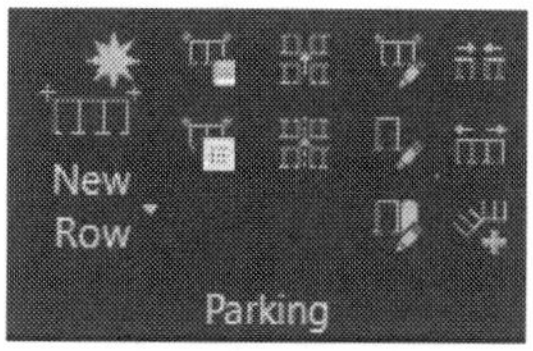

Figure 1–4

The Roundabouts panel, shown in Figure 1–5, includes:

- Access to roundabout settings
- Commands to create and edit roundabouts
- Report options

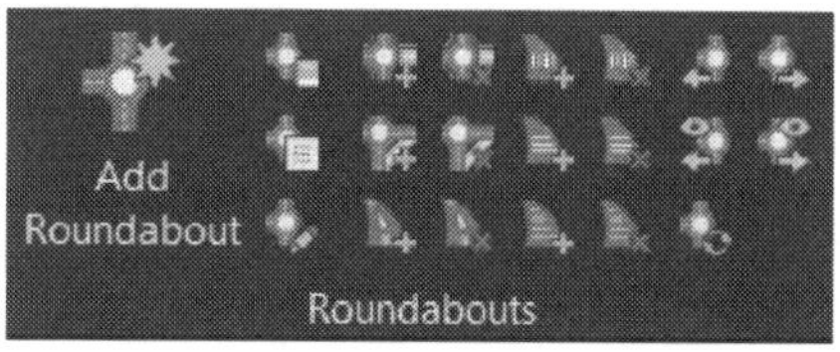

Figure 1–5

The Review panel, shown in Figure 1–6, includes:

- Animation tools
- Design Check options

Figure 1–6

1.3 Vehicle Tracking Settings

Before using the Vehicle Tracking software, make sure to set all the appropriate settings. There are many default settings already defined that can be used. To verify the Vehicle Tracking settings, use the **Settings** button in the *Vehicle Tracking* tab (shown in Figure 1–7).

Figure 1–7

When you click directly on the **Settings** button, a wizard is launched. The wizard includes the following tabs:

- *Scale:* Verify the drawing units match your drawing scale so that vehicles come in at the right size.
  - This will normally have a setting of 1 per unit.
- *Vehicle Editing Units:* Verify the distance, speed, and preferred angular units.
- *Layers:* Set up layer name conventions and create new layers as new objects are created.
- *Turn Spirals:* Set forward and reverse turn rates.
- *Design Speeds:* Set forward and reverse design speeds.
- *Steering Limits:* Limit the steering in three ways: percentage, angle, and radius.
- *Articulation Limits:* Limit articulation in two ways: percentage and angle.
- *Dynamic Effects:* Set dynamic effects.

A drop-down list is also available in the Settings panel to access more settings options. This includes the System Settings and Drawing Settings, as shown in Figure 1–8. Some of these settings are also available within the wizard.

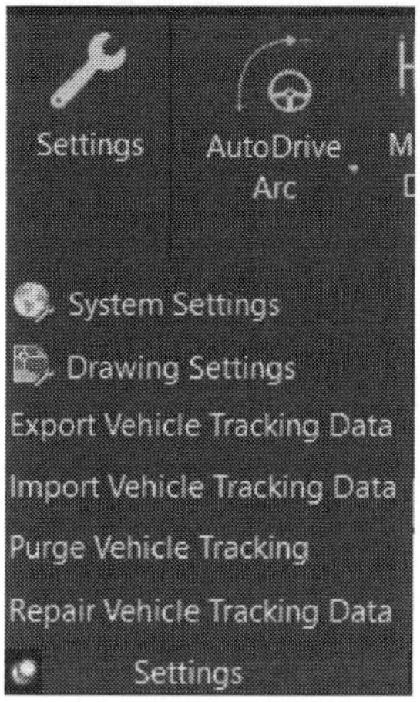

Figure 1–8

The System Settings include:

- Start Up
- Directories
- AutoLoad
- Language
- Skill Language
- View
- Paths
- ARCADY Link (ARCADY is an analysis tool used for traffic flow behavior at roundabouts)

The ARCADY analysis tools are not covered in this guide.

Drawing Settings include:

- Units
- Scale
- Surfaces
- Styles
- Paths
- Roundabouts

Hint: Settings

By default, all settings are stored in the Settings subdirectory of the application data directory.

In the System Settings and Drawing Settings dialog boxes, adjust colors, views, layering, and more within the View, Paths, and Roundabouts panels.

Chapter Review Questions

1. What software does Autodesk Vehicle Tracking run on? (Select all that apply.)
    a. Autodesk Civil 3D
    b. Revit Architecture
    c. AutoCAD Architecture
    d. Navisworks Manage
2. The Vehicle Library is limited to North American standard vehicles.
    a. True
    b. False
3. Which of the following is not part of Autodesk Vehicle Tracking?
    a. Parking Layout
    b. Roundabout Design
    c. Intersection Design
    d. Vehicle Path Analysis

Vehicle Library Explorer

Autodesk® Vehicle Tracking comes with an extensive Vehicle Library that contains design vehicle definitions. Existing vehicles can be edited and new vehicles can be created. Included in the standard Vehicle Tracking software are worldwide design standard vehicles and regional design standard vehicles, including AASHTO, Cal Trans, Main Roads, FTA, and DOT.

In this chapter, you will learn about the Vehicle Library. You will also learn how to create and edit vehicles within the library.

Learning Objectives in This Chapter

- Navigate the Vehicle Library Explorer dialog box.
- Edit existing vehicles from the library.
- Create new vehicles using templates.

2.1 Navigating the Vehicle Library

The Vehicle Library is found on the *Vehicle Tracking* tab>Swept Paths panel, as shown in Figure 2–1.

Figure 2–1

When the command is launched, two windows will open:

1. The Vehicle Library Explorer
2. The Vehicle Diagram

You can browse through the vehicle options in the Vehicle Library Explorer, as shown on the left in Figure 2–2. Select a vehicle and the dimensions will appear in the Vehicle Diagram window on the right.

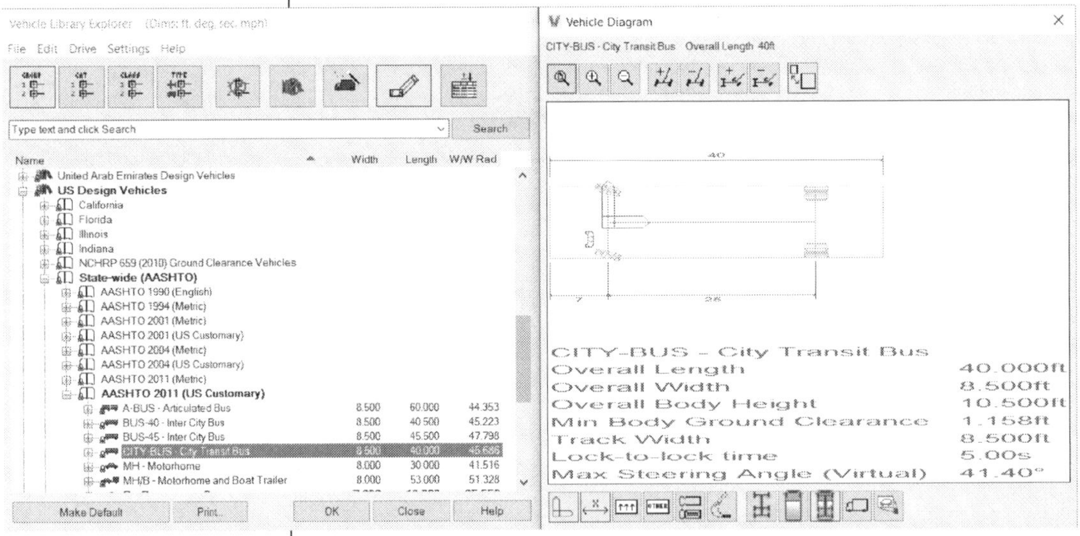

Figure 2–2

Within the Vehicle Library Explorer, you can search for and group vehicles, control the display of the window, and create and edit vehicles. Libraries and vehicles can also be imported and exported.

Figure 2–3 shows the buttons that are available in the Vehicle Library Explorer window.

Figure 2–3

1. Group by Vehicle Group
2. Group by Vehicle Category
3. Group by Vehicle Classification
4. Group by Vehicle Type
5. Do Not Group
6. Hide Library Level
7. Vehicle Wizard (used to create new vehicles)
8. Vehicle Diagram (used to control display of the Vehicle Diagram window)
9. Insert/Remove Columns: Approximately 25 columns are available for display, dimensions, and more

The Vehicle Diagram window has many visibility options and options for adjustments to angles in the design, as shown in Figure 2–4 and Figure 2–5.

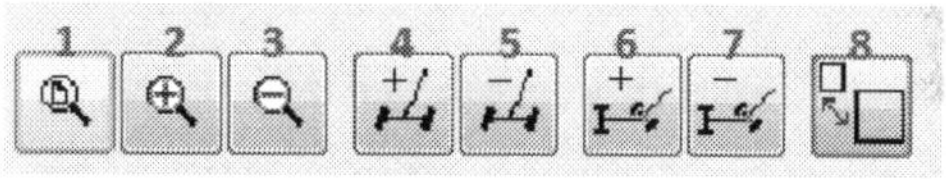

Figure 2–4

1. Zoom Extents
2. Zoom In
3. Zoom Out
4. Increase Steering Angle
5. Decrease Steering Angle
6. Increase Articulation Angle
7. Decrease Articulation Angle
8. AutoScale

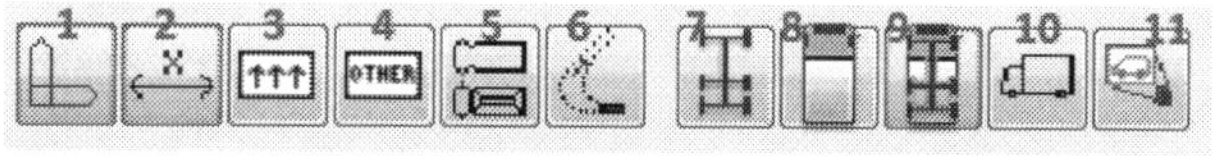

Figure 2–5

1. Show Datums
2. Show Dimensions
3. Show Loads
4. Show Other Outlines
5. Show Simple Body Outlines
6. Show Turn Template
7. Show Chassis
8. Show Body
9. Show All
10. Show Elevation
11. Show Image

Editing Vehicles

All vehicles can easily be copied and then modified for your specific design. A seven-page wizard can be used to adjust any vehicle. In the Vehicle Library Explorer, right-click on a vehicle and click **Edit a Copy...** to launch the wizard, as shown in Figure 2–6.

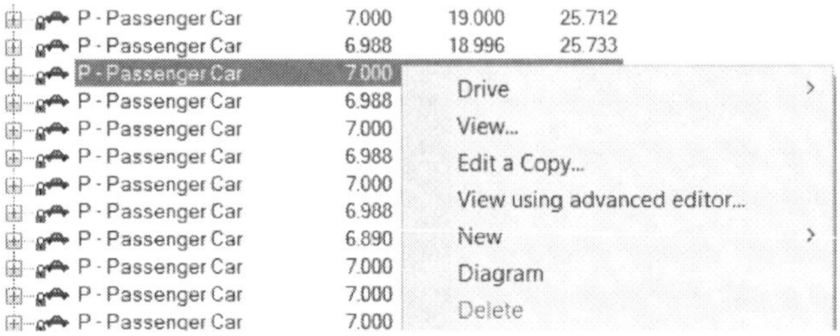

Figure 2–6

The following pages are included in the wizard.

- **Name:** Name, description, and type of vehicle (as shown in Figure 2–7)
- **Tractor Axles:** Front and rear axle information
- **Tractor Wheelbase:** Distance between the innermost front and rear axles
- **Tractor Steering:** Steering type and lock-to-lock time
- **Tractor Maneuverability:** Turning radius, wheel angle, and steering angle
- **Tractor Coupling:** Front and rear coupling information
- **Tractor Body:** Dimensions and body style

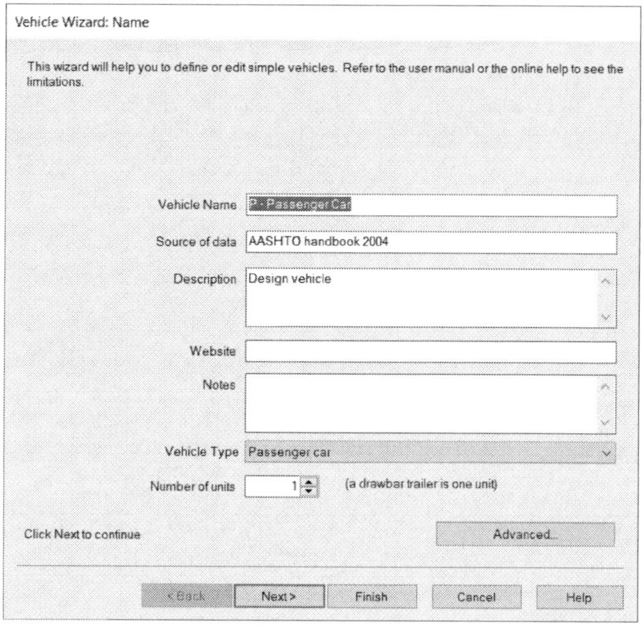

Figure 2–7

Within the wizard, you can also select the **Advanced** button on any page to fill out more settings and dimensions for the vehicle, as shown in Figure 2–8 and Figure 2–9.

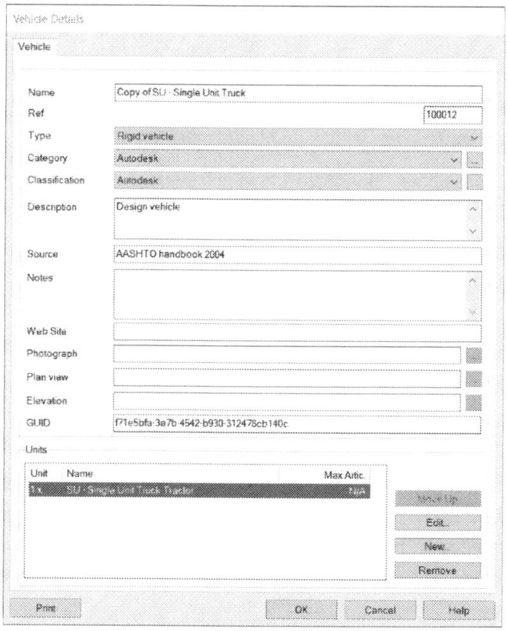

Figure 2–8

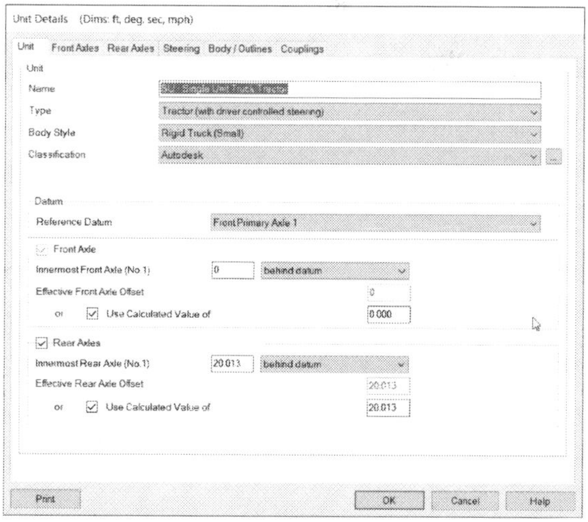

Figure 2–9

Creating Vehicles

If there is a need for a custom-made vehicle, it can be created using the Vehicle Wizard. The wizard can be launched by clicking the icon in the Vehicle Library Explorer window or by using the File drop-down list and selecting **New**, as shown in Figure 2–10. You can also select any vehicle in the library, right-click, and select **Edit a Copy...**. This wizard is the same as the edit wizard.

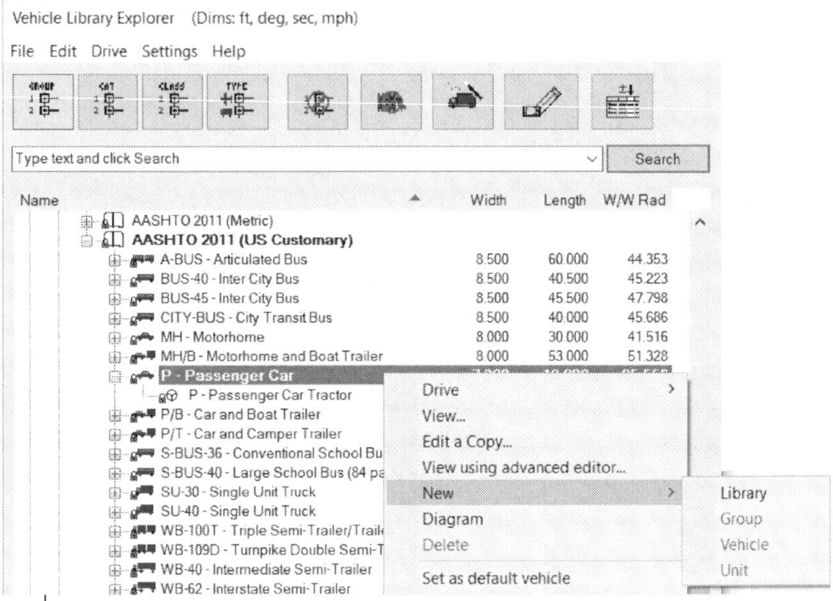

Figure 2–10

Practice 2a Edit an Existing Vehicle

Learning Objectives

- Examine the Vehicle Library Explorer.
- Make a copy of an existing vehicle for customizing.

In this practice, you will create a new vehicle by editing an existing passenger car. The new vehicle has different dimensions and requires modifications.

1. Start a new drawing using the standard drawing template.
2. Click the *Vehicle Tracking* tab on the ribbon.
3. On the Swept Paths panel, select **Vehicle Library Explorer**, as shown in Figure 2–11.

Figure 2–11

4. In the Vehicle Library Explorer window, select **Group by Vehicle Group** and verify that **Vehicle Diagram** is on, as shown in Figure 2–12.

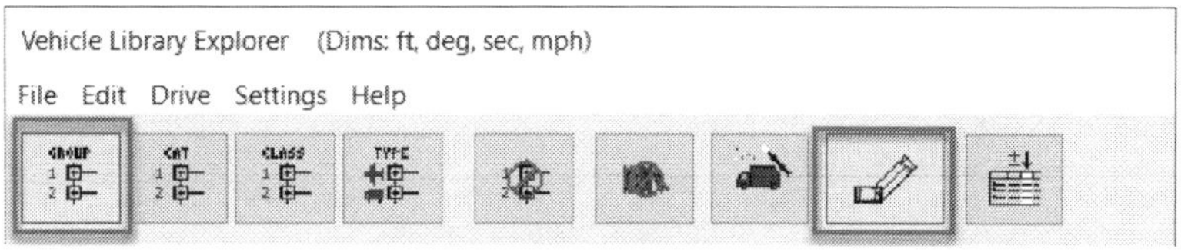

Figure 2–12

5. Scroll to the bottom of the vehicle list, expand *US Design Vehicles>State-wide (AASHTO)>AASHTO 2011 (US Customary)*, and select **P-Passenger Car**.

6. Right-click on **P-Passenger Car** and select **Edit a Copy...**, as shown in Figure 2–13. The Vehicle Wizard will launch.

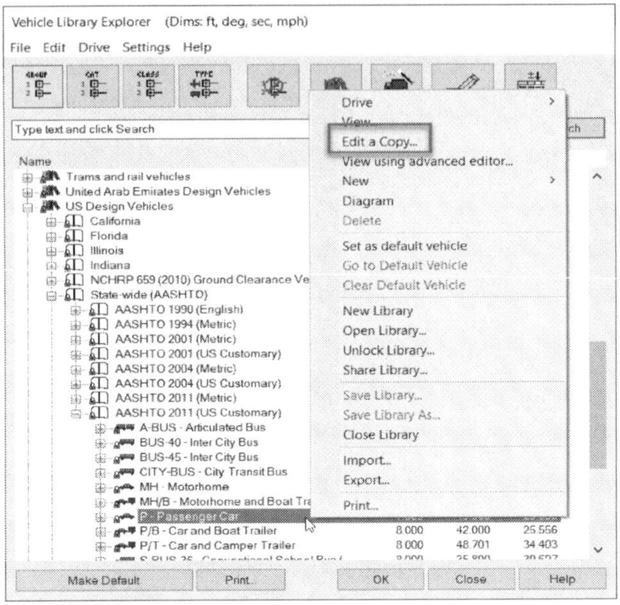

Figure 2–13

7. On the Name page, for the *Vehicle Name*, add **-Custom** to the name (as shown in Figure 2–14) and click **Next**.

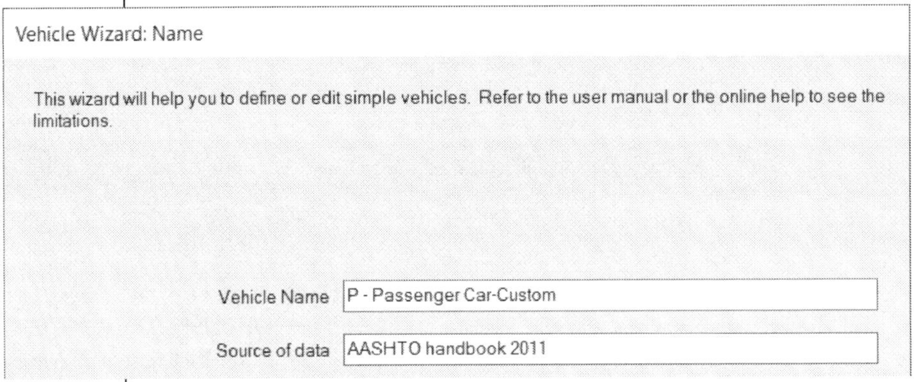

Figure 2–14

8. On the Tractor Axles page, adjust both the *Front track width* and the *Rear track width* to **8 ft**, as shown in Figure 2–15. Note the immediate change that occurs in the Vehicle Diagram window. Click **Next**.

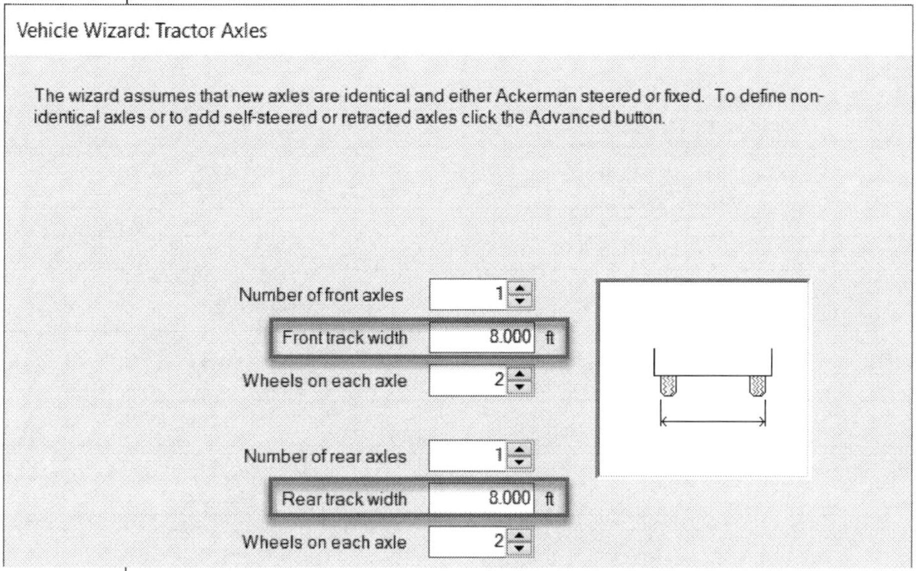
Vehicle Wizard: Tractor Axles
The wizard assumes that new axles are identical and either Ackerman steered or fixed. To define non-identical axles or to add self-steered or retracted axles click the Advanced button.
Number of front axles
1
Front track width
8.000
ft
Wheels on each axle
2
Number of rear axles
1
Rear track width
8.000
ft
Wheels on each axle
2

Figure 2–15

9. On the Tractor Wheelbase page, change the *Wheelbase* to **13 ft**, as shown in Figure 2–16. Click **Next**.

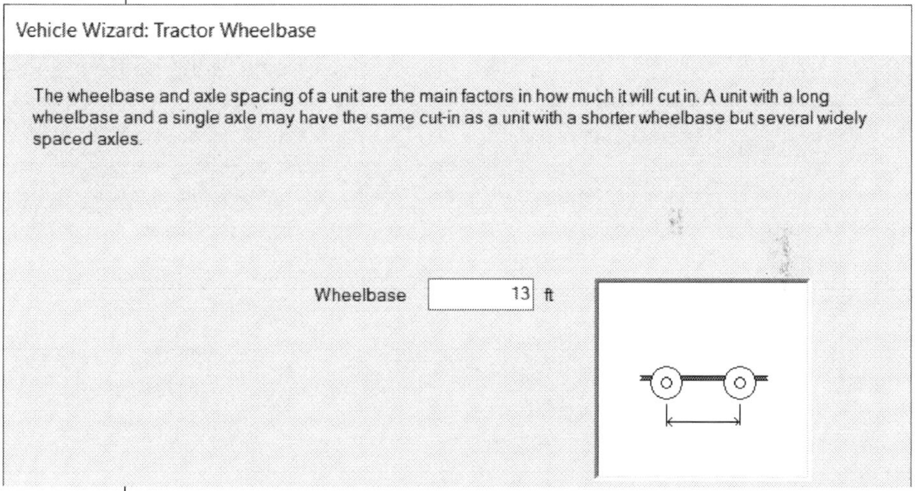
Vehicle Wizard: Tractor Wheelbase
The wheelbase and axle spacing of a unit are the main factors in how much it will cut in. A unit with a long wheelbase and a single axle may have the same cut-in as a unit with a shorter wheelbase but several widely spaced axles.
Wheelbase
13
ft

Figure 2–16

10. Continue to click **Next** on the following pages until you come to the *Tractor Body* page.

11. Adjust the parameters as shown in Figure 2–17.

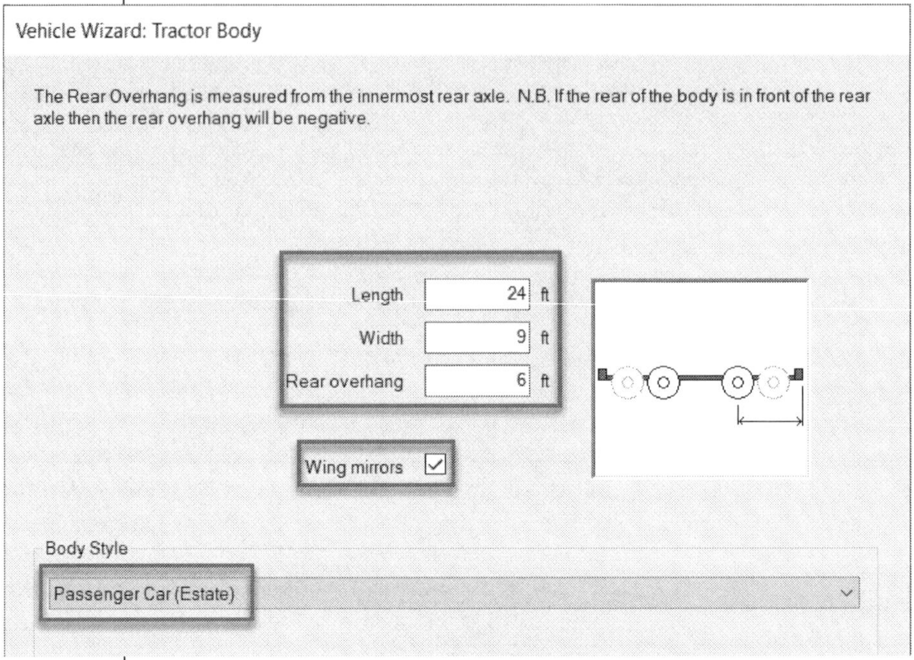
Vehicle Wizard: Tractor Body
The Rear Overhang is measured from the innermost rear axle. N.B. If the rear of the body is in front of the rear axle then the rear overhang will be negative.
Length
24
ft
Width
9
ft
Rear overhang
6
ft
Wing mirrors
Body Style
Passenger Car (Estate)

Figure 2–17

12. Review the adjustments being made to the Vehicle Diagram, as shown in Figure 2–18.

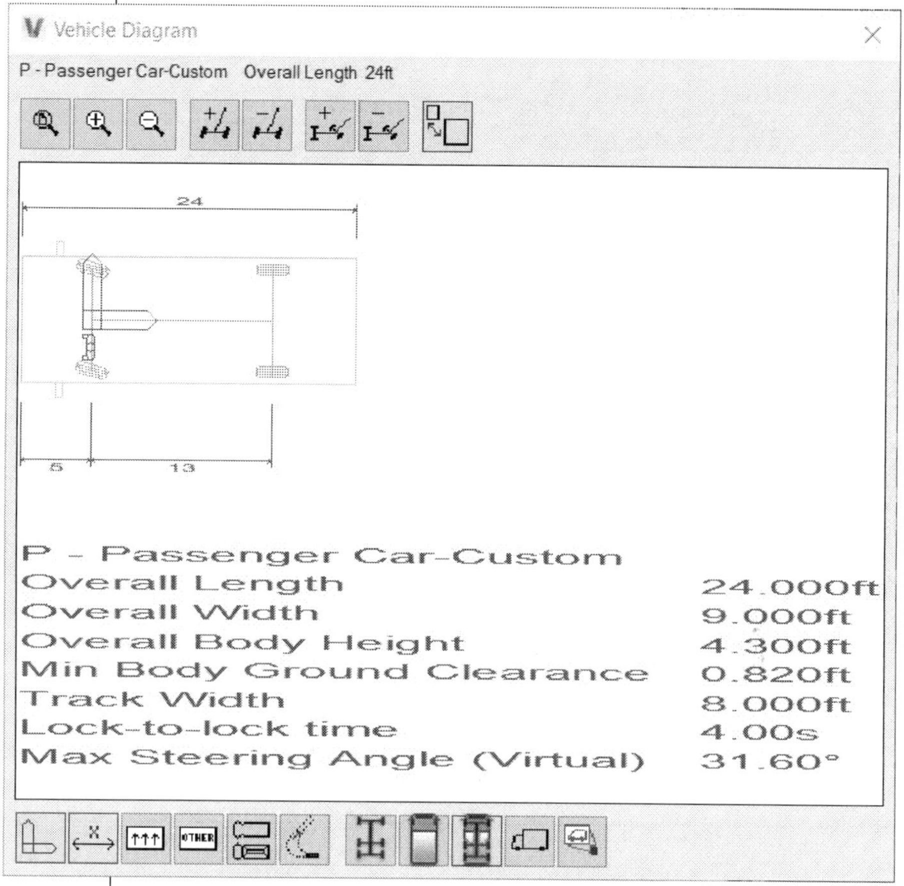

Figure 2–18

13. Click **Finish**. You will note that the vehicle is now listed in the bottom of the library under *Pool for Drawing*, as shown in Figure 2–19.

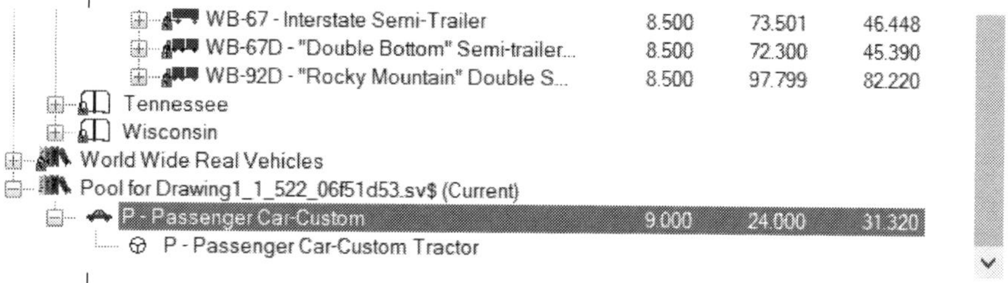

Figure 2–19

14. Save your drawing as **Vehicle.dwg** in the *Autodesk Vehicle Tracking\Working* practice files folder.

Practice 2b Create a Vehicle

Learning Objectives

- Create a new vehicle library.
- Create a new vehicle from scratch.

In this practice, you will create a new library within the Vehicle Library Explorer for all of your custom vehicles. Then, you will create a new vehicle based on dimensions given to you.

1. In the same drawing, launch the **Vehicle Library Explorer** again, as shown in Figure 2–20. Verify that the Vehicle Diagram also displays.

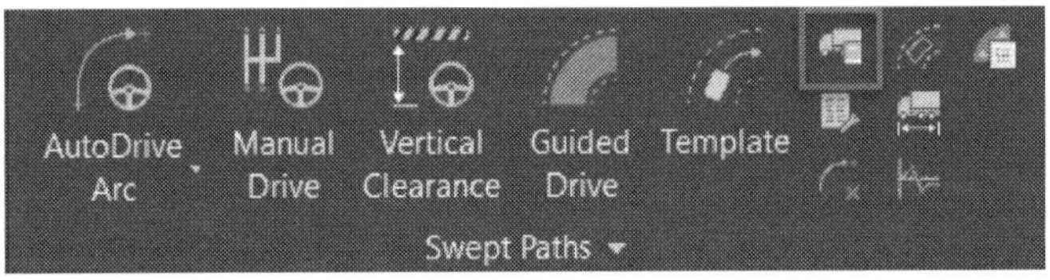

Figure 2–20

2. In the Vehicle Library Explorer, click *File* and select **New Library**, as shown in Figure 2–21. Name the library **Demo** and leave all the other fields as the default, then click **OK**.

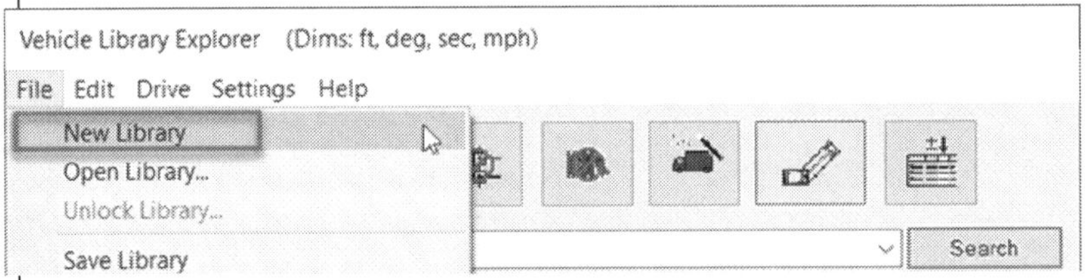

Figure 2–21

3. A new library will be created at the bottom of the Vehicle Library Explorer window. Right-click on the **Demo** library and select **New**, then select **Vehicle**, as shown in Figure 2–22.

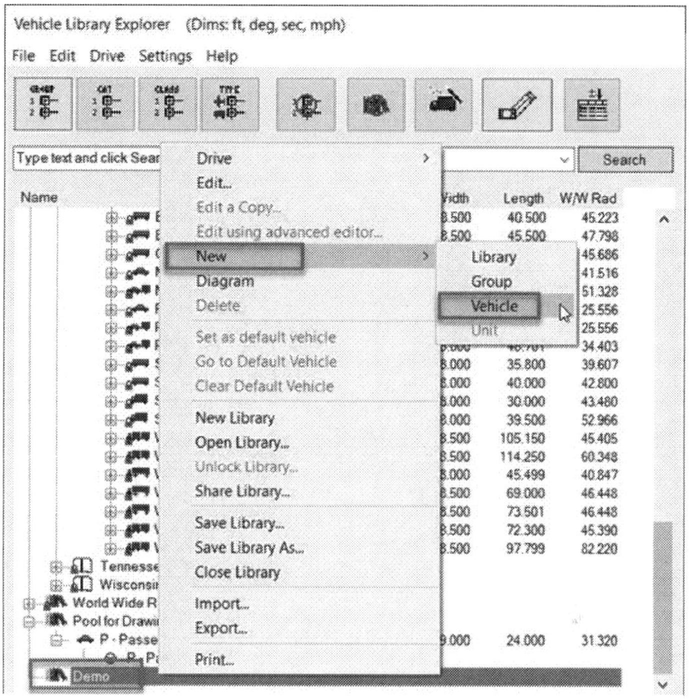

Figure 2–22

4. The Vehicle Wizard launches. Do the following, as shown in Figure 2–23:
   - Name the vehicle **Custom Bus**.
   - Set the *Vehicle Type* to **Bus**.
   - Click **Next**.

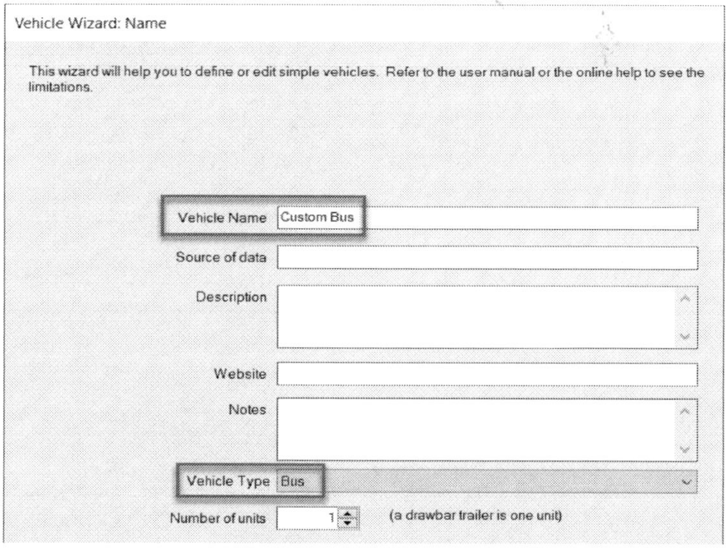

Figure 2–23

5. On the Tractor Axles page, assign the parameters shown in Figure 2–24 and click **Next**.

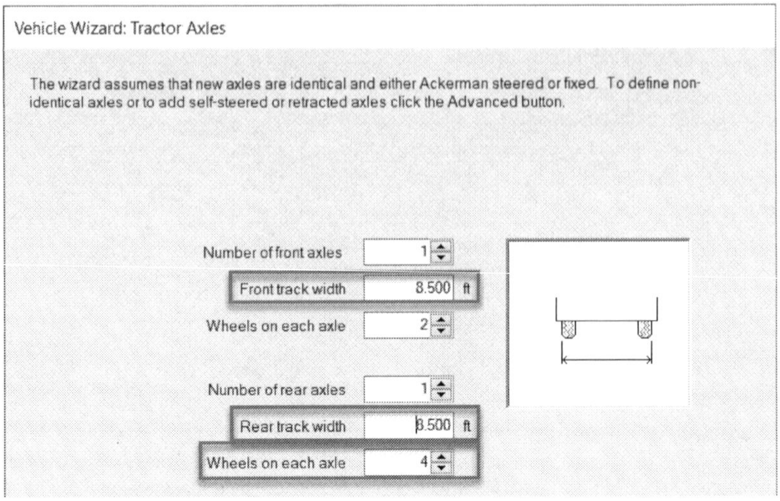
Vehicle Wizard: Tractor Axles
The wizard assumes that new axles are identical and either Ackerman steered or fixed. To define non-identical axles or to add self-steered or retracted axles click the Advanced button.
Number of front axles
1
Front track width
8.500
ft
Wheels on each axle
2
Number of rear axles
1
Rear track width
8.500
ft
Wheels on each axle
4

Figure 2–24

6. On the Tractor Wheelbase page, enter **25** for the *Wheelbase*, as shown in Figure 2–25. Click **Next**.

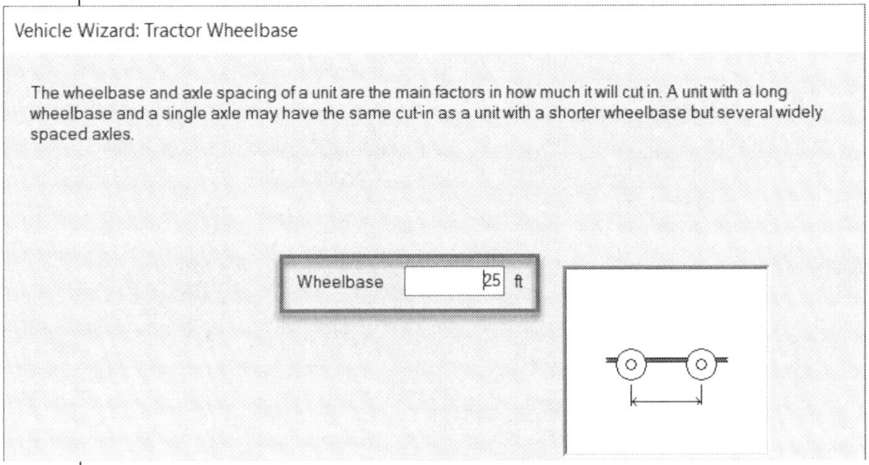
Vehicle Wizard: Tractor Wheelbase
The wheelbase and axle spacing of a unit are the main factors in how much it will cut in. A unit with a long wheelbase and a single axle may have the same cut-in as a unit with a shorter wheelbase but several widely spaced axles.
Wheelbase
25
ft

Figure 2–25

7. On the Tractor Steering page, enter **5** for the *Lock-to-lock time*, as shown in Figure 2–26. Click **Next**.

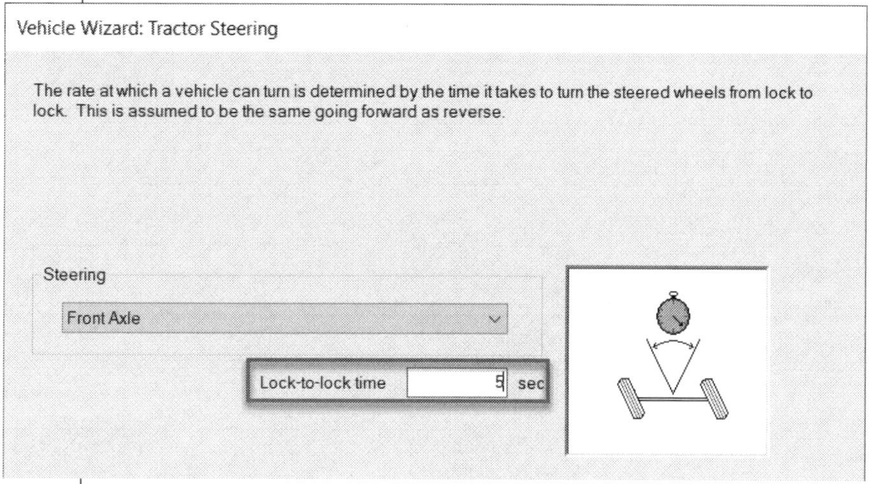
Vehicle Wizard: Tractor Steering
The rate at which a vehicle can turn is determined by the time it takes to turn the steered wheels from lock to lock. This is assumed to be the same going forward as reverse.
Steering
Front Axle
Lock-to-lock time
5
sec

Figure 2–26

8. On the Tractor Maneuverability page, enter **40** for the *Minimum turning circle radius*, as shown in Figure 2–27. Click **Next**.

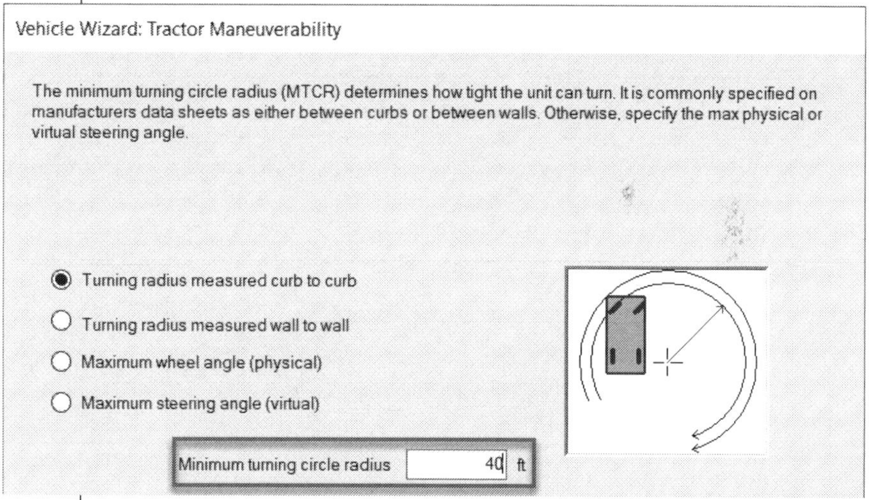
Vehicle Wizard: Tractor Maneuverability
The minimum turning circle radius (MTCR) determines how tight the unit can turn. It is commonly specified on manufacturers data sheets as either between curbs or between walls. Otherwise, specify the max physical or virtual steering angle.
Turning radius measured curb to curb
Turning radius measured wall to wall
Maximum wheel angle (physical)
Maximum steering angle (virtual)
Minimum turning circle radius
40
ft

Figure 2–27

9. On the Tractor Couplings page, uncheck all boxes, as shown in Figure 2–28. Click **Next**.

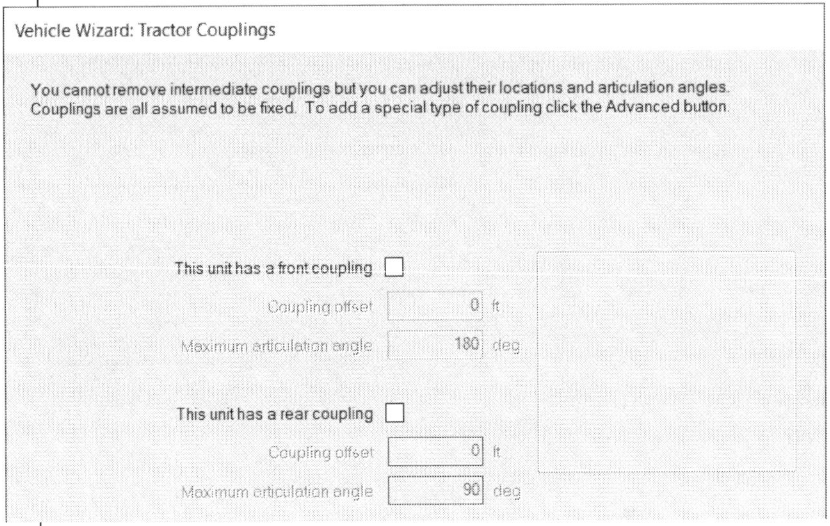
Vehicle Wizard: Tractor Couplings
You cannot remove intermediate couplings but you can adjust their locations and articulation angles. Couplings are all assumed to be fixed. To add a special type of coupling click the Advanced button.
This unit has a front coupling
Coupling offset
0
ft
Maximum articulation angle
180
deg
This unit has a rear coupling
Coupling offset
0
ft
Maximum articulation angle
90
deg

Figure 2–28

10. On the Tractor Body page, assign the parameters shown in Figure 2–29.

    Note: There may be a message at the bottom of the page that you will have to check to override.

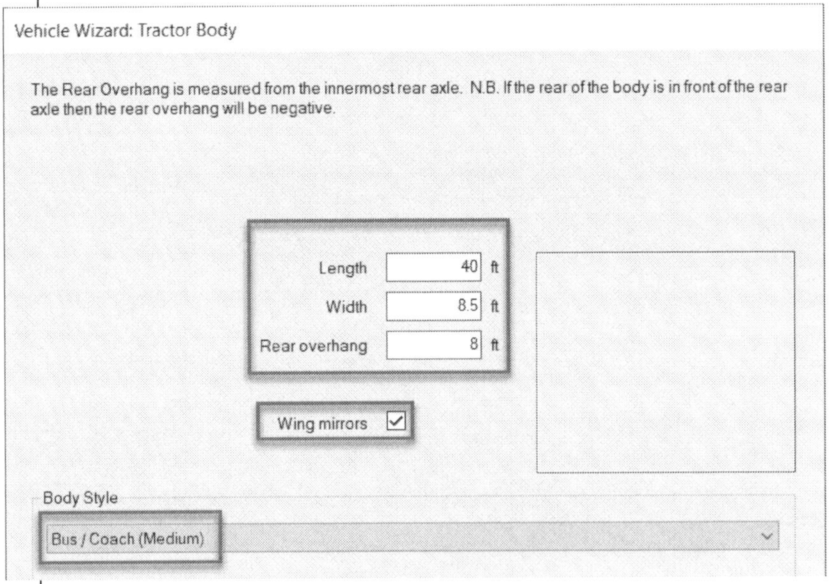
Vehicle Wizard: Tractor Body
The Rear Overhang is measured from the innermost rear axle. N.B. If the rear of the body is in front of the rear axle then the rear overhang will be negative.
Length
40
ft
Width
8.5
ft
Rear overhang
8
ft
Wing mirrors
Body Style
Bus / Coach (Medium)

Figure 2–29

11. Review the Vehicle Diagram (as shown in Figure 2–30) and click **Finish**. Note that the vehicle is added to the library.

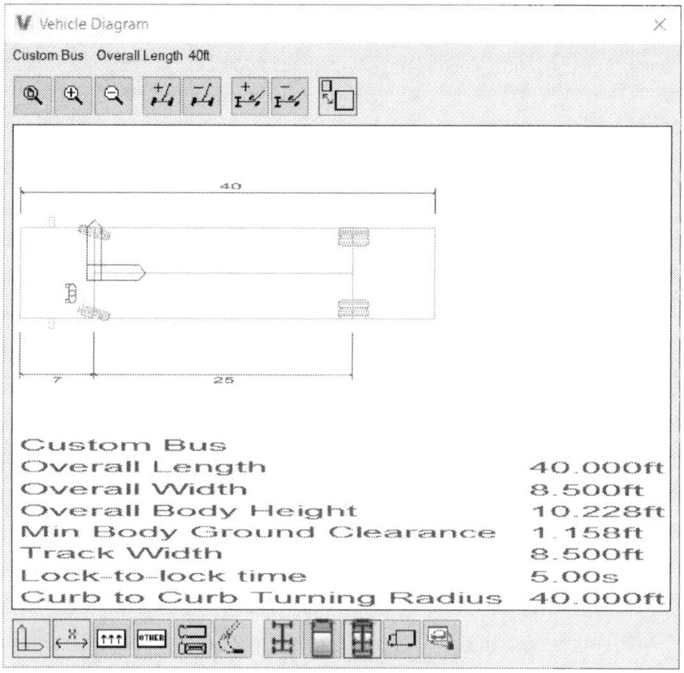

Figure 2–30

12. If the Vehicle Diagram is no longer displayed, select the new vehicle in the library.

13. In the Vehicle Diagram window, select **Show Turn Template** to see the turn radius, as shown in Figure 2–31.

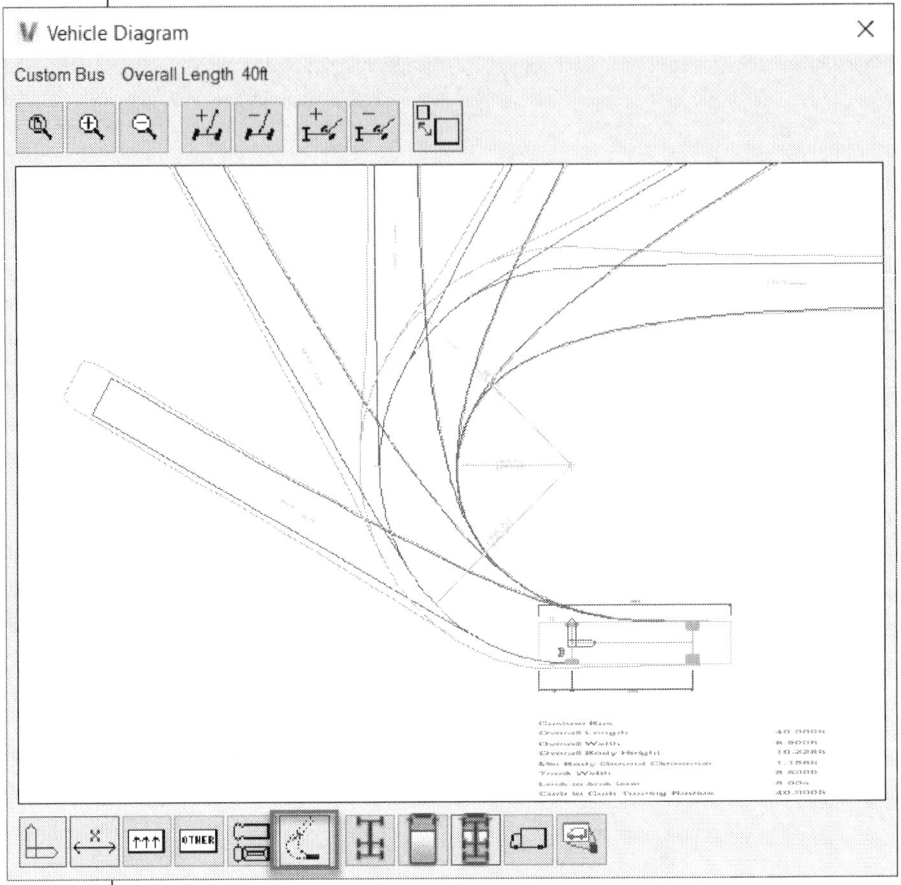

Figure 2–31

14. Save and close the drawing.

15. If you are prompted to update the library file, click **Yes**.

Chapter Review Questions

1. Can you edit a vehicle in the standard Vehicle Library Explorer? (Select all that apply.)
   a. No, the vehicles cannot be changed.
   b. Yes, any vehicle can be modified.
   c. No, you need to create a new vehicle from scratch.
   d. You need to make a copy of an existing vehicle, which you can then modify. The original remains unaltered.
2. Can you get visual feedback of the turning radii once the values have been altered?
   a. Yes
   b. No
   c. Only after regenerating the drawing

Swept Paths

A swept path represents the extents (or envelope) of a vehicle body, or any other part of the structure of the vehicle, swept along its path on all sides. One of the main features of Vehicle Tracking is creating swept paths to determine the full extent of the area required for any given vehicle to safely maneuver, not just the path of the wheels.

There are five options in Autodesk® Vehicle Tracking for creating swept paths: AutoDrive Arc, AutoDrive Bearing, Manual Drive, Guided Drive (used for streetcars and light rail), and Follow. In this chapter, you will learn about the different swept path options within Vehicle Tracking.

Learning Objectives in This Chapter

- Create paths using various options, such as Arc and Bearing mode or with a Guided Path tool.
- Edit paths that have been created.
- Use the library to set appropriate vehicles.
- Understand the importance of a path.

3.1 Using AutoDrive to Create a Vehicle Path

AutoDrive operates in two modes, as shown in Figure 3–1.

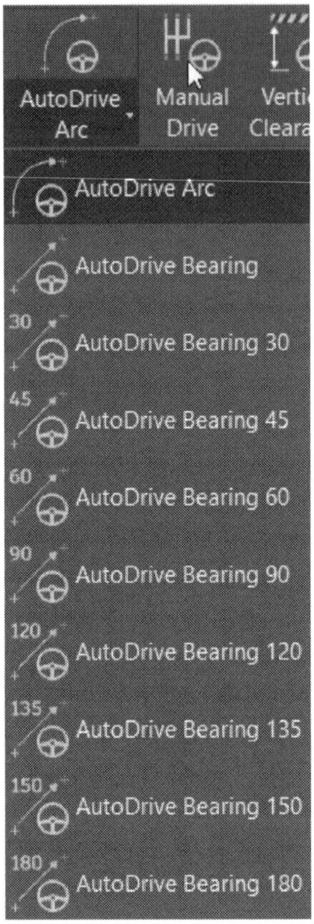

Figure 3–1

- **Arc Mode:** Arc mode displays the path the vehicle takes based on the picked points of the user. The calculated path consists of circular arcs running through those picked targets. The transitions between the arc segments are automatically generated.

- **Bearing Mode:** The vehicle turns as quickly as possible (as dictated by its allowable lock rate) until the steered wheels are on a bearing through the target point of the desired direction, and then continues on that bearing until the selected path point reaches its target.

When starting either of the modes, first pick your vehicle from the Vehicle Library Explorer. It is possible to set a default vehicle to be used on a regular basis.

Once a vehicle is accepted, position your vehicle on the road with two clicks. The first click is for its position and the second is for its starting direction.

With each click, you will see the front and rear tracking, as well as the envelope of the vehicle. As you click from point to point, note the adjustments made to the path, which incorporates the entire vehicle envelope.

- The envelope is a single line representing the maximum body or wheel movement. In the case of vehicle bodies, it is the outer limit of movement of any point on the body. In the case of wheels, it is the outer limit of travel of any of the wheels of the vehicle.

Arc Mode

How To: Create a Path Using Arc Mode

1. Start the **Arc Mode** option.
2. Click once to position the vehicle in the drawing.
3. Click again to assign the driving direction of the vehicle.
4. After the second click, the Position Vehicle dialog box appears.
5. Within the Position Vehicle dialog box, change the vehicle you are using, if necessary.
6. Adjust the orientation, path, and view, if necessary.
7. Once the vehicle is placed and the heading is set, click **Proceed**.
8. Continue to click in the drawing area to add the pass-through points. You will see a path preview before you click.
9. Once the path is created, it is considered a Vehicle Tracking Path and is placed on its specified layer.

The Position Vehicle dialog box is shown in Figure 3–2.

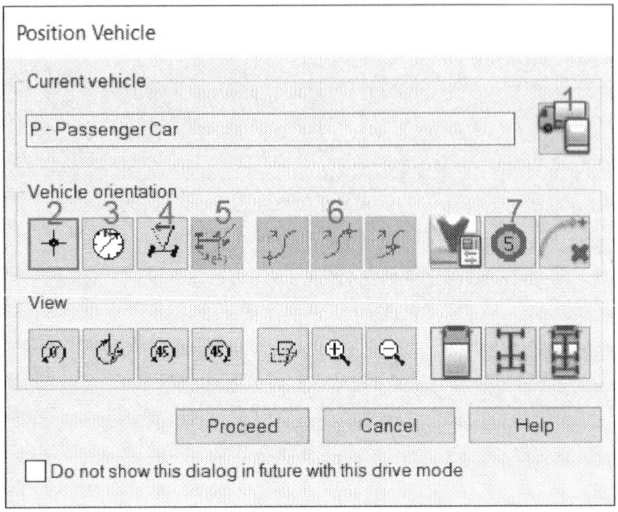

Figure 3–2

1. Change Vehicle
2. Location: Change Position of Vehicle
3. Heading: Rotate the Vehicle
4. Adjust Steering
5. Adjust Articulation
6. Adjust Paths
7. Adjust Settings

Two colors appear on the path:

- Green represents the path of the vehicle body.
- Red represents the path of the vehicle chassis.

These colors are the default settings. Later, you will learn how to adjust these colors.

Hint: When creating your path, click often on the turns for a more realistic turn.

As you continue to click, there is an option on the command line to **Remove Last Target**, which deletes the last point you picked. You can also hover over the last point (marked with a large **X**) and click on it to delete it. However, be careful to select right on the point; otherwise, you are selecting a new target point!

The Undo option within the AutoDrive command acts the same as <Enter> and finishes the command.

If you try to click and a red line appears, this signifies that the maneuver cannot be done. Move the cursor to a less severe turn to place the vehicle.

Note: Vehicles can also be moved in reverse by moving the cursor behind the vehicle. Continue to path in the same way as moving forward.

AutoDrive Settings

When you click to add your path, the AutoDrive dialog box appears, as shown in Figure 3–3. This dialog box allows you to set the minimum radius and clearance offset and toggle between Bearing and Arc mode. You also have the ability to select an object to align with the path by using the **Pick alignment** option. Adjustments in the dialog box can be made in real-time as you draw your path. When you exit the AutoDrive command, the dialog box closes.

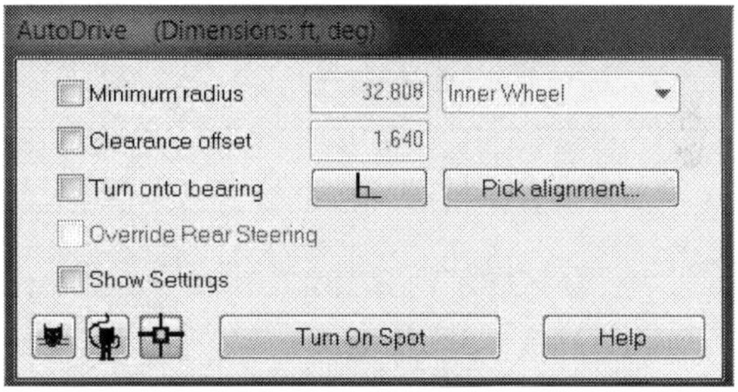

Figure 3–3

- **Clearance offset:** Select this option to shows a clearance zone around the vehicle. The clearance envelope applies to all of the body and chassis.

- **Pick alignment:** Use this option to specify the alignment by picking a line or line segment from the drawing.

Show Settings

The quickness of the turn is controlled by the design speed assigned. This setting (among many others) can be found by selecting **Show Settings** in the AutoDrive dialog box, as shown in Figure 3–4. As with the other AutoDrive options, any settings adjustments are made in real-time.

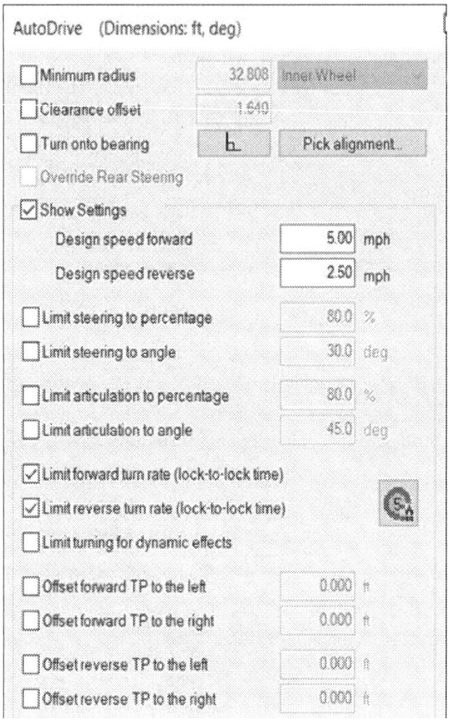

Figure 3–4

- **Limit steering to percentage** or **Limit steering to angle:** Limiting the steering by percentage is vehicle independent, whereas limiting to a specific angle is not.
- **Limit articulation to percentage** or **Limit articulation to angle:** Limiting the articulation angles by percentage is vehicle independent, whereas limiting by angle is not.
- **Limit forward turn rate** or **Limit reverse turn rate:** When such limits are disabled, you will see the steering pointer at the last picked position changing as you move the cursor to change the current position.
- **Limit turning for dynamic effects**: If you are modeling higher speed maneuvers (above 15 km/h or 9 mph), this limits the turn radius to compensate for comfort and safety.

Bearing Mode

Bearing mode can be used from the start of the path or turned on at any point while creating the path. The default angle is 90 degrees; however, the flyout toolbar of the **AutoDrive** command includes standard angles of 30, 45, 60, 90, 120, 135, 150, and 180 degrees, as shown in Figure 3–5.

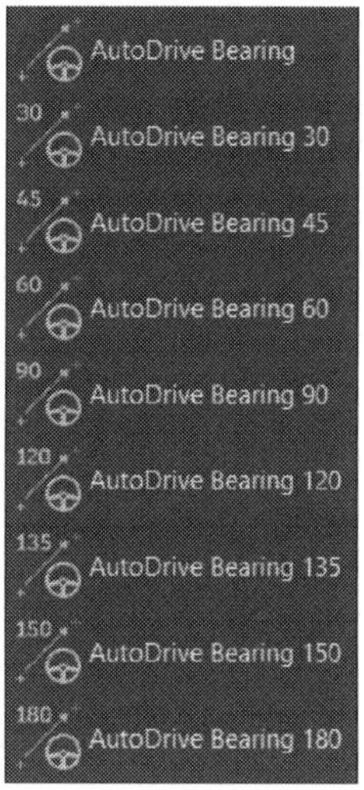

Figure 3–5

These angles can also be assigned in the AutoDrive dialog box by selecting **Turn onto bearing**, as shown in Figure 3–6.

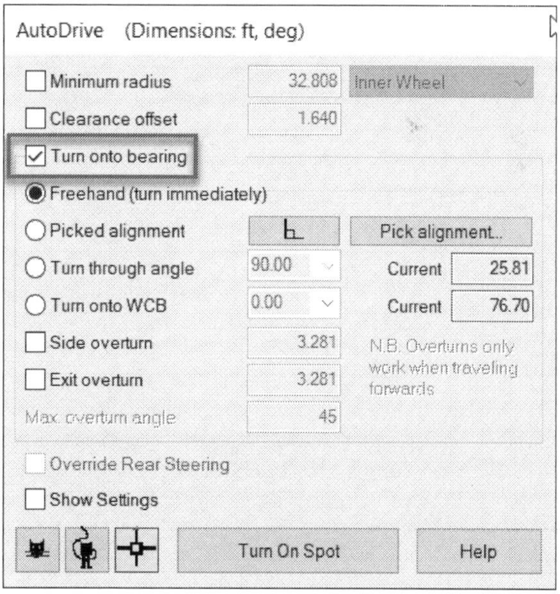

Figure 3–6

- **Freehand (turn immediately):** Turn the vehicle immediately and drive straight to the cursor.

When using Bearing mode to draft your path, you will notice a difference in how the arcs are created. Bearing will create immediate turns. Using the Freehand option, specific angles, or the Pick alignment option, you can enhance the path creation.

Note in the figures below the difference between using **AutoDrive Arc** and using **AutoDrive Bearing**.

Figure 3–7 shows AutoDrive: Arc Mode.

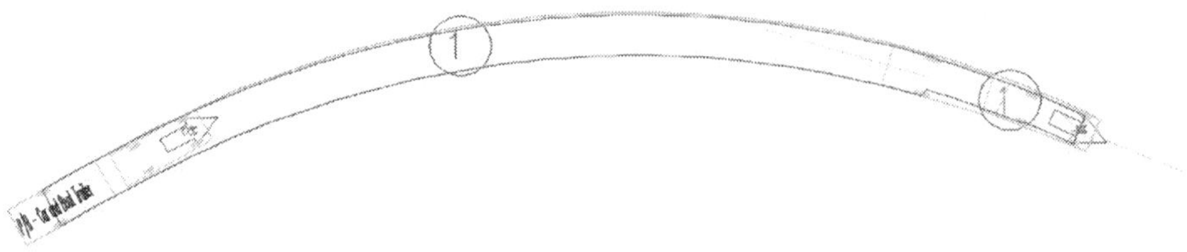

Figure 3–7

Figure 3–8 shows AutoDrive: Bearing Mode - Freehand.

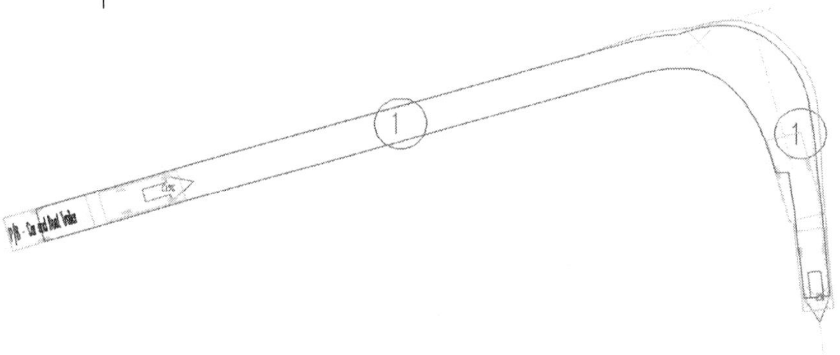

Figure 3–8

Figure 3–9 shows AutoDrive: Bearing Mode - Specific Angle.

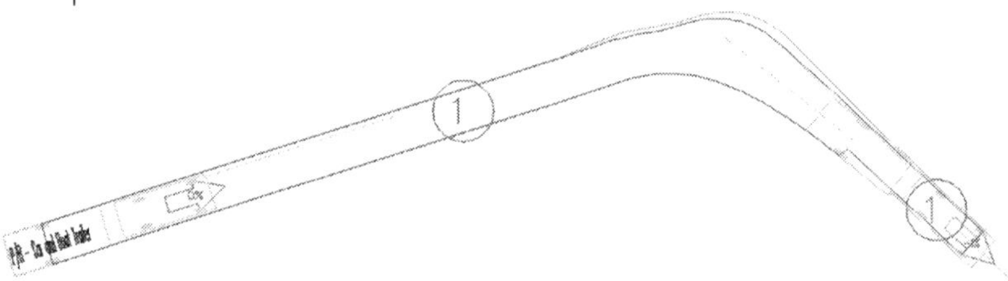

Figure 3–9

Practice 3a Create a Path Using Arc Mode

Learning Objectives

- Use the AutoDrive Arc mode to create the vehicle swept path.
- Place vehicle turn points and remove them if necessary.

In this practice, you will examine how best to travel between two points, as shown in Figure 3–10, and learn if the chosen vehicle can maneuver safely.

Figure 3–10

1. Open **Arc Mode.dwg** in the *Autodesk Vehicle Tracking\Working\Swept Paths* folder.

2. In the *View* tab>Named Views panel, expand the drop-down list and select **ArcMode**.

3. On the *Vehicle Tracking* tab>Swept Paths panel, click **AutoDrive Arc**, as shown in Figure 3–11.

Figure 3–11

4. If the Drawing Settings dialog box comes up, click **OK** to accept the default settings. It is a good idea to check the **Don't ask me this again** checkbox to prevent this message from reappearing, as shown in Figure 3–12.

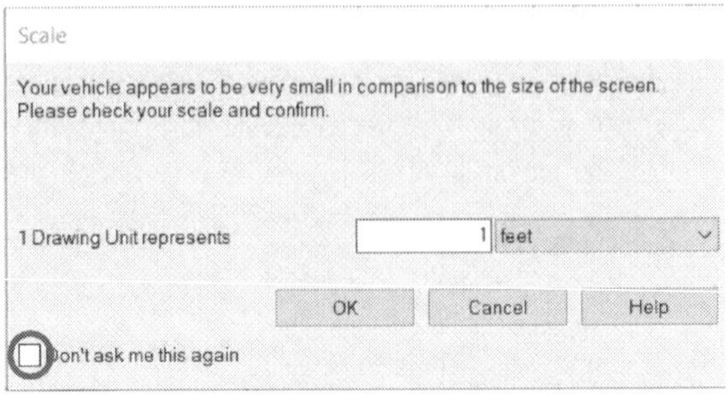
Scale
Your vehicle appears to be very small in comparison to the size of the screen.
Please check your scale and confirm.
1 Drawing Unit represents
1
feet
OK
Cancel
Help
Don't ask me this again

Figure 3–12

5. If the Vehicle Library Explorer pops up, scroll to the bottom of the vehicle list and expand *US Design Vehicles>State-wide (AASHTO)>AASHTO 2011 (US Customary)* and select **P-Passenger Car**.

6. If you are prompted to set this as a default, click **Yes**.

7. Place the vehicle in the center of the target block marked **A**. Position the vehicle to face south towards the roundabout, as marked with the purple arrow in Figure 3–13.

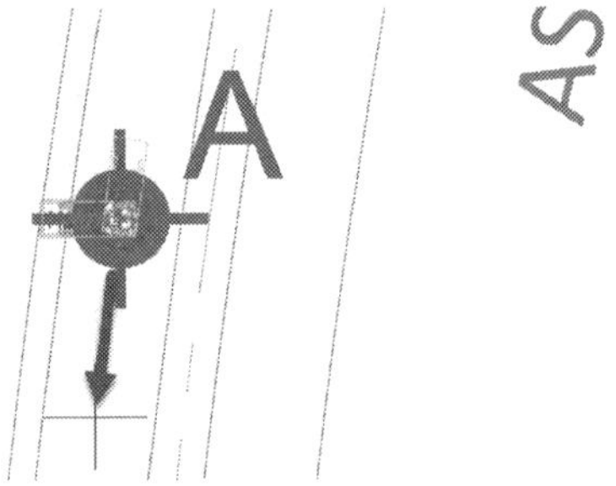
A

Figure 3–13

8. In the Position Vehicle dialog box, verify that the *Current vehicle* is **P-Passenger Car**, as shown in Figure 3–14. Click **Proceed**.

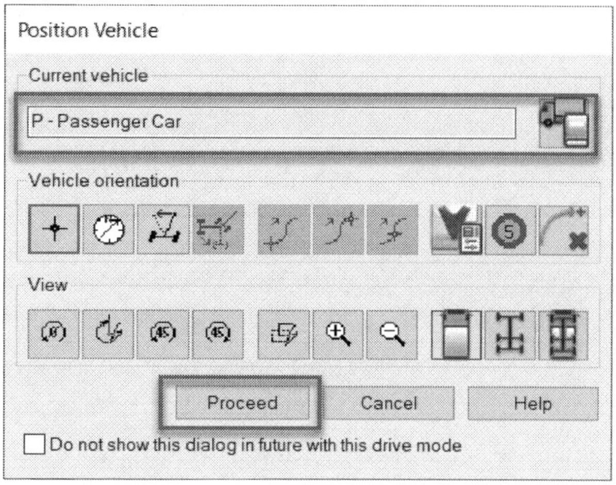

Figure 3–14

Note: If Passenger Car is not set as the vehicle, click the **Change Vehicle** button. Pick the **Passenger Car** from the AASHTO 2011 US drop-down list. Double-click on the option. Click **Proceed** in the Position Vehicle dialog box.

9. Create the Arc mode path by using single clicks to set the path. Click often and watch the path as you create it. Also, remember that you have a **Remove Last Target** option in the command line if you click a wrong point.

10. Follow the path from **A** to **B**, as shown in Figure 3–15. Watch the curves and use the **Remove Last Target** option as needed. The final result should look like Figure 3–15.

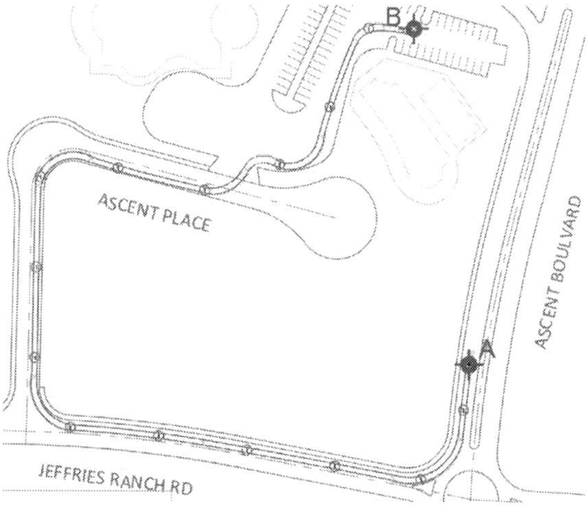

Figure 3–15

11. Save and close the drawing.

Practice 3b

Create a Path Using Bearing Mode

Learning Objectives

- Use the AutoDrive Bearing mode to examine how vehicles can be maneuvered.
- Create vehicle swept paths with restrictive parameters.

In this practice, you will examine how best to travel among multiple points, as shown in Figure 3–16, by using multiple methods within Bearing mode.

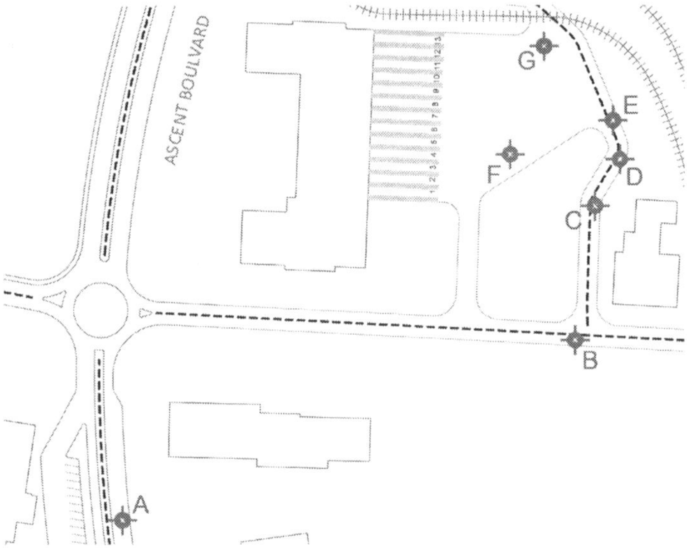

Figure 3–16

1. Open **Bearing Mode.dwg** in the *Autodesk Vehicle Tracking\ Working\Swept Paths* folder.
2. In the *View* tab>Named Views panel, expand the drop-down list and select **BearingMode**.
3. On the *Vehicle Tracking* tab>Swept Paths panel, click **AutoDrive Arc**, as shown in Figure 3–17.

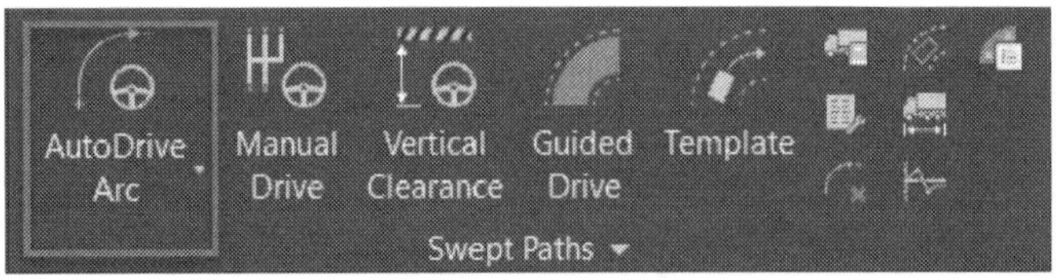

Figure 3–17

4. If the Drawing Settings dialog box appears, click **OK** to accept the default settings.

5. Place the vehicle in the center of the target block marked **A**. Position the vehicle to face north towards the roundabout, as marked with the purple arrow in Figure 3–18.

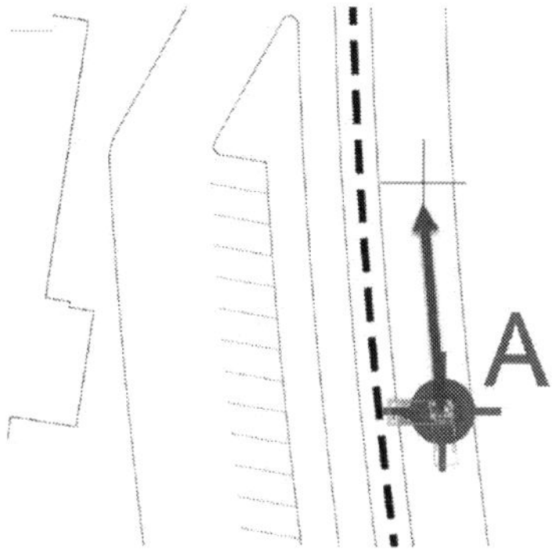

Figure 3–18

6. In the Position Vehicle dialog box, verify that the *Current vehicle* is **P-Passenger Car**, as shown in Figure 3–19. Click **Proceed**.

   Note: If Passenger Car is not set as the vehicle, click the **Change Vehicle** button. Pick the **Passenger Car** from the AASHTO 2011 US drop-down list. Double-click on the option. Click **Proceed** in the Position Vehicle dialog box.

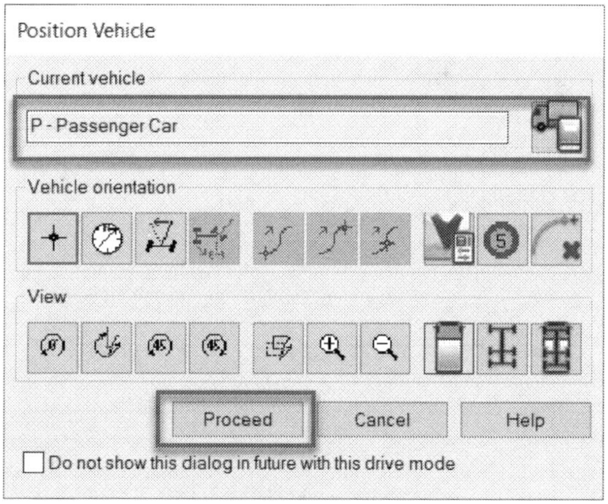

Figure 3–19

7. Create the Arc mode path by using single clicks until you get near the center of the target marked **B** (3 or 4 clicks should get you there).

8. In the AutoDrive dialog box, select **Turn onto bearing**. Select **Freehand** as the option, as shown in Figure 3–20.

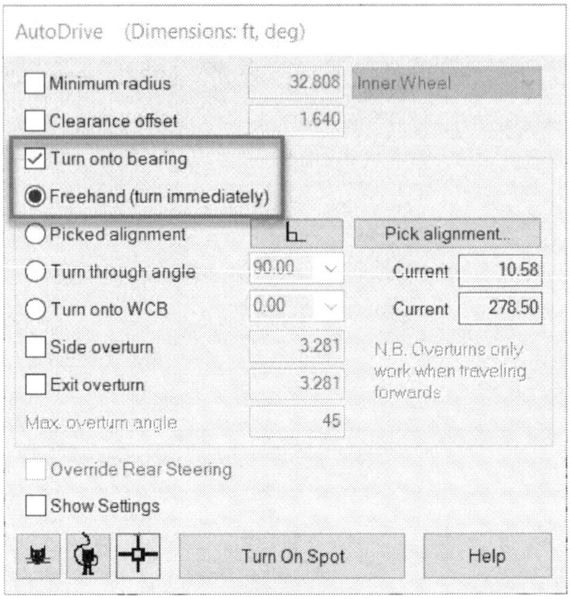

Figure 3–20

9. Move your cursor to make the right turn, as shown in Figure 3–21. Straighten the arrow and click the mouse to enter the chosen point.

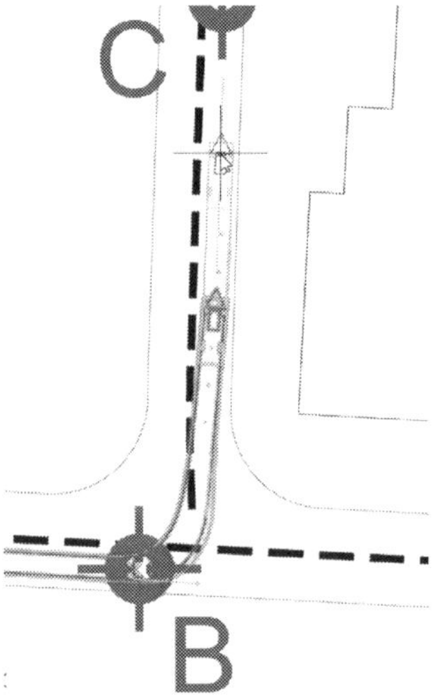

Figure 3–21

10. Move the cursor up to target **C** and click in the middle of the target.

11. Select the **Turn through angle** option in the AutoDrive dialog box. Set the angle to **30**, as shown in Figure 3–22.

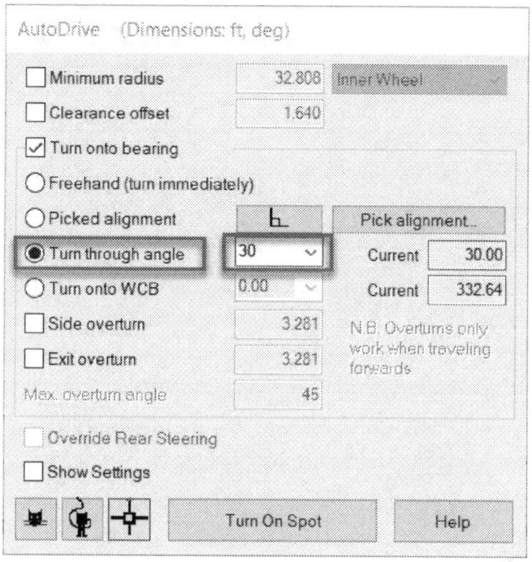

Figure 3–22

12. Move the cursor towards target **D.** Click in the center of the target marked **D**, as shown in Figure 3–23.

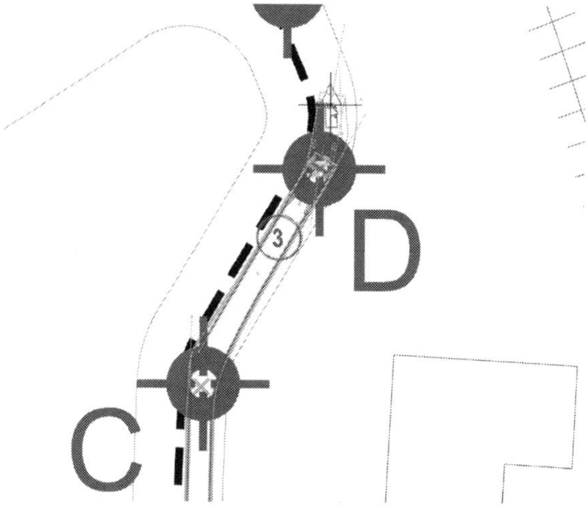

Figure 3–23

13. In the AutoDrive dialog box, set the angle to **150**, as shown in Figure 3–24.

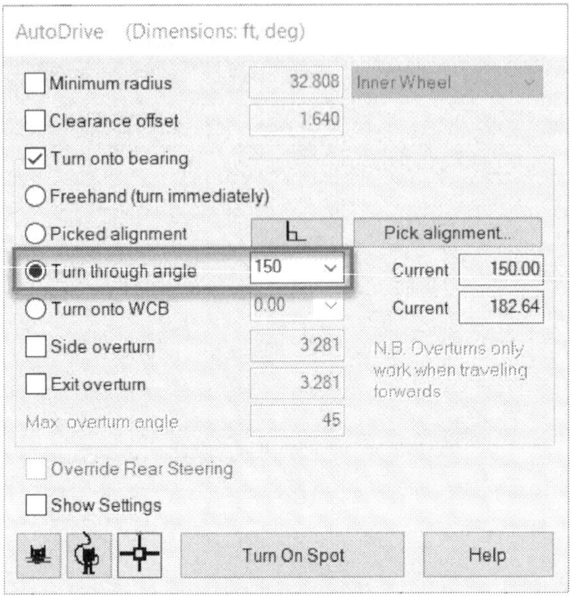

Figure 3–24

14. As you move your cursor, you will note that the angle adjusts quickly. Move the cursor just slightly up until the arrow is parallel to the road, then click to add the target point, as shown in Figure 3–25.

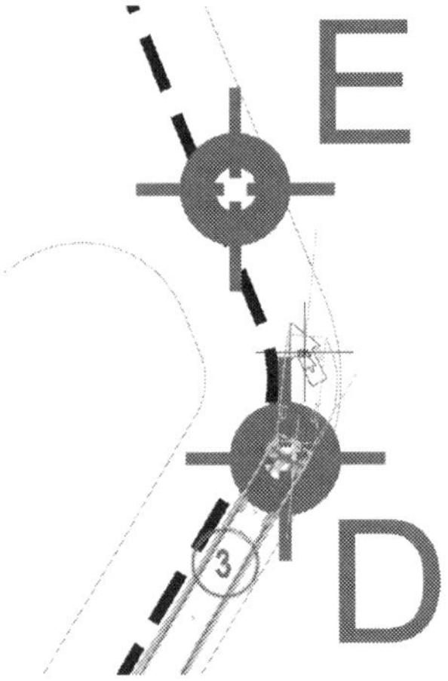

Figure 3–25

15. With the arrow paralleling the road, click in the center of the target marked **E**. If the path tries to rotate too much, temporarily uncheck the **Turn onto bearing** option.

16. Once you have clicked on the target marked **E**, turn the bearing back on and set the angle to **90**, as shown in Figure 3–26.

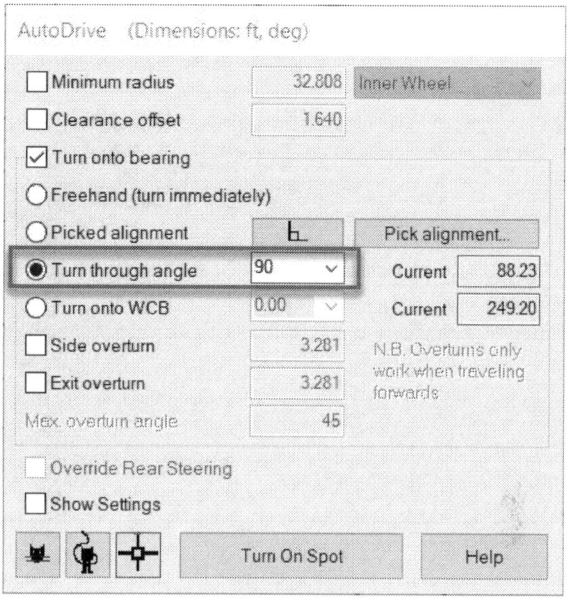

Figure 3–26

17. Move the cursor to the west and click on the center of the target marked **F**. Press <Enter> to end the command.

18. The final path should look like the one shown in Figure 3–27.

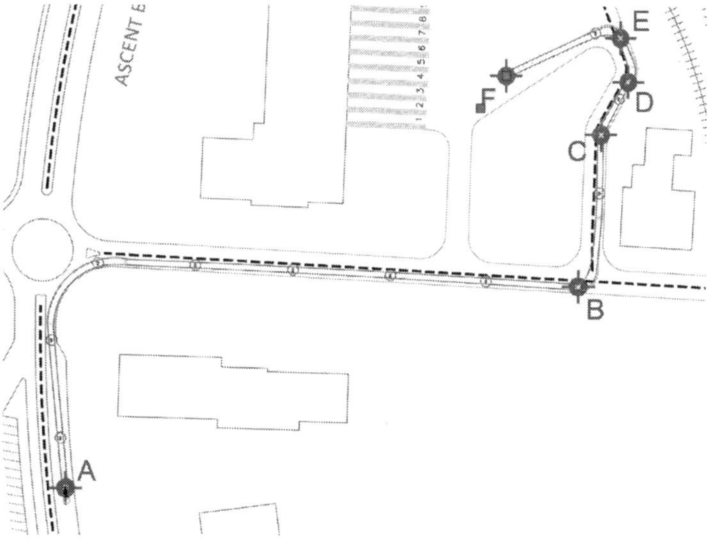

Figure 3–27

19. To continue the path, click on the plus symbol of the vehicle.

20. Move the cursor west and slightly north-west as you will need to click slightly off a straight line to be able to go around the curve.

21. Make sure the path is still selected.

22. On the Swept Paths panel, use the AutoDrive drop-down list to assign **AutoDrive Bearing 150**, as shown in Figure 3–28.

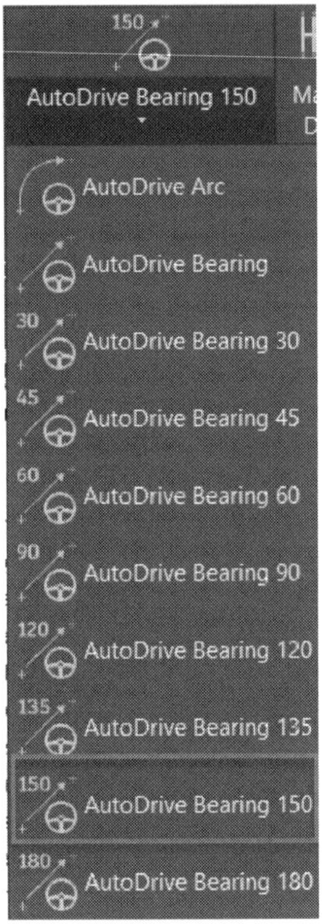

Figure 3–28

23. Move the cursor and click near the center of the target marked **G**, as shown in Figure 3–29.

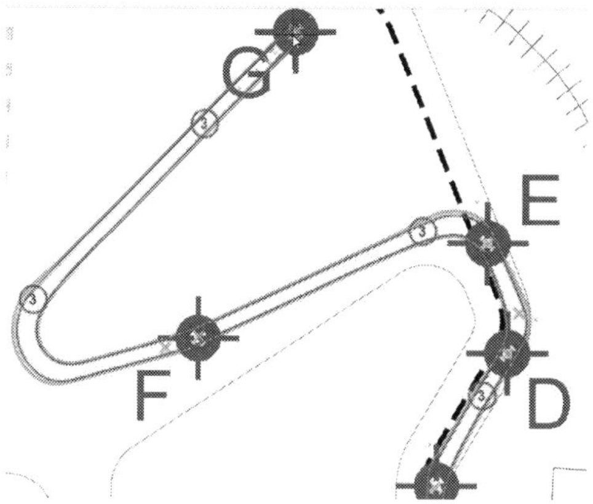

Figure 3–29

24. In the AutoDrive dialog box, click **Pick alignment...**, as shown in Figure 3–30.

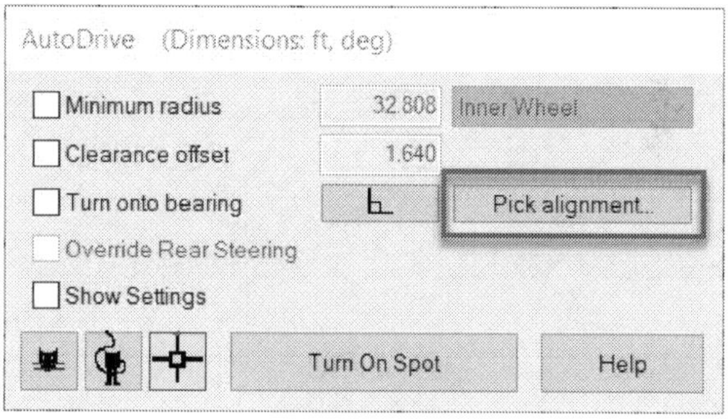

Figure 3–30

25. Select any of the cyan lines of the loading bays shown in Figure 3–31. Since they all have the same bearing, it does not matter which one you pick.

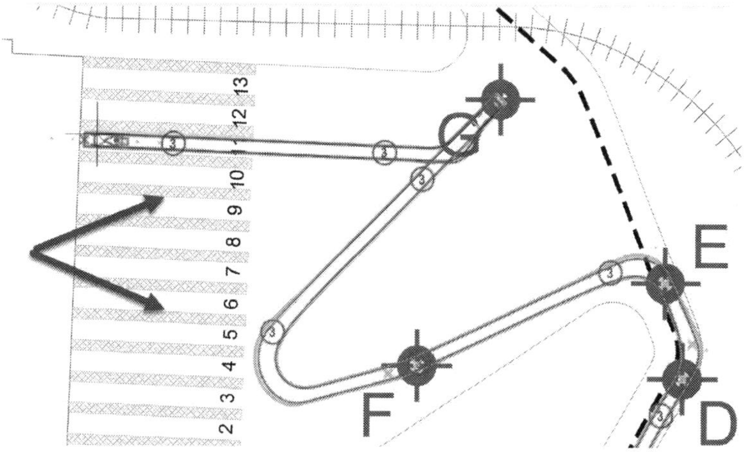

Figure 3–31

26. Note from your current position that you can safely navigate to bays 1 through 11, but for bays 12 and 13 you would need to move up beyond marker **G**.

27. Click to place the vehicle.

28. Press <Esc> to clear the path, as shown in Figure 3–32.

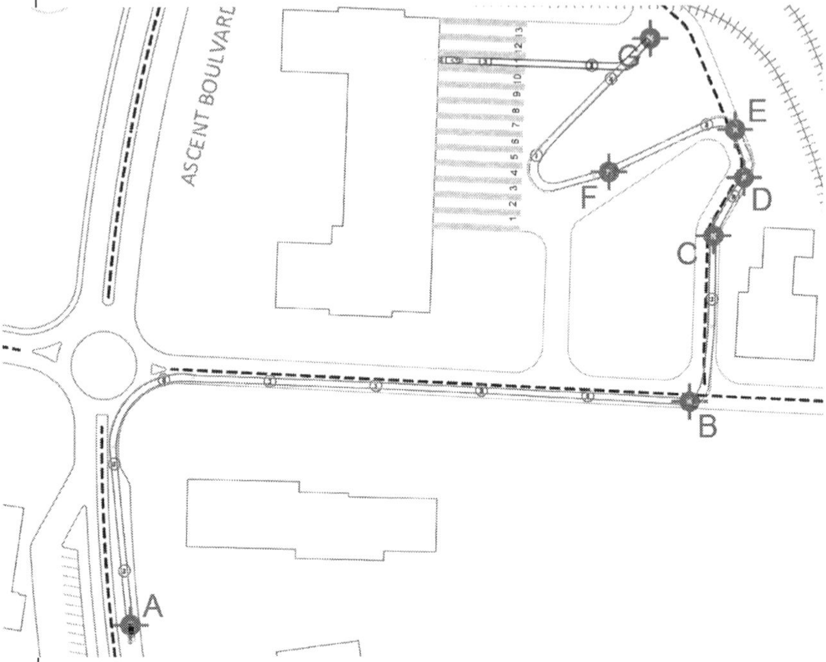

Figure 3–32

29. Save and close the file.

30. (Optional) This analysis was done with a passenger vehicle. It would be different if you were to test this with transport trucks of varying sizes. Test out multiple vehicle types and create the same path.

3.2 Manual Drive and Guided Drive

Manual Drive

Manual Drive (shown in Figure 3–33) allows you to control the vehicle interactively, much like a video game would do. Move the cursor up and down to make the car move fast or slow. Move the cursor to the right or left to turn or shift direction.

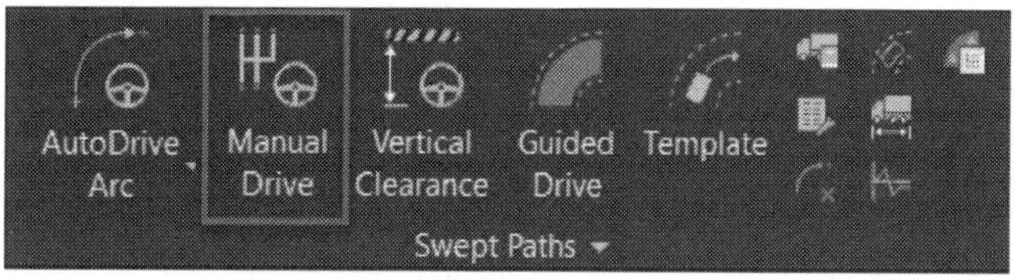

Figure 3–33

How To: Use the Manual Drive Option

1. Launch the command from the Swept Paths panel of the *Vehicle Tracking* tab.
2. Position the vehicle as you would using AutoDrive.
3. Once you click **Proceed** in the AutoDrive dialog box, a driving window appears, as shown in Figure 3–34.

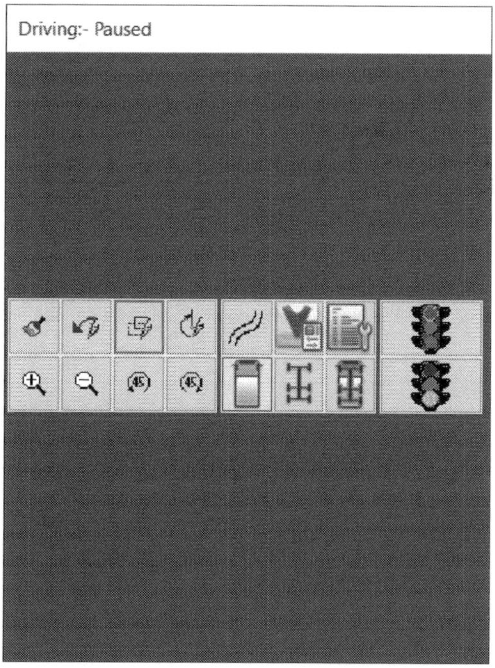

Figure 3–34

4. Click the **Go** button. The buttons will disappear and the cursor now represents the requested steering angle and rate at which the path is generated.
5. Keep the cursor within the Driving dialog box. The vehicle will start to move when you move the cursor beyond the stop zone.
6. Move the cursor between the two center horizontal bands to stop moving. Move the cursor above the bands to go progressively faster forward, or move the cursor below the bands to go progressively faster in reverse.
7. Move the cursor left or right to turn the steered wheels left or right, respectively.
8. Click anywhere on the overlay to pause the vehicle and redisplay the buttons.

Guided Drive

Guided Drive (shown in Figure 3–35) is generally used for trams (streetcars) and light rails. Using Guided Drive, the vehicle position is entirely dictated by the rail layout.

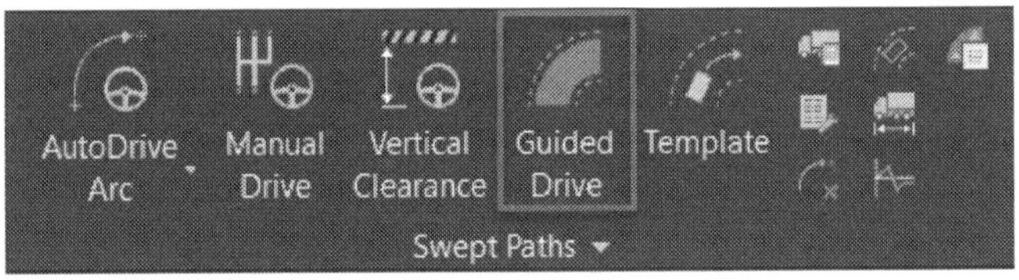

Figure 3–35

How To: Use the Guided Drive Option

1. Launch the command from the Swept Paths panel of the *Vehicle Tracking* tab.
2. Select the appropriate vehicle. If you choose something other than a tram or light rail, an error message will appear stating you must use a vehicle that can work with Guided Drive. Select one of those choices as your vehicle.
3. Select an AutoCAD polyline that represents the path. The polyline can be 2D, 3D, splined, straight, or with arc segments. If the polyline is closed, the closing segment of the polyline will be ignored.
4. The swept path is immediately created without any more input required.

Practice 3c Investigations Through Guided Drive

Learning Objectives

- Examine if a streetcar can maneuver around a chosen path that represents tracks.
- Adjust the track path and test the streetcar maneuverability.

In this practice, you will study if a streetcar can safely drive along tracks laid out and make the necessary adjustments for it to maneuver.

1. Open **Guided Drive.dwg** in the *Autodesk Vehicle Tracking\Working\Swept Paths* folder.
2. In the *View* tab>Named Views panel, expand the drop-down list and select **Guided**.
3. The red curving polyline represents the tracks of a streetcar (also known as a tram). You need to check to ensure the selected streetcar can safely navigate the tracks.

The polyline has the AutoCAD Tracks linetype assigned to it.

4. On the *Vehicle Tracking* tab>Swept Paths panel, select **Vehicle Library Explorer**, as shown in Figure 3–36.

Figure 3–36

5. In the Vehicle Library Explorer, expand the tree to *Trams and rail vehicles* and select **Dallas Streetcar**.

6. Click **Make Default**, as shown in Figure 3–37, and then click **OK** to dismiss the window.

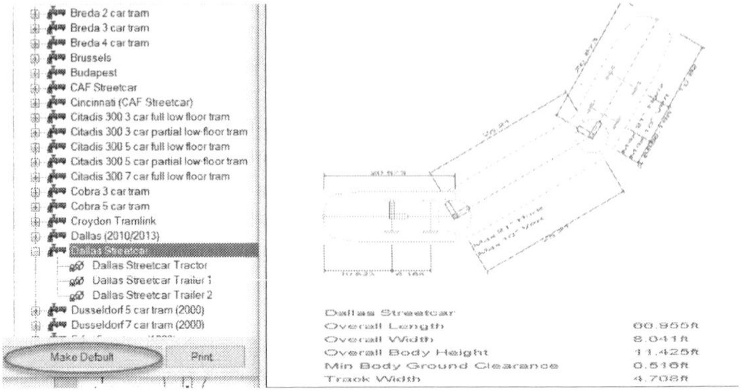

Figure 3–37

7. On the Swept Paths panel, click **Guided Drive**, as shown in Figure 3–38.

Figure 3–38

8. In the ensuing dialog box about using the default vehicle, click **Yes**.

9. Select the red track polyline near the target **A** point as the object to follow.

10. In the Settings dialog box, click **Speed** in the left panel and ensure the design speeds are set for **5 mph** for forward and **2.5 mph** for reverse, as shown in Figure 3–39.

Figure 3–39

11. Click **OK**.

12. The path of the Dallas streetcar is traced, but it ends near target **B**, as shown in Figure 3–40. The reason is the radius of the path near this point is too narrow for the streetcar to safely navigate at the chosen speed.

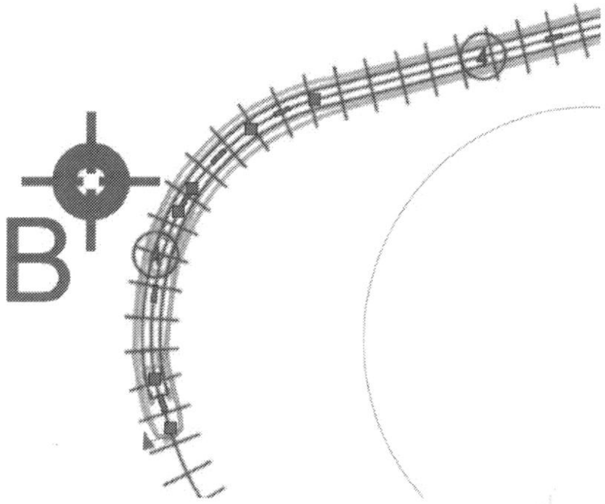

Figure 3–40

13. You need to adjust the path and try again. Erase the path Vehicle Tracking has just traced. Do not erase the red track polyline.

14. Select the red track polyline and note the grips that appear.

15. Delete the vertices (blue square grips) shown in Figure 3–41 following these steps:

    a. Hover over a blue square grip (do not select it!).

    b. The grip turns red. In the tooltip, select **Remove Vertex**.

    c. Repeat for the other three vertices as indicated.

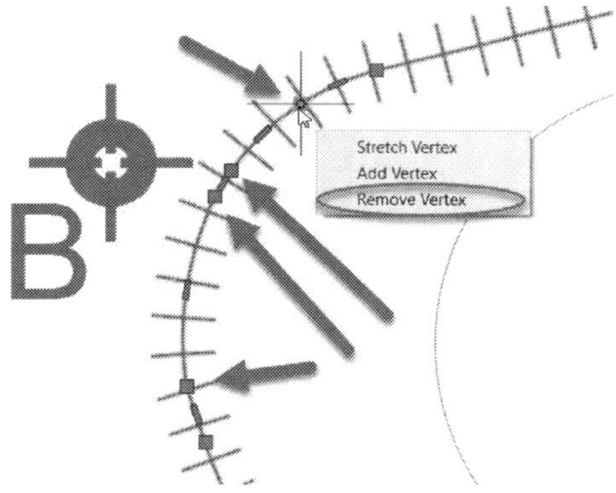

Figure 3–41

16. Change the straight polyline segment to an arc, as shown in Figure 3–42, by hovering over the blue narrow rectangular grip in the middle of the segment. Once the grip turns red, select **Convert to Arc** in the tooltip.

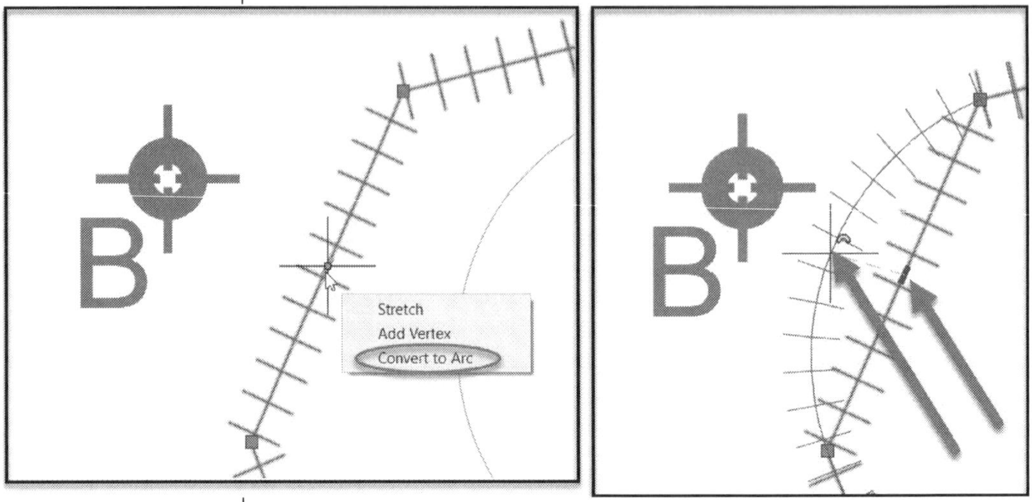

Figure 3–42

17. Position the arc's midpoint as indicated in Figure 3–42 above.

18. Try the Guided Drive again by repeating the procedure outlined in Steps 9 to 11. This time, the streetcar should make it through all the way. If it does not, you will need to erase the path and adjust the polyline's grips again.

19. Zoom in near target **B**. You will note that the body of the tram is visible, but not the tracks.

20. To correct this, select the Guided Drive path you just created and go the **Report Wizard** on the Swept Paths panel, as shown in Figure 3–43.

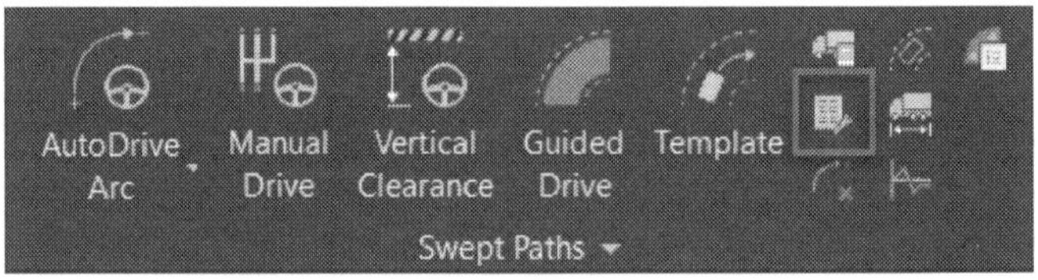

Figure 3–43

21. In the Report Wizard: Start dialog box, click **Advanced...** in the lower right corner.

22. In the Report Settings dialog box, ensure that **Chassis outlines** is checked.

23. Select **Chassis outlines** and click **Edit**, as shown in Figure 3–44.

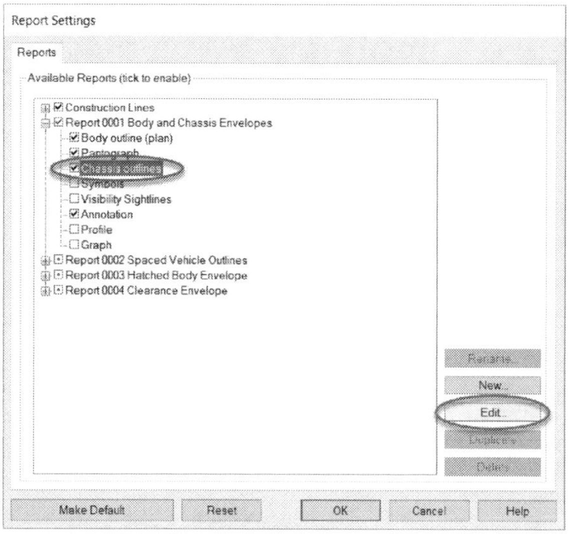

Figure 3–44

24. In the Chassis outlines dialog box, click on the *Loci* tab and select the checkbox for the **Show Loci / Tracks** option, as shown in Figure 3–45.

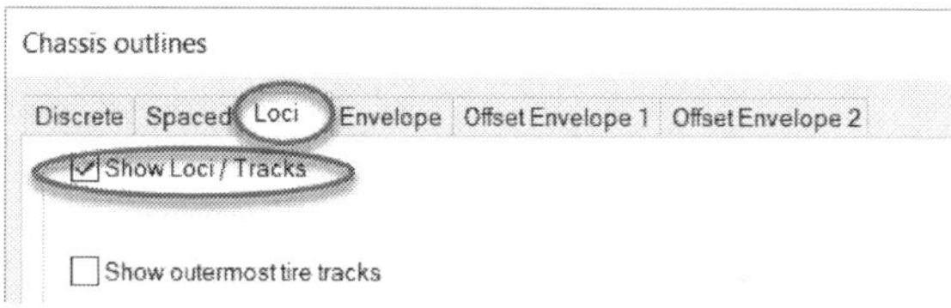

Figure 3–45

25. Click **OK** twice and then click **Finish** in the Report Wizard dialog box to close all dialog boxes. Now you can see the tracks in the path, as shown in Figure 3–46.

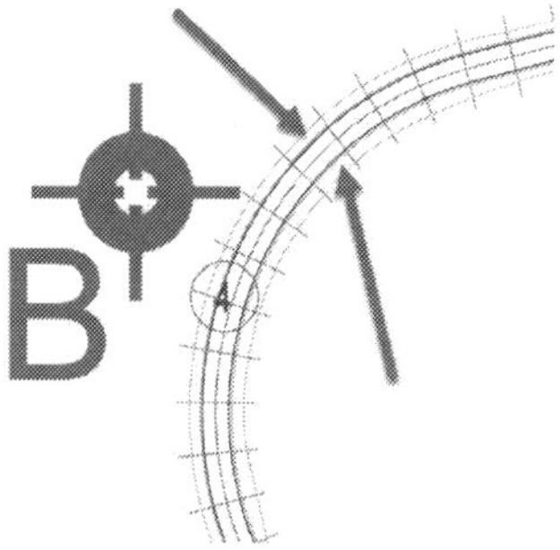

Figure 3–46

26. Save and close the drawing.

3.3 Following and Editing Paths

Follow Tool

The **Follow Tool** (shown in Figure 3–47) allows you to track a vehicle along a predefined path consisting of a polyline or a spline. It works in the same way as the Guided Drive, but you select non-guided vehicles when using this option.

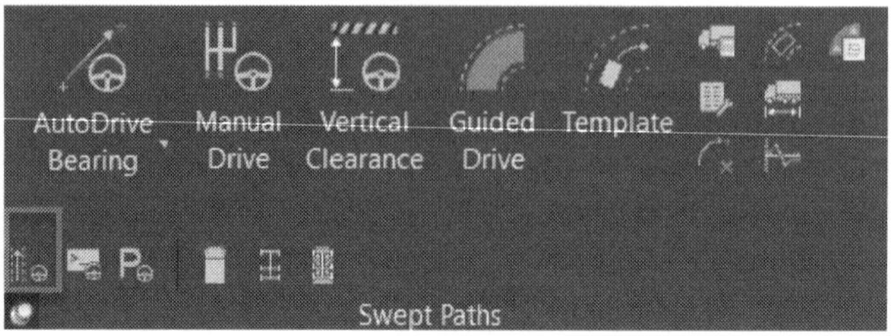

Figure 3–47

How To: Use the Follow Tool

1. Launch the command from the Swept Paths panel of the *Vehicle Tracking* tab.
2. Select the appropriate vehicle.
3. Select an AutoCAD polyline that represents the path. The polyline can be 2D, 3D, splined, straight, or with arc segments. If the polyline is closed, the closing segment of the polyline will be ignored.
4. On the Follow Drive page in the Settings dialog box, make sure that the *Start Direction* is set to the correct direction, as shown in Figure 3–48.
    - Select **Forward** or **Reverse** to force the direction of travel.
    - Select **Keep Current** to continue in the current direction.

Figure 3–48

- Select **Automatic** to determine the direction of travel based upon the orientation of the vehicle relative to the starting vertex of the polyline, as shown in Figure 3–49.

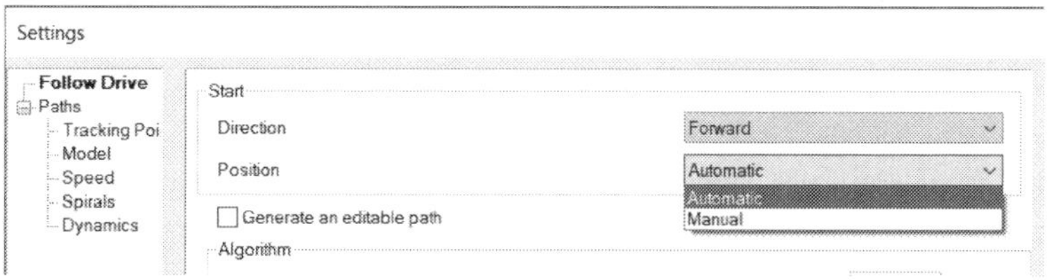

Figure 3–49

5. The swept path is created.

Editing Paths

Swept paths can be edited as long as they have not been exploded. See Figure 3–50 for examples of the many grips available to use. Hover over any grip in the drawing to see what the individual grip does.

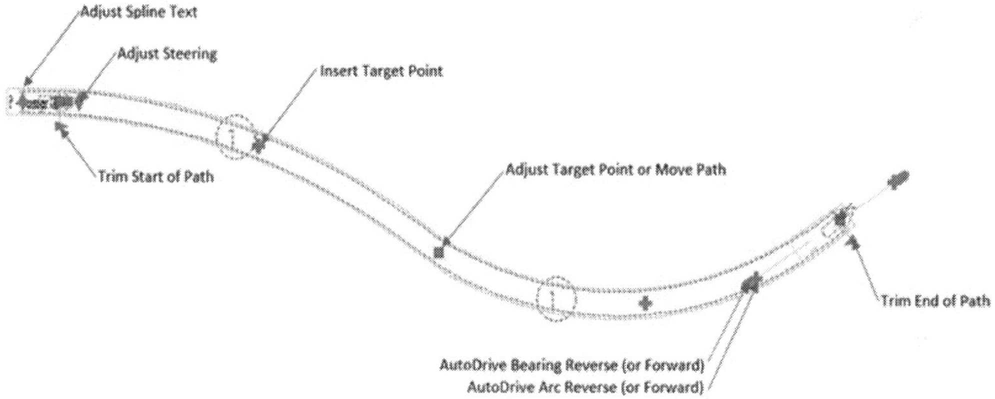

Figure 3–50

The **Vehicle Tracking Properties** command lets you edit a single path. You can adjust the path alignment using the Edit Tools toolbar. Practically speaking, however, the majority of your editing will be done using grips.

All paths, except those created using Guided Drive, create a series of target points. These target points can be moved, dynamically updating the path to reflect changes in position.

Practice 3d Edit the Vehicle Path

Learning Objectives

- Tweak existing paths.
- Move target points of paths.

In this practice, you will edit existing paths to fine-tune the swept paths and make minor adjustments.

1. Open **EditPath.dwg** in the *Autodesk Vehicle Tracking\ Working\Swept Paths* folder.
2. In the *View* tab>Named Views panel, expand the drop-down list and select **EditPath**.
3. Note that the path goes through the center line. Select the target point around the target marked **B**, as shown in Figure 3–51. Move the target point to be in the middle of the target marked **B**.

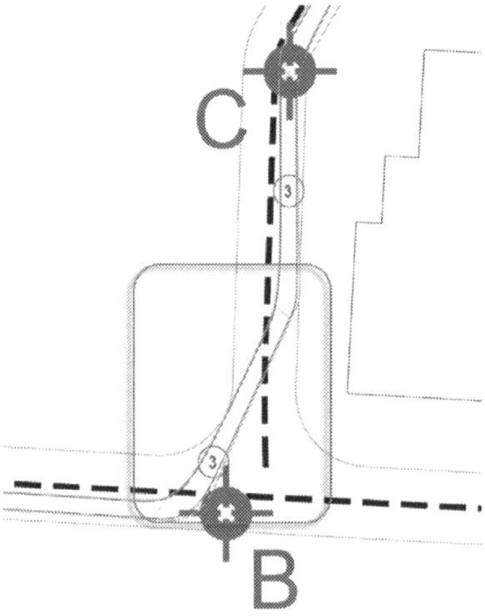

Figure 3–51

4. Scroll up to the target marked **D**, as shown in Figure 3–52. Note that the path here also moves out of its lane. This section will not be as easy to fix. Play with various options to adjust the path.

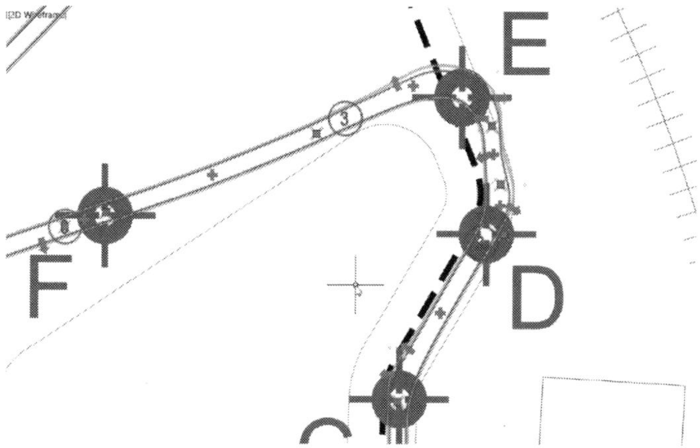

Figure 3–52

5. Try adding more target points and shifting the path.
6. Figure 3–53 shows an example of changes that can be made. Note the many target points that have been added.

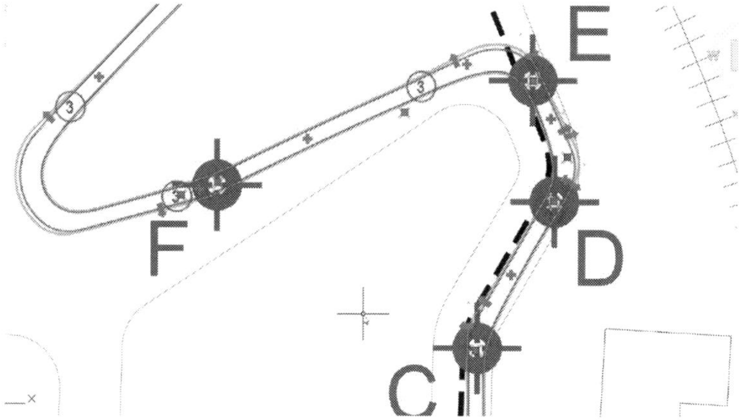

Figure 3–53

Chapter Review Questions

1. Which of the following is NOT a swept path analysis option?
    a. AutoDrive Arc
    b. Polyline Converter
    c. AutoDrive Bearing
    d. Manual Drive
    e. Guided Drive
2. Which method for swept path analysis would you use to turn as sharply as allowed by the vehicle specifications?
    a. AutoDrive Arc
    b. AutoDrive Bearing
    c. Manual Drive
3. What is the Guided Drive method used for? (Select all that apply.)
    a. Aircraft
    b. Light rail
    c. Transport trailers
    d. Streetcars (trams)
4. How can you check to see how a vehicle can follow parallel to an object?
    a. Use the Manual method and the **Parallel** AutoCAD object snap.
    b. Use the **Pick alignment** option.
    c. Estimate the path by picking points.
    d. Determine the bearing of the object and type it in.

Settings and Analysis

In this chapter, you will learn about the many settings and analysis tools within the Autodesk® Vehicle Tracking software. Each section of Vehicle Tracking has settings and “reports” within the individual panel of the ribbon. In Vehicle Tracking, the term *reports* is used as a collection of settings and defaults, as well as regular, informational reports.This includes settings for swept paths, parking lots, roundabouts, and more.

Learning Objectives in This Chapter

- Use Design Check to further analyze the design.
- Run Vertical Clearance to check for clash locations.
- Create animations for a full visual of the path.

4.1 Settings and Tools

Report Wizard

The **Report Wizard** is found on the Swept Paths panel, as shown in Figure 4–1. This wizard allows you to set up your Autodesk Vehicle Tracking reports correctly. The name is a bit misleading, as this is really a settings or properties dialog box, rather than a report of information.

AutoDrive Arc
Manual Drive
Vertical Clearance
Guided Drive
Template
Swept Paths

Figure 4–1

Within the report, the following information can be set:

- Display of the vehicle path
- Display of the vehicle profile
- Display of the graph

Multiple reports (or settings) can be used in the drawing. Individual reports can be modified or reports can be swapped (made current) at any time.

The first page of the Report Wizard allows you to adjust which report is being used, as shown in Figure 4–2.

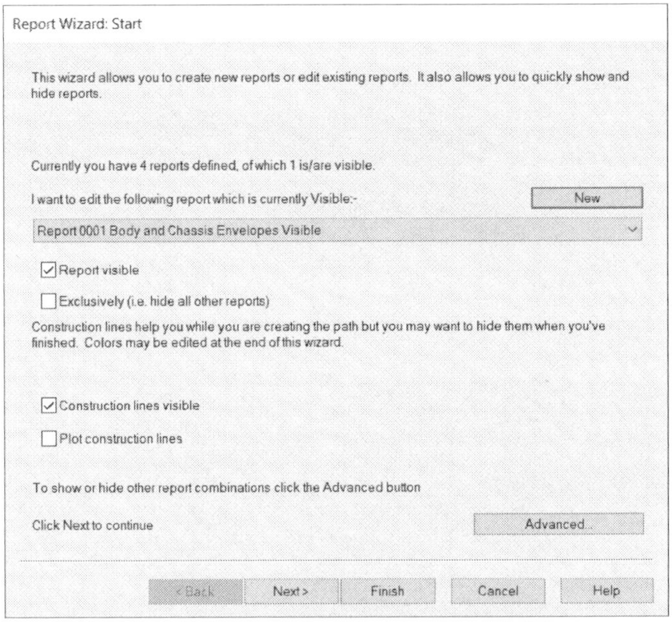
Report Wizard: Start
This wizard allows you to create new reports or edit existing reports. It also allows you to quickly show and hide reports.
Currently you have 4 reports defined, of which 1 is/are visible.
I want to edit the following report which is currently Visible:-
New
Report 0001 Body and Chassis Envelopes Visible
Report visible
Exclusively (i.e. hide all other reports)
Construction lines help you while you are creating the path but you may want to hide them when you've finished. Colors may be edited at the end of this wizard.
Construction lines visible
Plot construction lines
To show or hide other report combinations click the Advanced button
Click Next to continue
Advanced...
< Back
Next >
Finish
Cancel
Help

Figure 4–2

Note: Make sure the proper vehicle path is selected if you want changes to be reflected on an existing vehicle path.

Figure 4–3 shows examples of different reports (with different settings). Note how the report can affect the display of the vehicle path. In the previous Guided Path exercise, you used the Report Wizard to display the tracks of the tram path.

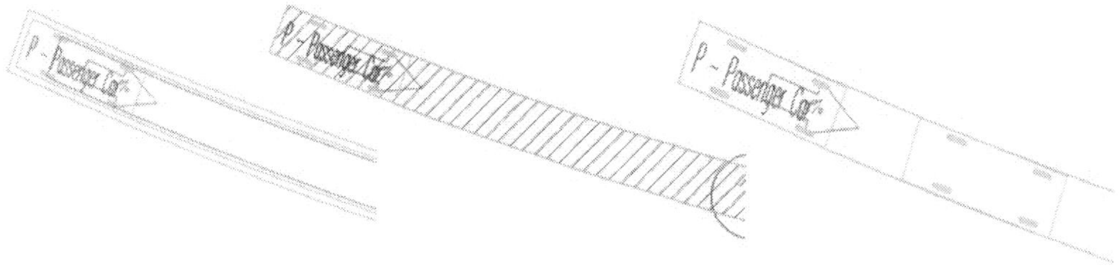

Figure 4–3

There are many options in the Report Wizard to control the look of the path:

- Body Outlines
- Chassis Outlines
- Load Outlines
- Vertical Clearance
- Profiles
- Steering and Articulation Graphs
- Construction Lines

An example of *Body Outlines* listed in the wizard is shown in Figure 4–4.

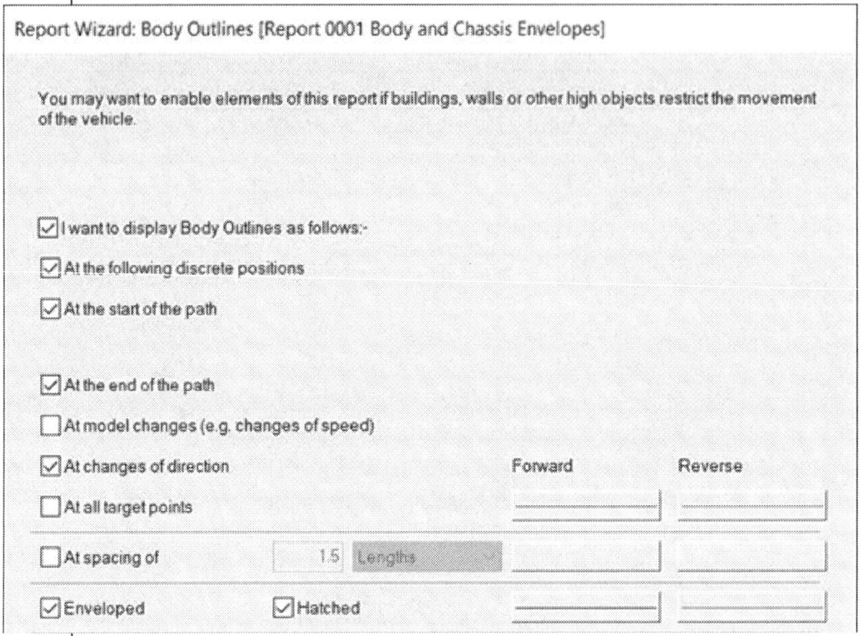

Figure 4–4

Use the **Advanced** button to control the report options to show in the Report Wizard, as shown in Figure 4–5.

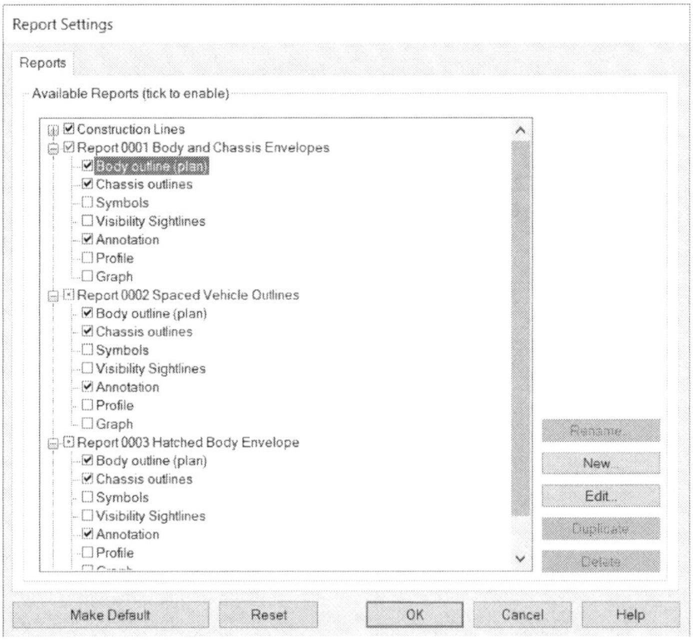

Figure 4–5

If you want more control over the layering of the objects, adjust the report settings in the Drawing Settings dialog box, as shown in Figure 4–6.

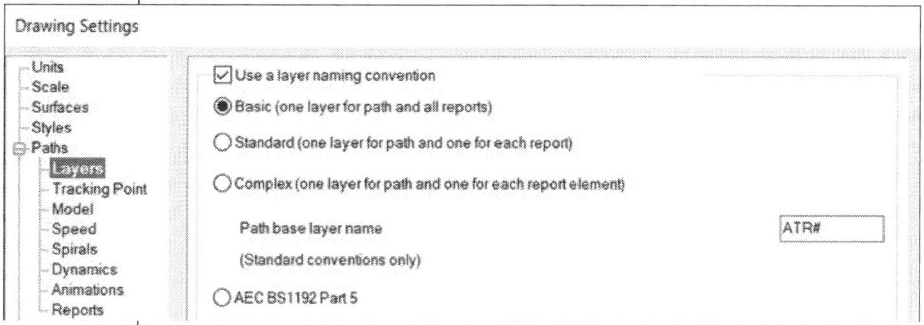

Figure 4–6

Insert Profile

A *profile* is a Vehicle Tracking object that lets you display a side or plan view of a vehicle, along with dimensions. The **Insert Profile** command is found on the Swept Paths panel of the ribbon (shown in Figure 4–7) and is used to verify the vehicle and vehicle properties being used for the path, as shown in Figure 4–8.

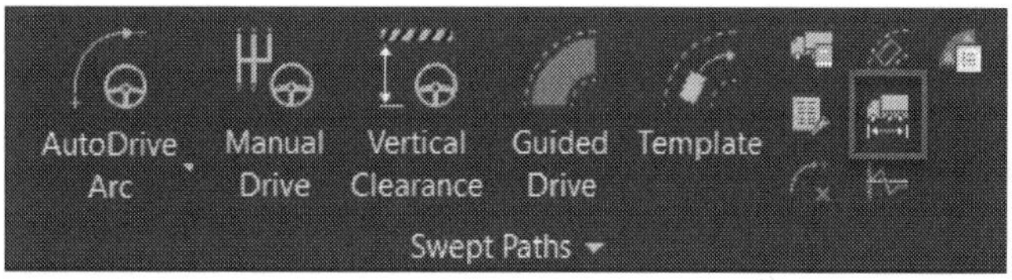

Figure 4–7

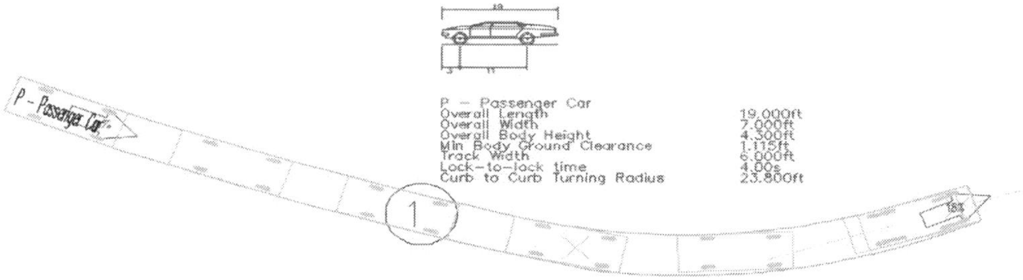

Figure 4–8

The visibility of the profile is controlled within the Report Wizard. See Figure 4–9 for the settings that can be adjusted. There are default settings for the placement of the profile in the drawing and size of dimensions, but the profile can be moved at any time.

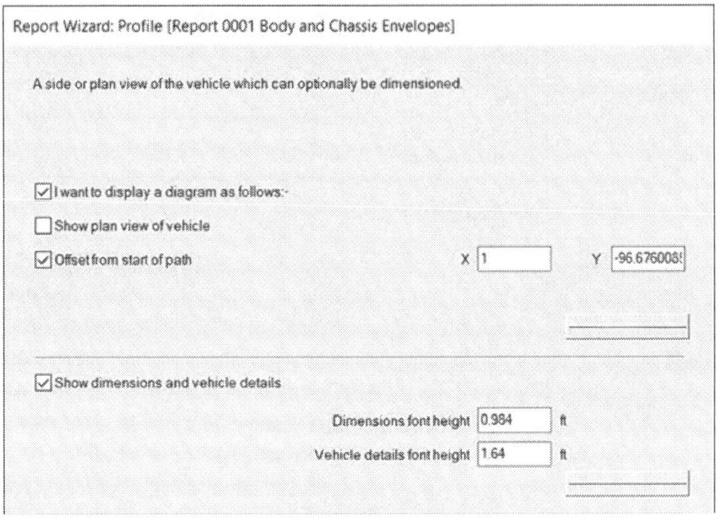

Figure 4–9

Design Checks

The Design Check tool lets you check your Autodesk® Vehicle Tracking objects for basic errors. The **Design Check** command is found on the Review panel of the ribbon (shown in Figure 4–10).

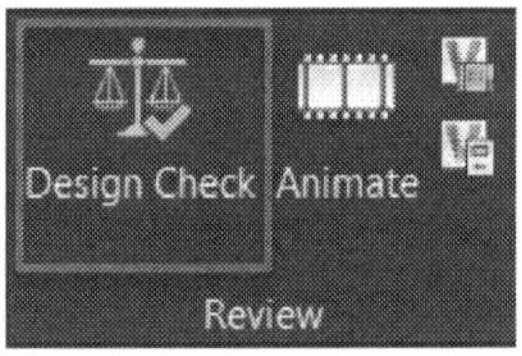

Figure 4–10

Once the command is launched, a dialog box appears with any errors found on the path. All paths will be reviewed in the design check. One common warning will be *Severe Steering*, as shown in Figure 4–11. Click on the warning to identify the issue. Within the Design Check Exceptions dialog box, the designer can justify, then assess the issue. Comments can also be left in this dialog box.

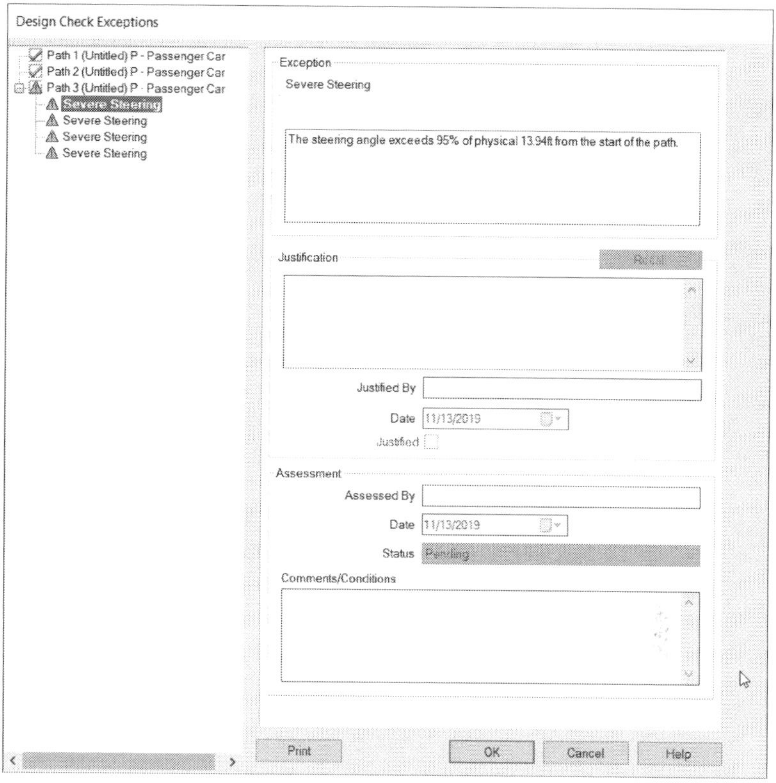

Figure 4–11

Design checks are a great precursor to inserting graphs. For example, if it is determined that excessive steering was used, you can create a graph to easily identify the location of the issue.

Insert Graph

A *graph* is a Vehicle Tracking object that lets you display the steering and articulation limits and angles and how they change along a path. This command is used to highlight potential problems along a path. The **Insert Graph** command is found on the Swept Paths panel of the ribbon (shown in Figure 4–12).

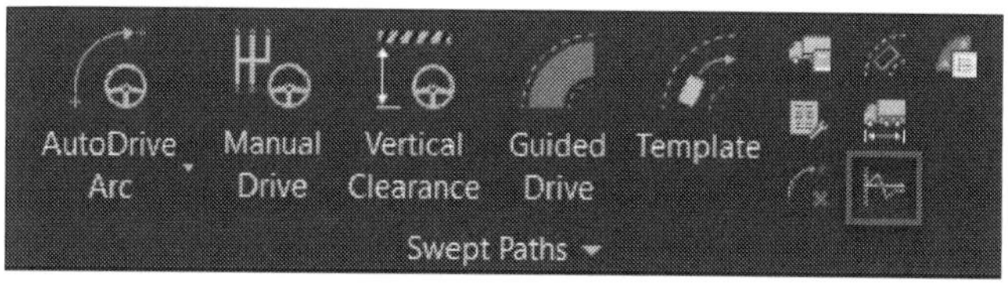

Figure 4–12

Once you launch the command, select the path and the graph will display, as shown in Figure 4–13. The graph can be placed anywhere in the drawing and moved at any time.

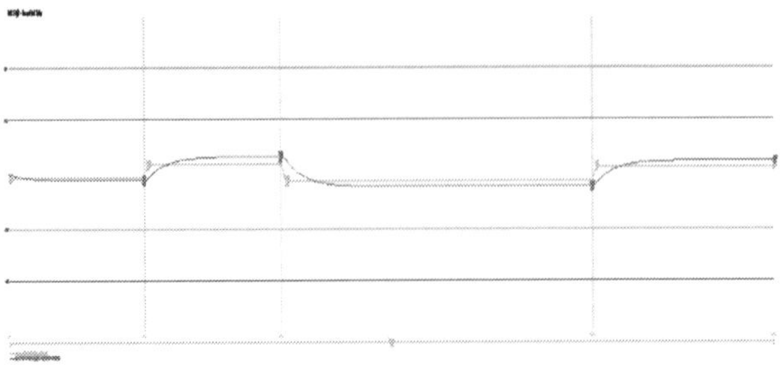

Figure 4–13

Within the graph, the steering and articulation lines display and text identifies the areas in excess. The graph is dynamic: as you adjust your path or add target points, the graph updates to reflect the changes. Zoom in to the graph to see where steering and articulation values are in excess, as shown in Figure 4–14.

Note: Use design checks along with graphs to highlight potential issues.

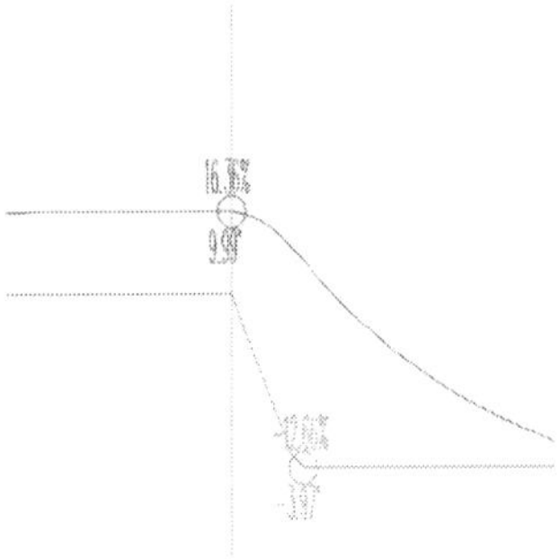

Figure 4–14

The visibility of the graph is controlled within the Report Wizard, as shown in Figure 4–15.

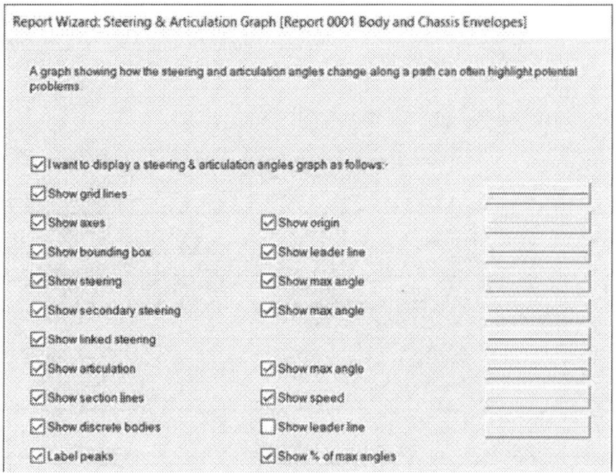

Figure 4–15

Place Outline

An *outline* is a Vehicle Tracking object that displays various boundary outlines along a path. Outlines can be very helpful when reviewing vertical and ground clearance. The **Place Outline** command is found on the Swept Paths panel of the ribbon (as shown in Figure 4–16).

Figure 4–16

Once the command is launched, select the path and a dialog box displays, allowing you to control which outlines and objects to display along the path.

Note: Removing outlines uses the same process as placing outlines. Launch the **Place Outline** command and uncheck what you do not want to see.

The following options are available in the Place / Remove Outline dialog box, as shown in Figure 4–17.

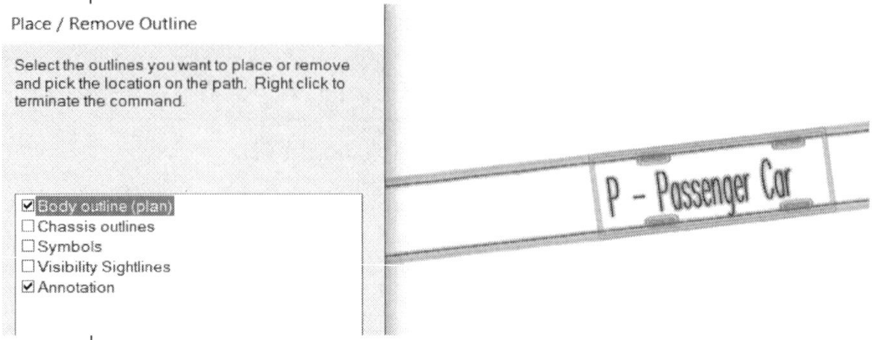
Place / Remove Outline
Select the outlines you want to place or remove and pick the location on the path. Right click to terminate the command.
Body outline (plan)
Chassis outlines
Symbols
Visibility Sightlines
Annotation
P - Passenger Car

Figure 4–17

- **Body outline (plan):** Select this option to see the vehicle move along the path. Use the cursor to move the vehicle. You can also click at any point along the path to leave a vehicle outline at that point.

- **Chassis outlines:** Select this option to see the internal framework of the vehicle move along the path. Use the cursor to move the framework. You can also click at any point along the path to leave the framework outline at that point.

- **Symbols:** Select this option to display arrows showing the direction of the path.

- **Visibility Sightlines:** Select this option to display linework representing the visibility the driver has at any point.

- **Annotation:** Select this option to display the type of vehicle being used.

Note: If you currently have a graph showing in the drawing, linework will display in the graph to represent the outlines being displayed in the path. Each outline has a letter that corresponds to the graph linework.

Hint: To remove a single outline, move the cursor completely over the outline and click like you are adding a new one. This should remove the existing outline.

Practice 4a

Settings and Analysis

Learning Objectives

- Examine and modify a report for a chosen vehicle path.
- Insert a profile and a graph in the drawing.
- Add outlines of vehicles in critical areas of their paths.

In this practice, you will go through the various settings and tools available for swept paths within the Vehicle Tracking software.

Task 1 - Create reports.

1. Open **Reports.dwg** in the *Autodesk Vehicle Tracking\Working\Settings and Analysis* folder.
2. In the *View* tab>Named Views panel, expand the drop-down list and select **ArcMode**.
3. Select the path in the drawing.
4. On the *Vehicle Tracking* tab>Swept Paths panel, click **Report Wizard**, as shown in Figure 4–18.

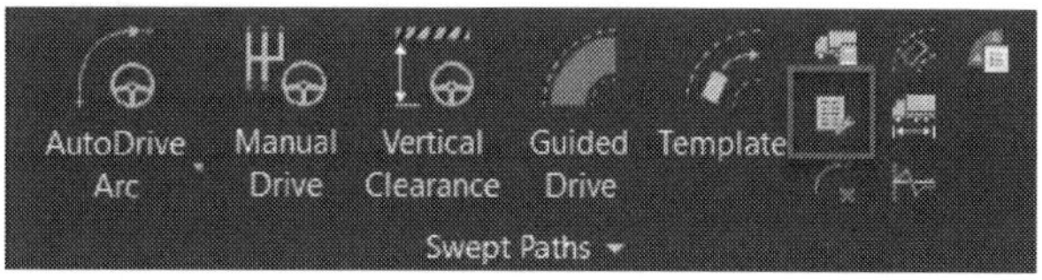
AutoDrive Arc
Manual Drive
Vertical Clearance
Guided Drive
Template
Swept Paths

Figure 4–18

5. Only one report is currently visible in the drawing. Click **New** in the Report Wizard: Start dialog box. Name it **With Hatch** and click **OK**, as shown in Figure 4–19.

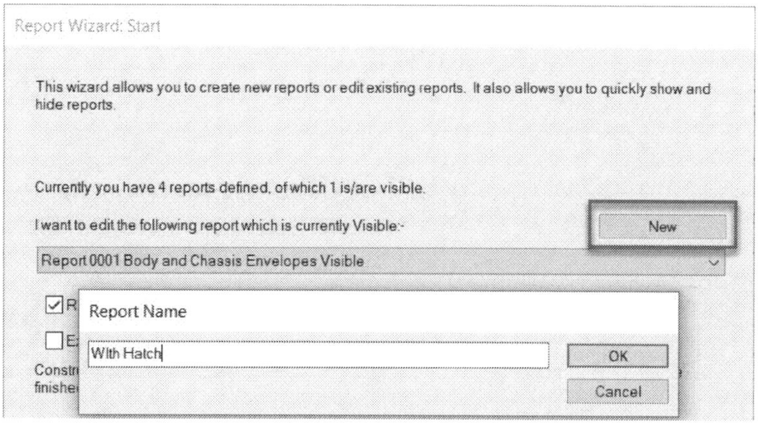
Report Wizard: Start
This wizard allows you to create new reports or edit existing reports. It also allows you to quickly show and hide reports.
Currently you have 4 reports defined, of which 1 is/are visible.
I want to edit the following report which is currently Visible:-
New
Report 0001 Body and Chassis Envelopes Visible
Report Name
WIth Hatch
OK
Cancel

Figure 4–19

6. Click **Next** in the Report Wizard.

7. On the Body Outlines page, select **Hatched**, as shown in Figure 4–20. Click the color box and change it to **Pen 5** (Blue). Click **OK**.

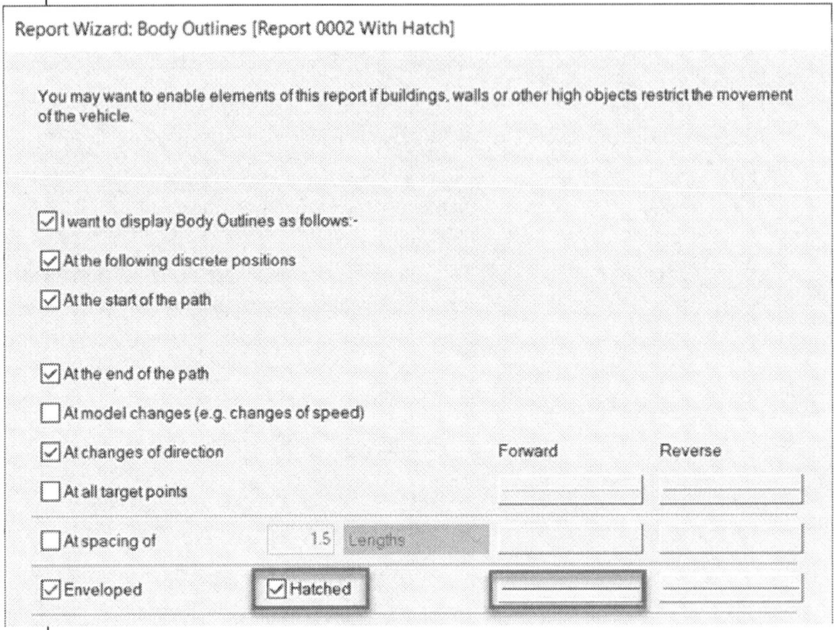

Figure 4–20

8. Click **Next** several times until you land on the Symbols page. Pay attention to each page's contents and options as you go.

9. On the Symbols page, select the **I want to display Symbols as follows** checkbox. Adjust the *At spacing of* to **20** and change the color to **Pen 1** (Red), as shown in Figure 4–21. Click **OK**.

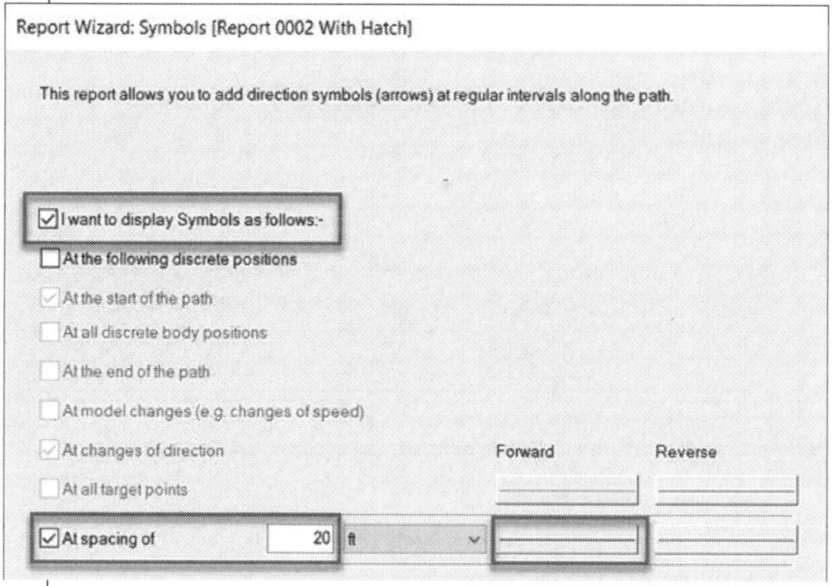

Figure 4–21

10. Click **Next**.

11. Continue to review the rest of the pages, noting what each page offers in contents and options and clicking **Next** to move forward.

12. At the last page, named Finish (when the **Next** button is grayed out), click **Finish**.

13. If you are prompted to make these changes the default, click **No**. This prompt may not show up, depending on your settings.

14. Note the changes made, as shown in Figure 4–22.

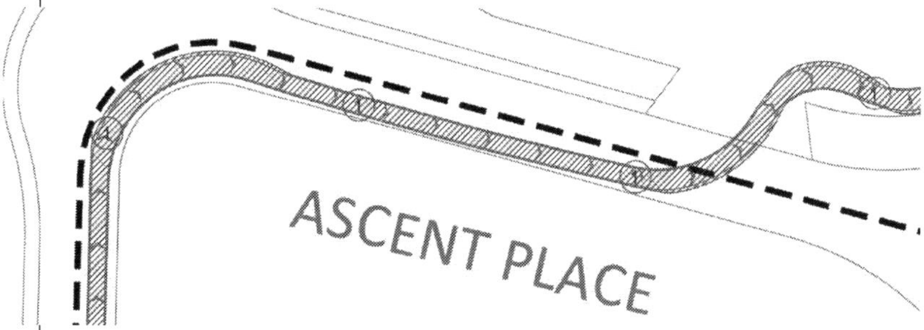

Figure 4–22

15. Select the path again.

16. Launch the **Report Wizard** command again and switch to the original report in the drawing. Verify that the **Report visible** and **Exclusively** options are checked, as shown in Figure 4–23.

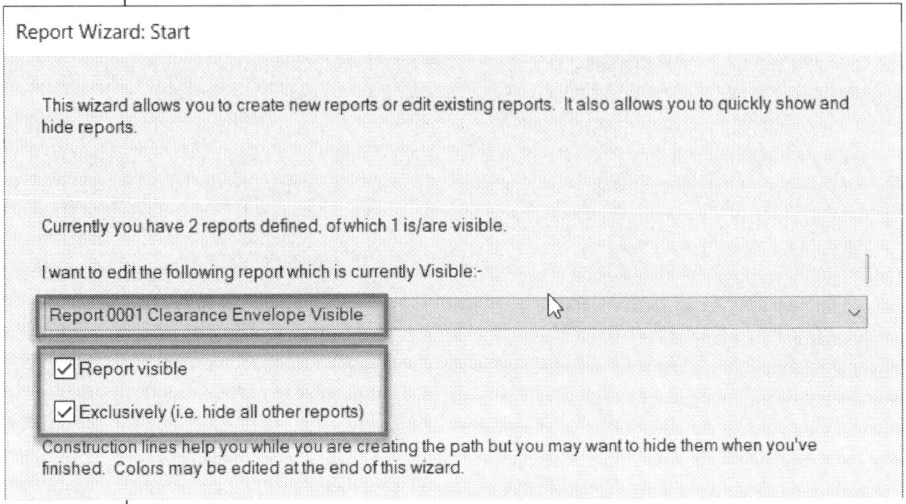
Report Wizard: Start
This wizard allows you to create new reports or edit existing reports. It also allows you to quickly show and hide reports.
Currently you have 2 reports defined, of which 1 is/are visible.
I want to edit the following report which is currently Visible:-
Report 0001 Clearance Envelope Visible
Report visible
Exclusively (i.e. hide all other reports)
Construction lines help you while you are creating the path but you may want to hide them when you've finished. Colors may be edited at the end of this wizard.

Figure 4–23

17. Click **Finish** and say **No** if a dialog box pops up confirming if you want to use this report as a default. Note that the path changed, as shown in Figure 4–24.

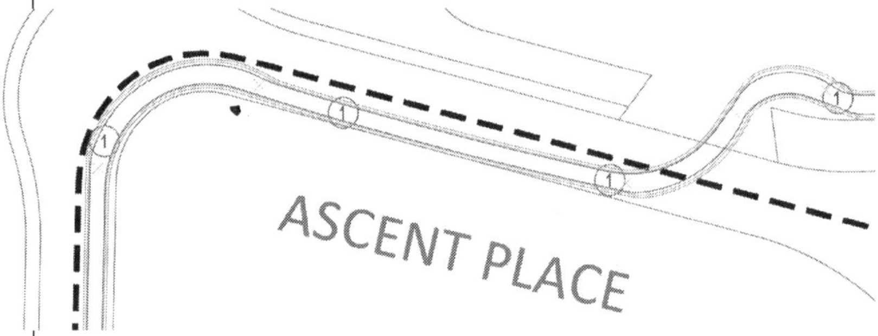
ASCENT PLACE

Figure 4–24

18. (Optional) Repeat this process with a new report and settings of your choosing.

Task 2 - Insert a profile.

1. With the same drawing open, on the Swept Paths panel, click **Insert Profile**, as shown in Figure 4–25.

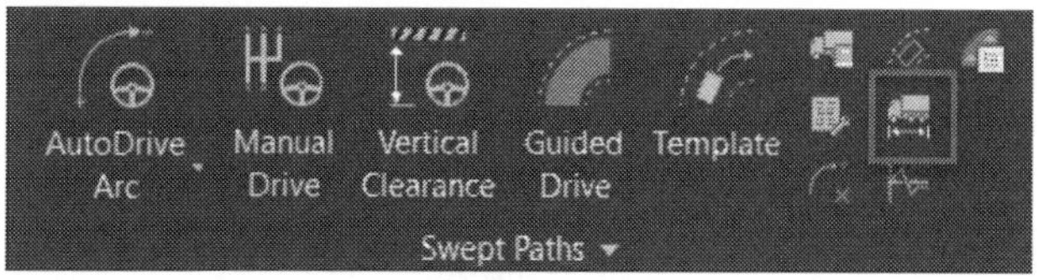

Figure 4–25

2. Select the path in the drawing.
3. When asked to select a location, click inside the rectangle shown in Figure 4–26.

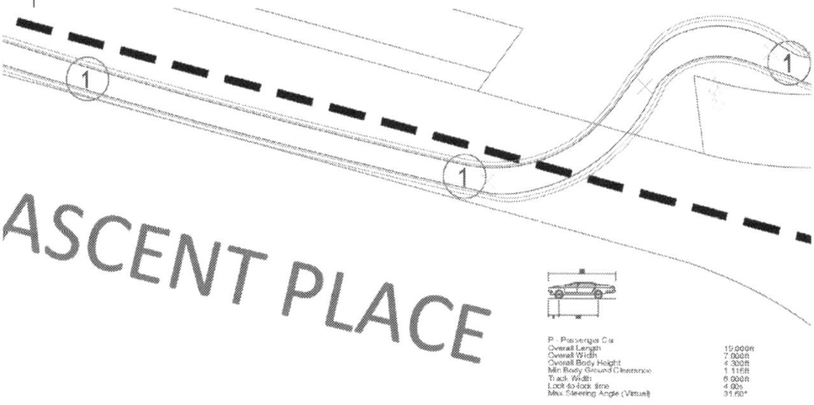

Figure 4–26

4. Review the profile.
5. Press <Esc> to clear the selection.

Task 3 - Insert a graph.

1. With the same drawing open, on the Swept Paths panel, click **Insert Graph**, as show in Figure 4–27.

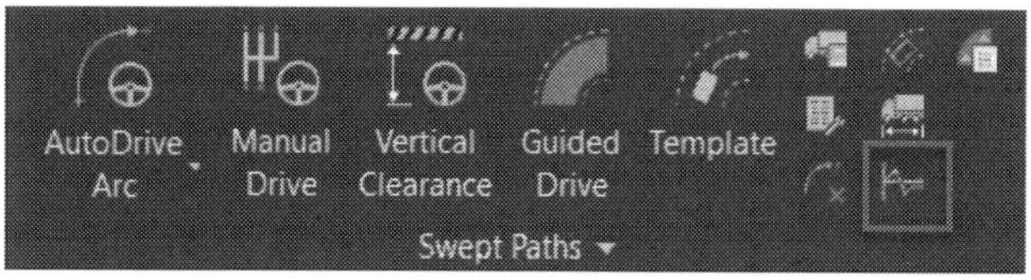

Figure 4–27

2. Select the path in the drawing.

3. When asked to select a location, place the graph in the upper section of the drawing. The graph is drawn, as shown in Figure 4–28.

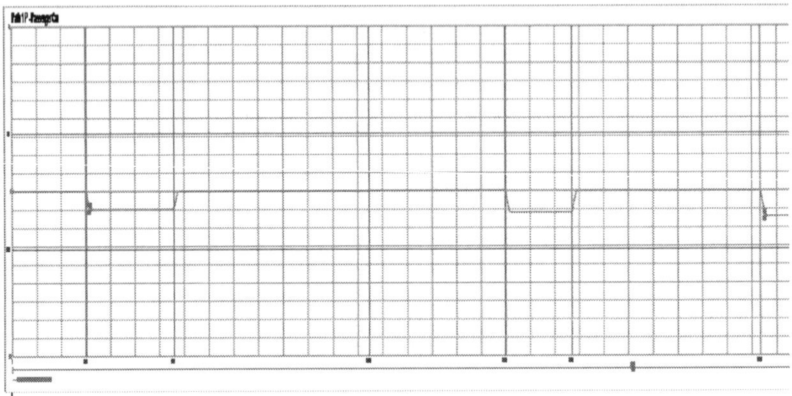

Figure 4–28

4. Zoom in to the graph and review the grips to adjust size and location.

5. Click the minus symbol on the in-canvas controls of the model space viewport. Click **Viewport Configuration List> Two: Horizontal**, as shown in Figure 4–29.

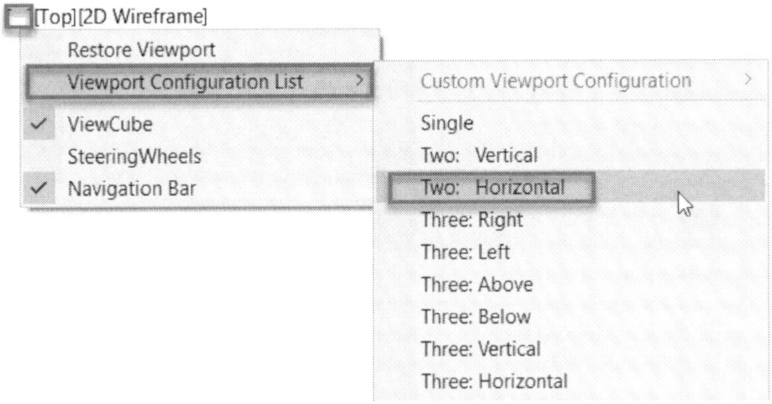

Figure 4–29

6. Two viewports will appear in the model space. Zoom to the top of the path for the top viewport and zoom to the graph for the bottom viewport, as shown in Figure 4–30.

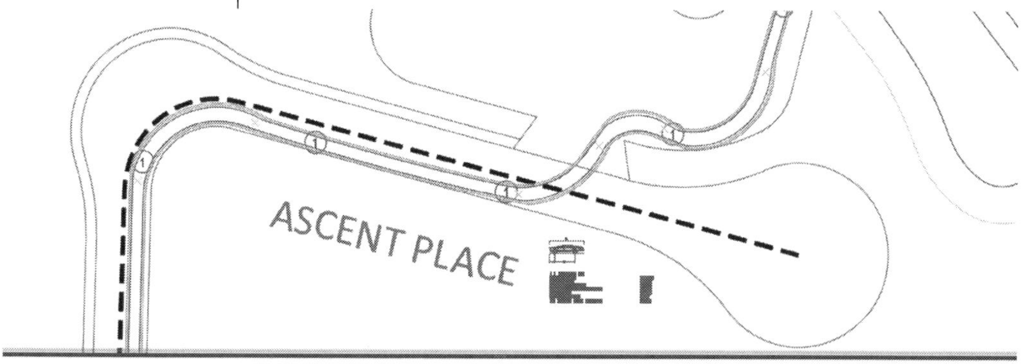

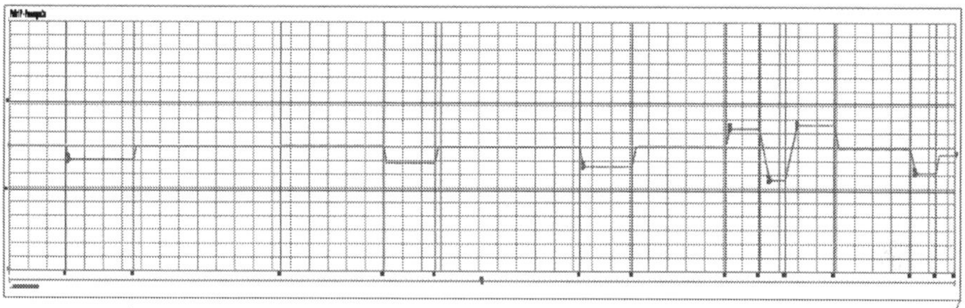

Figure 4–30

7. Modify the path in the top viewport and review the changes in the graph in the bottom viewport.

Task 4 - Add outlines.

1. With the same drawing open, on the Swept Paths panel, click **Place Outlines**, as shown in Figure 4–31.

Figure 4–31

Note: If the viewports are still set as split, click inside the upper viewport, double-click on the (**+**) symbol of the in-canvas controls, and select **Maximize Viewport**.

2. Select the path. The Place / Remove Outline dialog box displays.

3. Select **Body outline (plan)**, as shown in Figure 4–32, and move the cursor to see the outline of the vehicle.

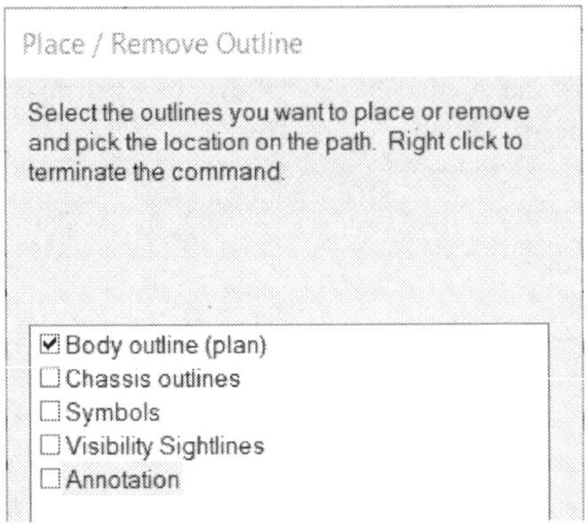

Figure 4–32

4. Uncheck **Body outline (plan)** and turn on one outline type at a time, moving the cursor to see the objects appear on the path.

5. Turn on all outlines and click on the path to hold the settings, as shown in Figure 4–33. Press <Esc>.

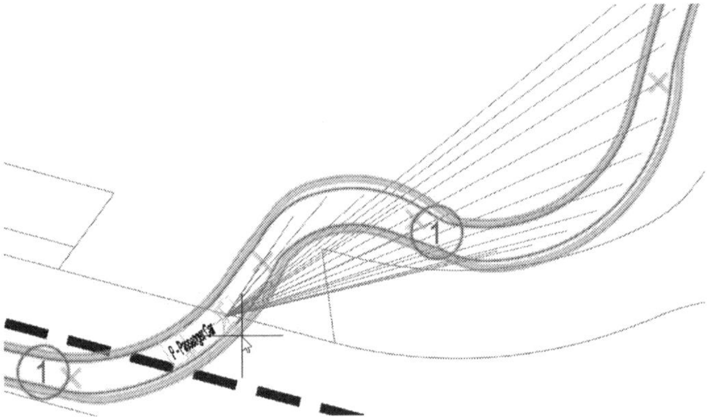

Figure 4–33

6. With the path still selected, launch the **Report Wizard**.

7. Note the changes to the report. As you click through the wizard, click off **Symbols**, **Sightlines**, and **Annotation**, as shown in Figure 4–34.

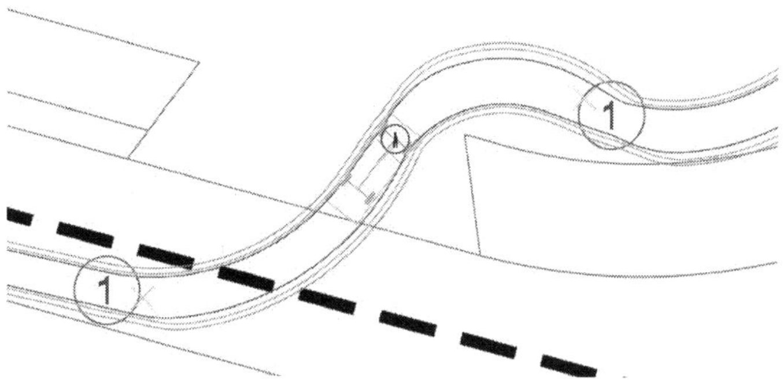

Figure 4–34

8. Click **Finish**. Click **No** if a dialog box pops up confirming if you want to use this report as a default.

4.2 Clearance Check

Vertical Clearance

The **Vertical Clearance** command is used to verify that vehicles can follow a path vertically. So far, we have only looked at whether the vehicle stays within a horizontal region; now we need to verify that the vehicle does not hit the ground and stays within vertical constraints. The **Vertical Clearance** command is found on the Swept Paths panel of the *Vehicle Tracking* tab (shown in Figure 4–35).

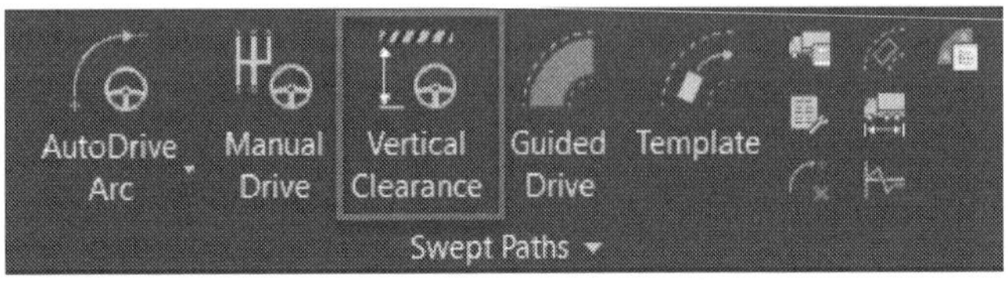

Figure 4–35

A Civil 3D profile will need to be used to execute this command. Once the command is launched, select the profile and a vertical representation of the path is placed along the profile, as shown in Figure 4–36. It is helpful to place a vehicle outline and move the car down the profile to identify problem spots.

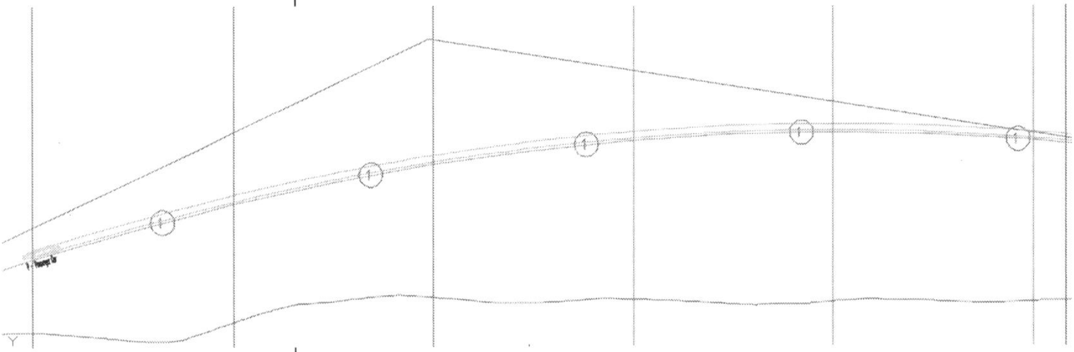

Figure 4–36

As you zoom in, you will note any grounding or overhead impacts with other structures. Warning symbols will also display. As you can see in Figure 4–37, the vehicle is running into the ground. This vehicle will not work along this profile.

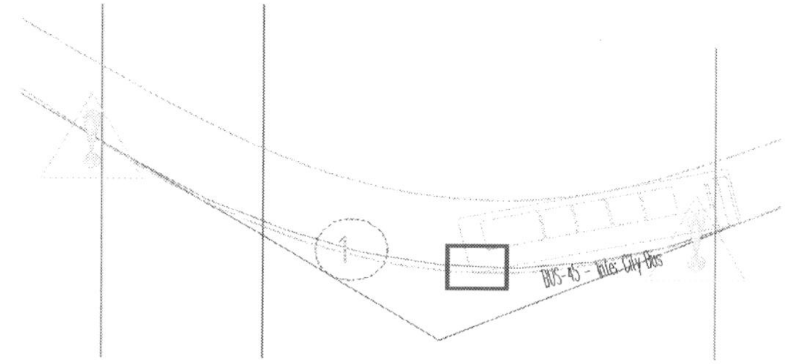

Figure 4–37

Note: The Civil 3D profile must be set to 1:1 for the path to show correctly within the profile. No vertical exaggeration shall be added.

Ground Clearance

The **Ground Conflict** report is used to verify that you have proper ground clearance in your design. Consider the fact that a transport truck has a wide width turn. Even though the horizontal clearance is acceptable, there might be an issue with ground clearance. The transport truck may be crossing the crown of the road as well as the outside lane at the same time. Will the transport truck hit the ground at this point?

The **Insert Ground Conflict Report** command is found on the *Vehicle Tracking* tab>Swept Paths panel (shown in Figure 4–38). After launching the command, select the path and hatch patterns will appear, identifying problems spots.

Figure 4–38

Note: A CAD system that supports surfaces, such as Civil 3D, should be used to use this tool accurately. Otherwise, the analysis will be performed on a flat plane. If no surface is along the path, a dialog box will prompt for a surface to be used.

Vehicle Tracking will clearly identify the locations that are in danger of hitting or have hit the ground. These will be indicated with ground proximity contours, as shown in Figure 4–39. The contours are drawn 50mm (2 inches) apart and use the following color scheme:

- More than 100mm ground clearance: clear
- Between 50mm and 100mm ground clearance: green
- Between zero and 50mm ground clearance: yellow
- Between zero and 50mm ground penetration: orange
- Between 50mm and 100mm ground penetration: magenta
- More than 100mm ground penetration: red

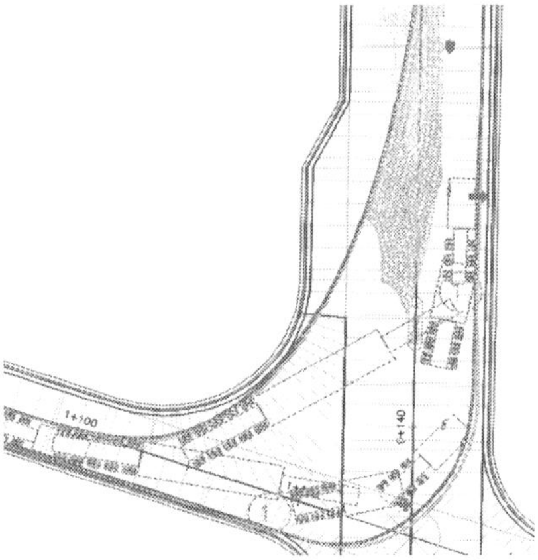

Figure 4–39

At each critical point of maximum ground penetration or minimum ground clearance, a label will be placed with the value of penetration or clearance.

A profile, or cross-section, will also automatically be generated at each critical point, as shown in Figure 4–40. The precise critical point will also be indicated on these profiles.

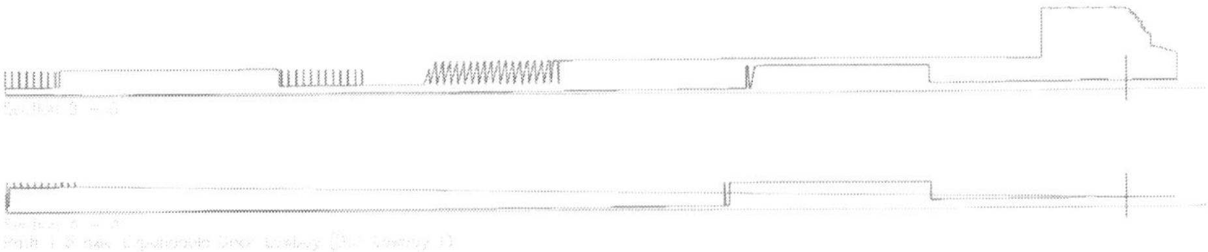

Figure 4–40

Note: The profiles are usually found in the far right corner of the drawing's extents.

Practice 4b Checking Clearance

Learning Objectives

- Check for vertical clearance in vertical profiles or simple polylines representing a profile.
- Determine if there is adequate ground clearance when surfaces are present.

In this practice, you will investigate if certain vehicles have enough clearance to pass over a vertical change in slope. Then, you will check if there is enough clearance when a finish ground surface exists.

Note: Civil 3D is required for this practice. If you do not have access to Civil 3D, skip this practice.

Task 1 - Check vertical clearance.

1. Open **Clearance.dwg** in the *Autodesk Vehicle Tracking\Working\Settings and Analysis* folder.
2. In the *View* tab>Named Views panel, expand the drop-down list and select **Vert Clearance**.
3. On the *Vehicle Tracking* tab>Swept Paths panel, click **Vertical Clearance**, as shown in Figure 4–41.

Figure 4–41

4. In the dialog box asking if you want to use the default vehicle, click **No**.

5. In the Vehicle Library Explorer, select the **P/B - Car and Boat Trailer** (as shown in Figure 4–42) and click **Proceed**.

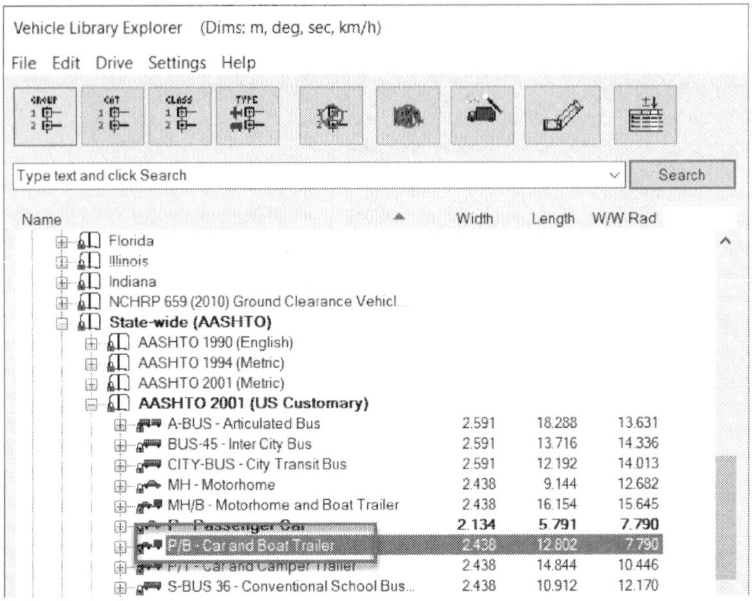

Figure 4–42

6. Select the level part of the polyline shown in the view, as shown in Figure 4–43.

Figure 4–43

7. Click **OK** and **Yes** in the next two dialog boxes that appear.

8. You will note that the path does not fully create because the vehicle runs ground before reaching the curve, as shown in Figure 4–44.

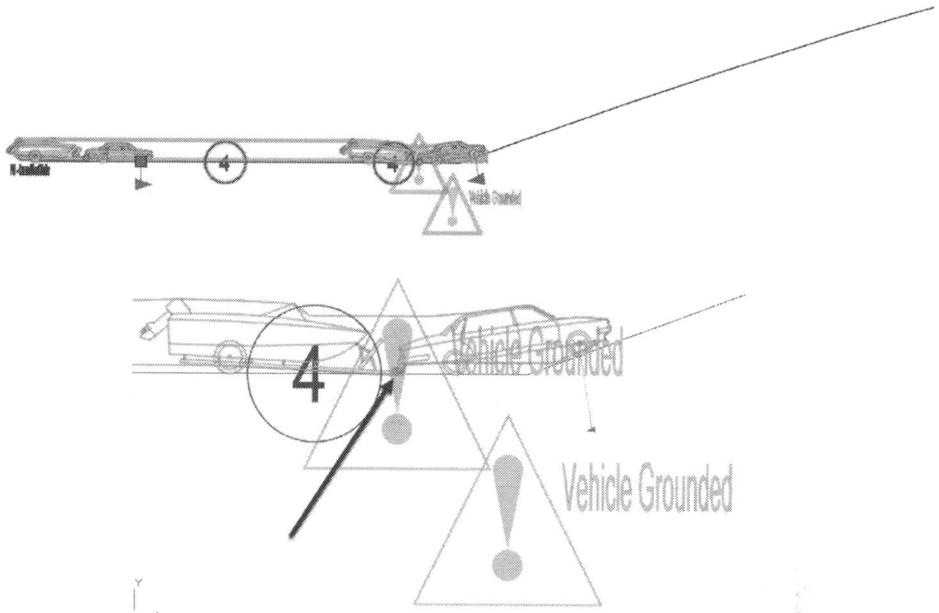

Figure 4–44

9. Delete the path and launch the **Vertical Clearance** command again.

10. Click **No** for using the default vehicle. In the Vehicle Library Explorer, select the **City Transit Bus** under *US Design Vehicles>Indiana>INDOT IDM 2013*, as shown in Figure 4–45. Click **Proceed**.

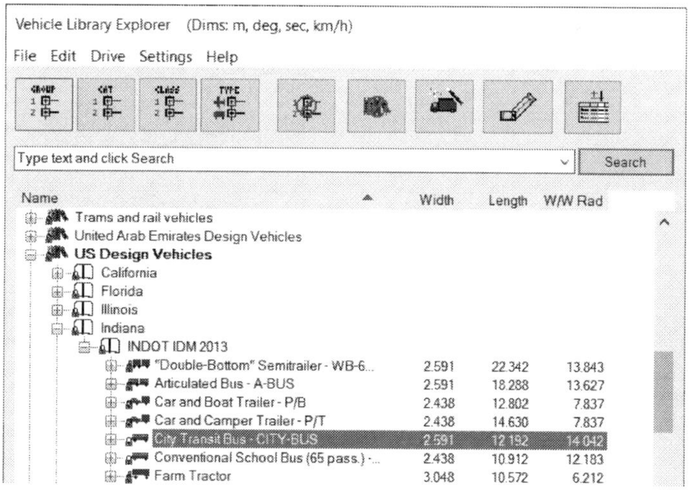

Figure 4–45

11. Select the polyline and click **Yes** in the dialog box that opens.

12. This time, the path created fully; however, you will note that there are warnings at the start of the curve, as shown in Figure 4–46.

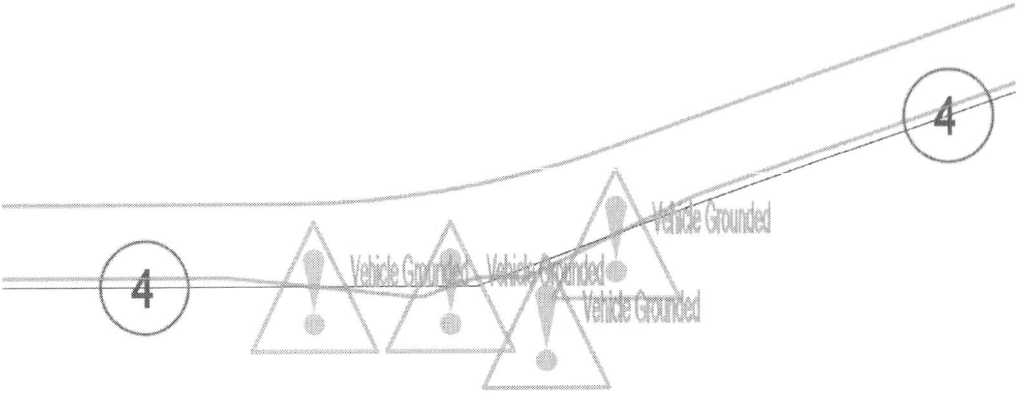

Figure 4–46

13. Launch the **Place Outline** command and move the outline along the path to see where the vehicle hits or comes close to hitting ground, as shown in Figure 4–47.

Figure 4–47

Task 2 - Check ground clearance.

1. Continue working in the same drawing.
2. In the *View* tab>Named Views panel, expand the drop-down list and select **Conflict**.
3. Select Path #4 in the drawing, as shown in Figure 4–48.

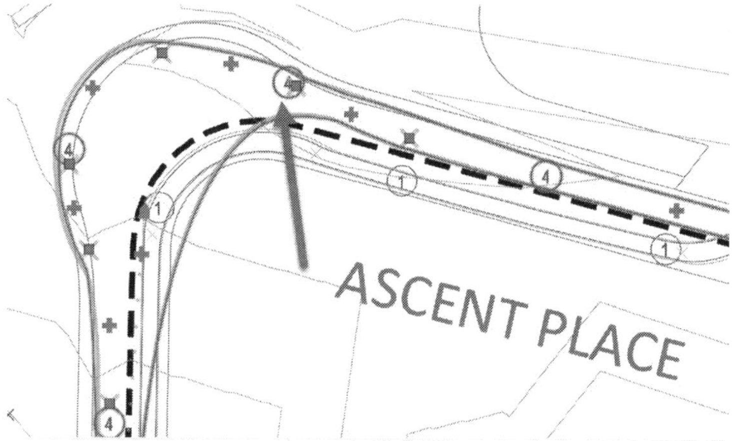

Figure 4–48

4. On the *Vehicle Tracking* tab>Swept Paths panel, click **Place Outline**, as shown in Figure 4–49.

Figure 4–49

5. In the Place / Remove Outline dialog box, select only **Body outline (plan)** and **Annotation**; leave the other options unchecked.

6. Move the vehicle outline along the path. Note the wide turn the semi must make, as shown in Figure 4–50.

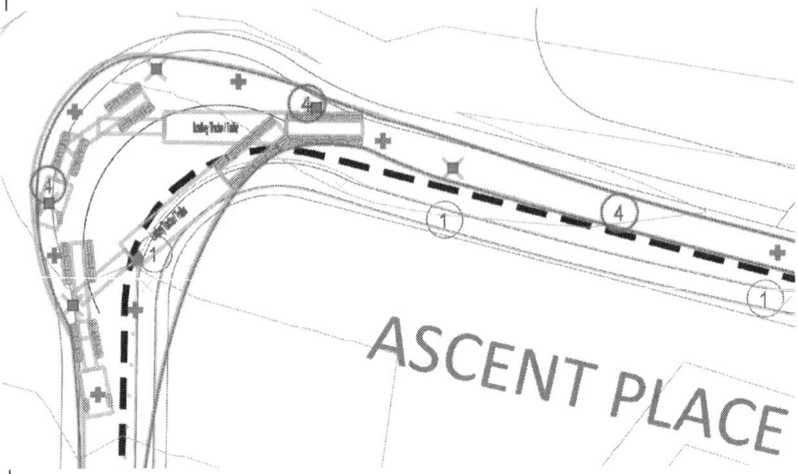

Figure 4–50

7. Press <Esc>.

8. On the *Vehicle Tracking* tab>Swept Paths panel, click **Insert Ground Conflict Report**, as shown in Figure 4–51.

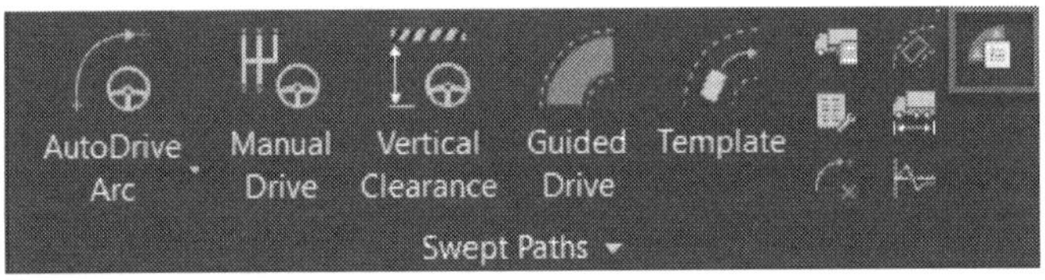

Figure 4–51

9. Select Path #4 again.

10. In the Assign Surfaces to Path dialog box, select **Existing-Site** for the *Existing Surface* and **FG** for the *Final Surface*, as shown in Figure 4–52.

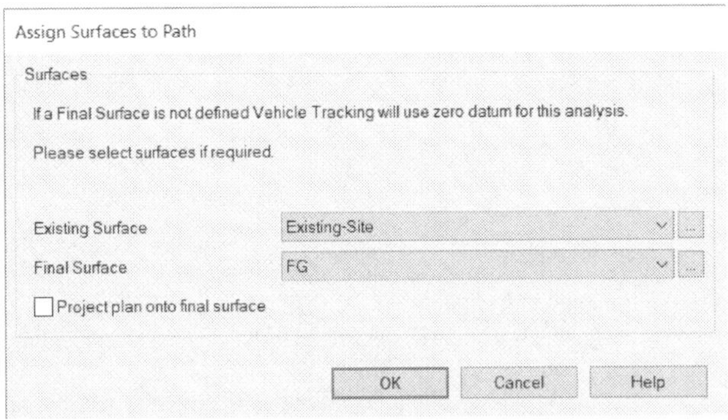

Figure 4–52

11. Click **Yes** in the ensuing dialog box.

12. Press <Esc> to clear the selection.

13. Zoom to the area with green and yellow hatching, as shown in Figure 4–53, and review the labels.

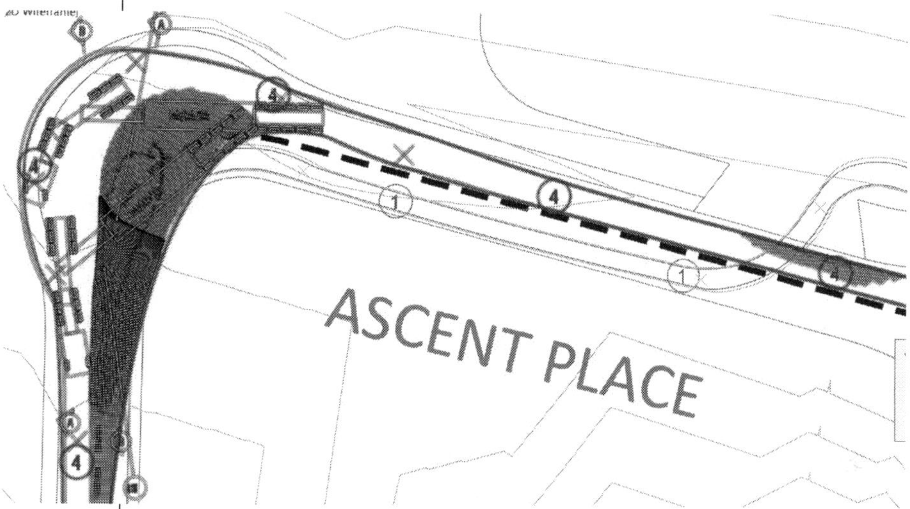

Figure 4–53

14. In the *View* tab>Named Views panel, expand the drop-down list and select **Conflict-Profile**.

15. Review the profiles, as shown in Figure 4–54.

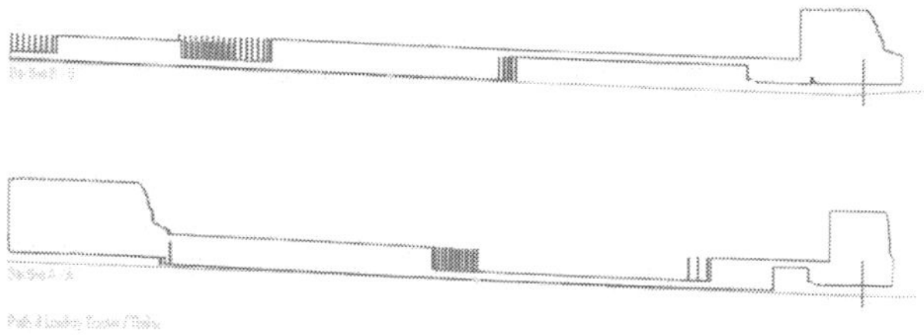

Figure 4–54

4.3 Animation Tools

The visualization tools within Vehicle Tracking provide a means to analyze and present our vehicle maneuvers from any vantage point the project requires, including the driver's side mirrors.

The **Animate** command is found on the Review panel of the ribbon, as shown in Figure 4–55.

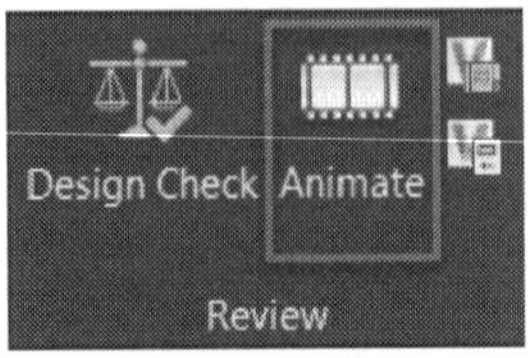

Figure 4–55

When the command is launched, a dialog box displays with all of the controls used to produce animations, as shown in Figure 4–56.

Figure 4–56

1. Reset
2. Play Backward (click to start and stop command)
3. Single Step Backward
4. Single Step Forward
5. Play (click to start and stop command)
6. Fast Forward
7. Loop Indefinitely
8. Record (creates an .AVI movie)
9. Settings
10. Snapshot (creates a .JPEG file)
11. Animate in 3D
12. Fly-By Camera

When creating a .AVI, whether in 2D or 3D, a dialog box displays with frame, length, and view settings, as shown in Figure 4–57.

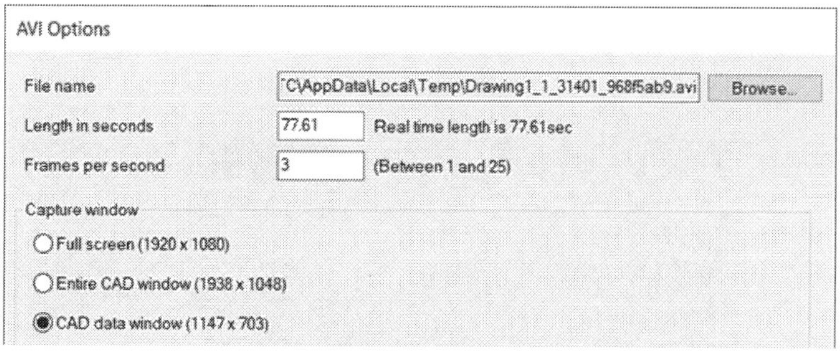

Figure 4–57

Several settings are available for 3D visualization and speed control. See Figure 4–58 for setting options.

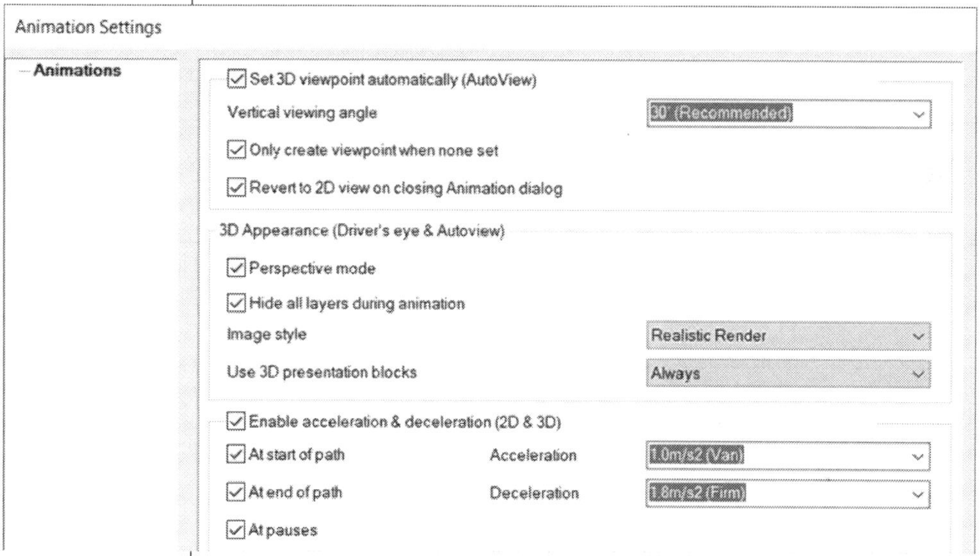

Figure 4–58

The **Animation** command can be used to visualize the movement of the car in 2D and 3D. Many times, a 2D representation is hard for people to visualize. You can present your analysis in a more lifelike fashion by quickly creating an animation. Once the path is completed, you can take the results vertical, showing a drive-through of the approach in 3D.

Click the **Animate in 3D** button or **Fly-By Camera** options to switch to a 3D environment. Click the **Animate in 3D** button again to move back to 2D.

A typical view in 3D is shown in Figure 4–59.

Figure 4–59

When using the Fly-By Camera, the Camera Control dialog box will launch, as shown in Figure 4–60. This dialog box lets you control the view of the vehicle as it moves. Adjust the settings as the vehicle is moving.

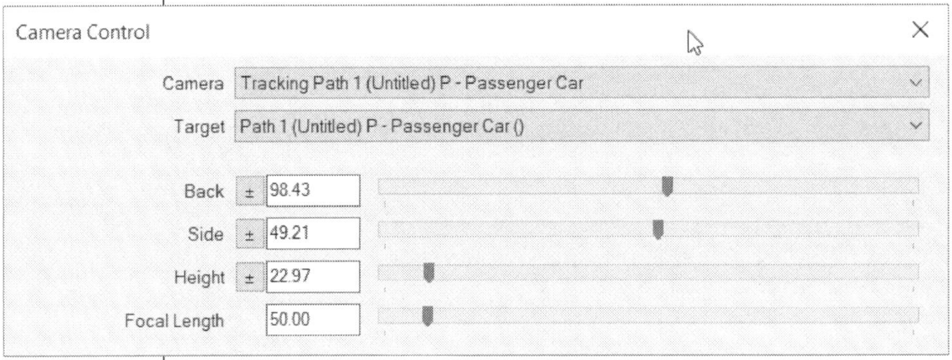

Figure 4–60

The adjustments are done in real-time. You can even adjust the *Back* to have a rearview mirror effect, as shown in Figure 4–61.

View from the front

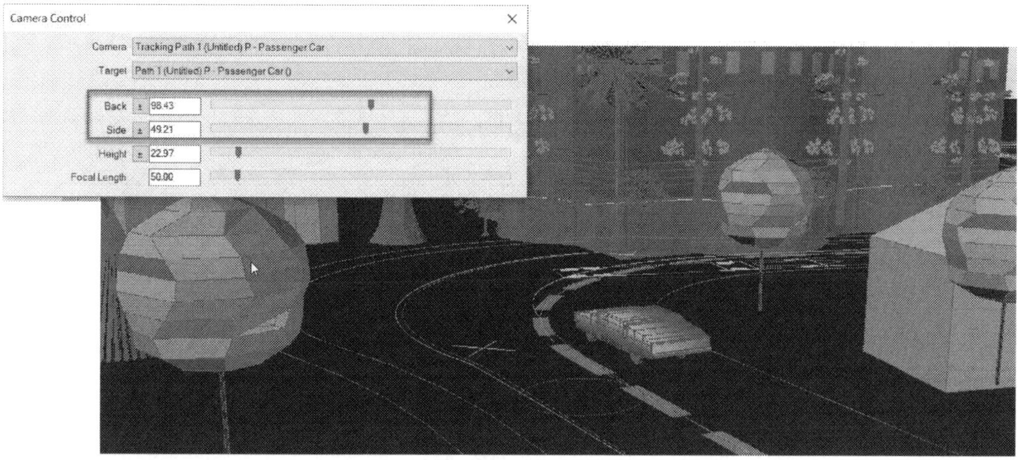

View from the rear (car in same position)

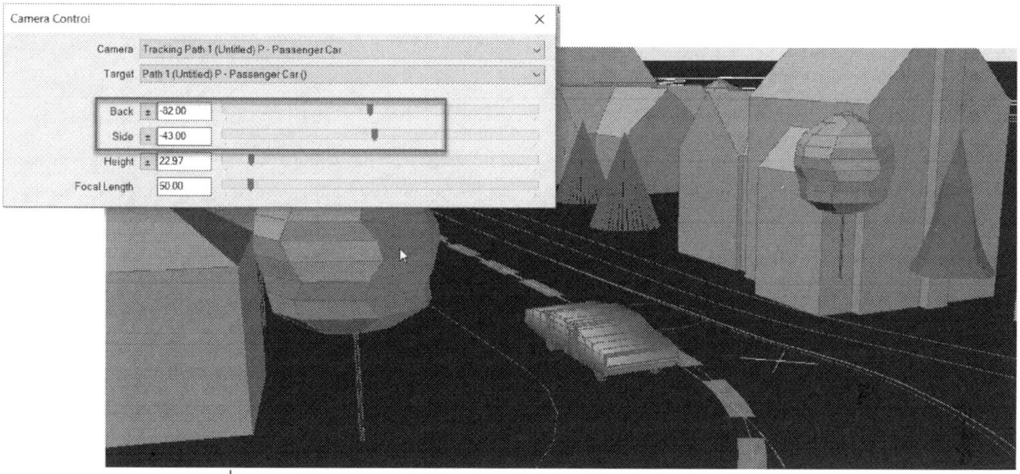

Figure 4–61

Click the **Advanced** button of the Vehicle Tracking Animation dialog box (shown in Figure 4–62) for more options.

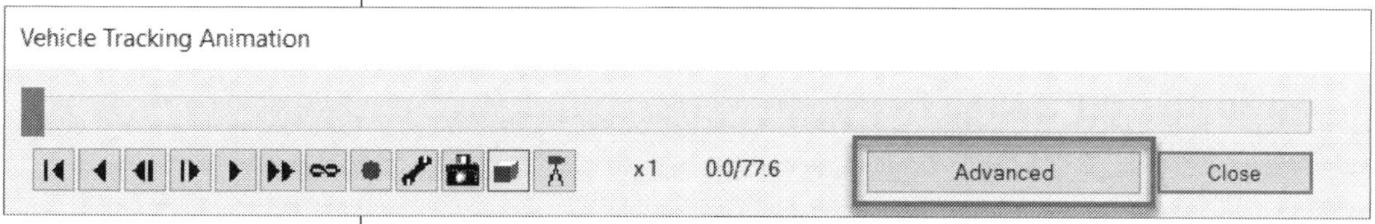

Figure 4–62

Paths will be displayed in rows once the **Advanced** button is selected, as shown in Figure 4–63. Each row represents the movement of the vehicle, which is represented by the following color scheme:

- Blue: Acceleration
- Green: At Speed
- Yellow: Slowing Down
- Red: Stopped

Note: To display multiple paths in the dialog box, make sure all paths are selected.

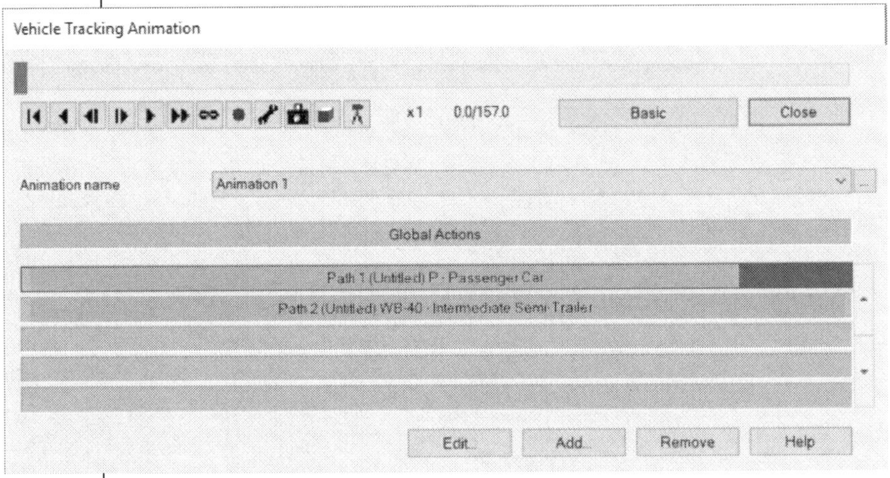

Figure 4–63

Click **Add** or **Edit** to adjust the movement of the vehicle. Add acceleration, deceleration, stops, and starts at any point along the path. If you have multiple paths, this tool can be used to resolve conflicts of vehicles passing within the same path area at the same time during animation, as shown in Figure 4–64.

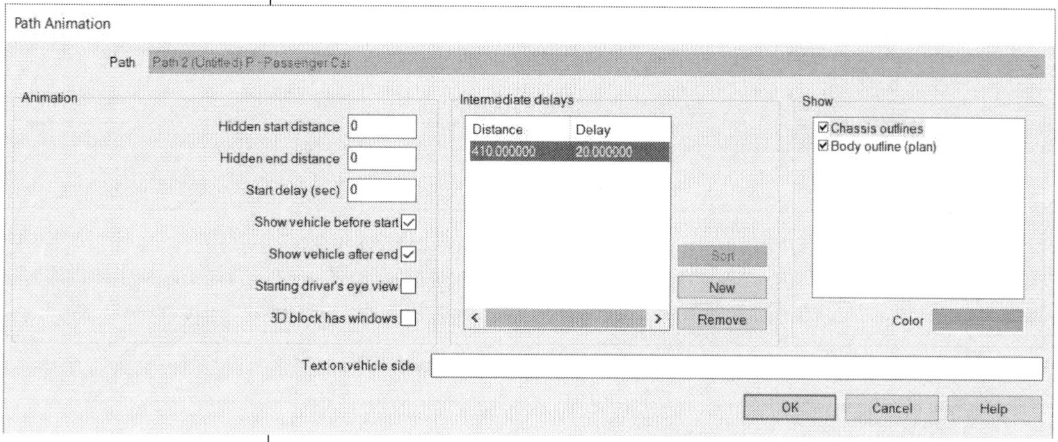

Figure 4–64

Note that Figure 4–65 shows a collision between two vehicles. This will need to be corrected.

Figure 4–65

Practice 4c Working with Animations

Learning Objectives

- Create a simple animation of a vehicle driving.
- Study the effect of two vehicles traveling along the same road.

In this practice, you will examine a vehicle driving along a path in real-time from a variety of vantage points. Then, you will take note of a second vehicle to study their interactions.

1. Open **Animations.dwg** in the *Autodesk Vehicle Tracking\ Working\Settings and Analysis* folder.

2. In the *View* tab>Named Views panel, expand the drop-down list and select **ArcMode**.

3. On the *Vehicle Tracking* tab>Review panel, click **Animate**, as shown in Figure 4–66.

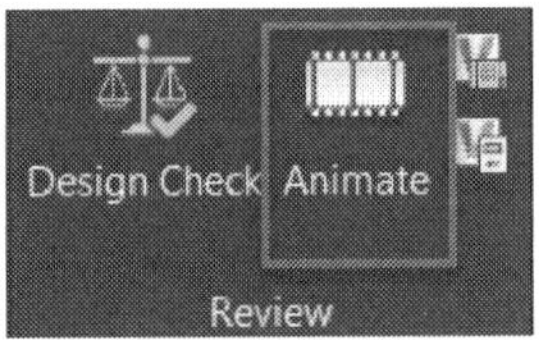

Figure 4–66

4. Click the **Settings** button in the Vehicle Tracking Animation dialog box, as shown in Figure 4–67.

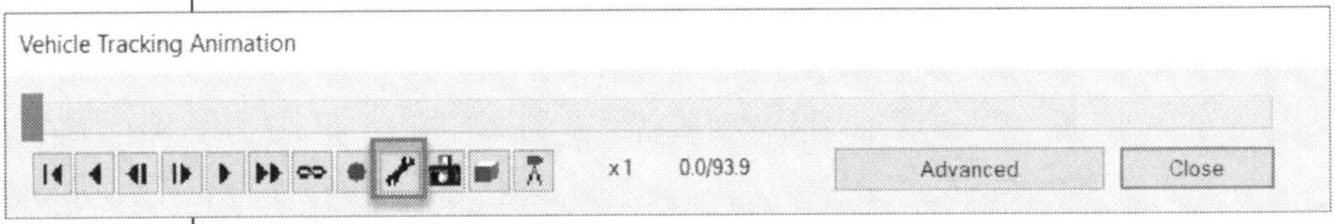

Figure 4–67

5. In the Animation Settings dialog box, change the *Acceleration* to **Car** (as shown in Figure 4–68) and click **OK**.

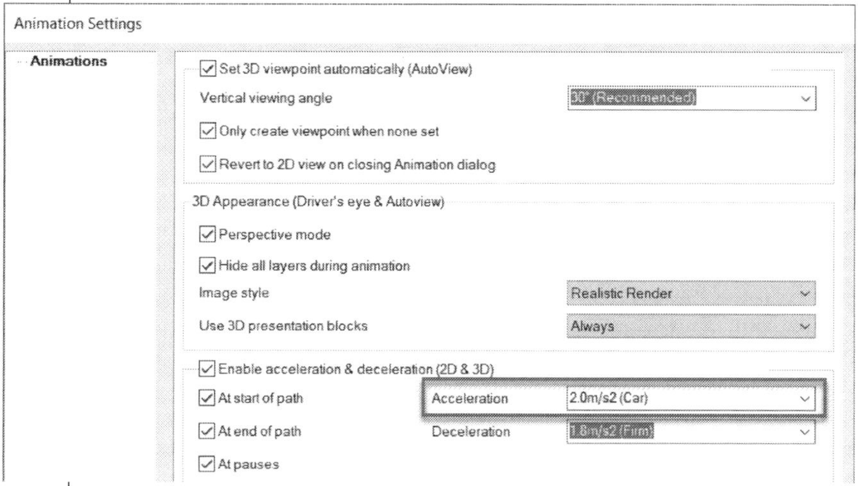

Figure 4–68

6. In the Vehicle Tracking Animation dialog box, click **Fly-By Camera**, as shown in Figure 4–69.

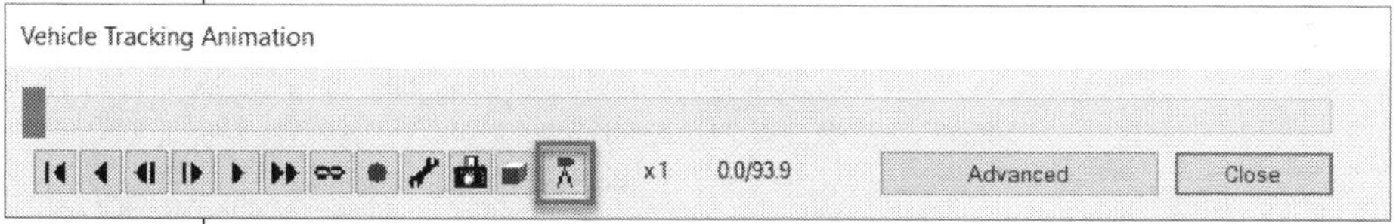

Figure 4–69

7. Adjust the camera control as follows (as shown in Figure 4–70):
   - *Back:* **134**
   - *Side:* **35**
   - *Height:* **15**
   - *Focal Length:* **90**

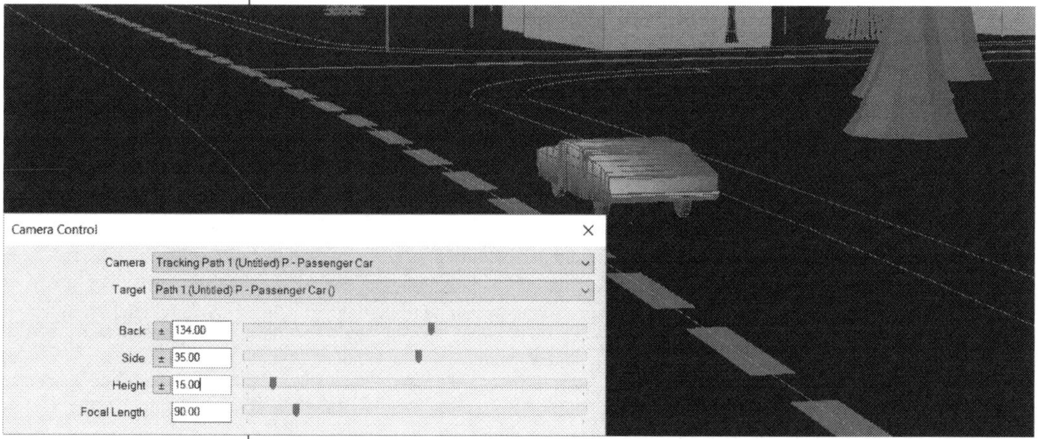

Figure 4–70

8. Click **Play** in the Vehicle Tracking Animation dialog box, as shown in Figure 4–71. Control the speed using the **Fast Forward** button.

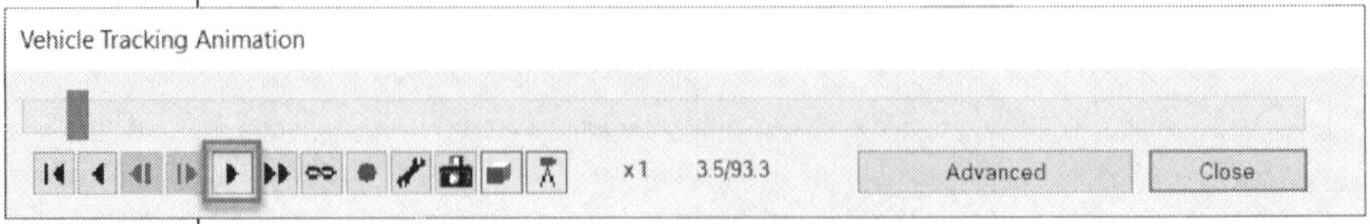

Figure 4–71

9. As you follow the car, around the **88** mark, you will collide with the oncoming truck, as shown in Figure 4–72.

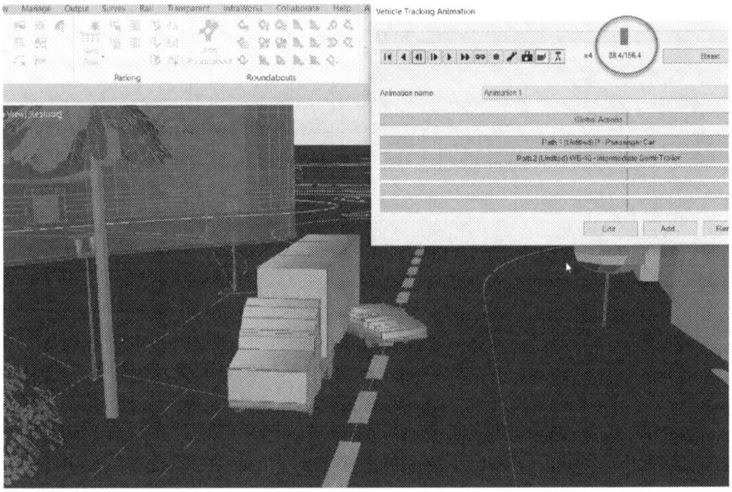

Figure 4–72

10. Pause the playback at that moment (or use the slider to move to that time frame) and adjust the camera controls to have a better view of the collision.

11. In order to avoid the collision, you will need to delay the start of either the truck or the car or have the car yield for the oncoming truck. You will use the yield method.

12. In the Vehicle Tracking Animation dialog box, click **Advanced**, as shown in Figure 4–73.

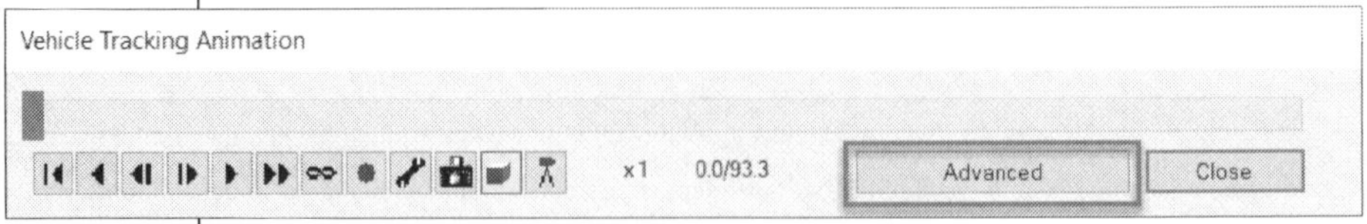

Figure 4–73

13. Move the cursor to be set near the **85** mark. Select the passenger car path (**Path 1**), then click **Edit**, as shown in Figure 4–74.

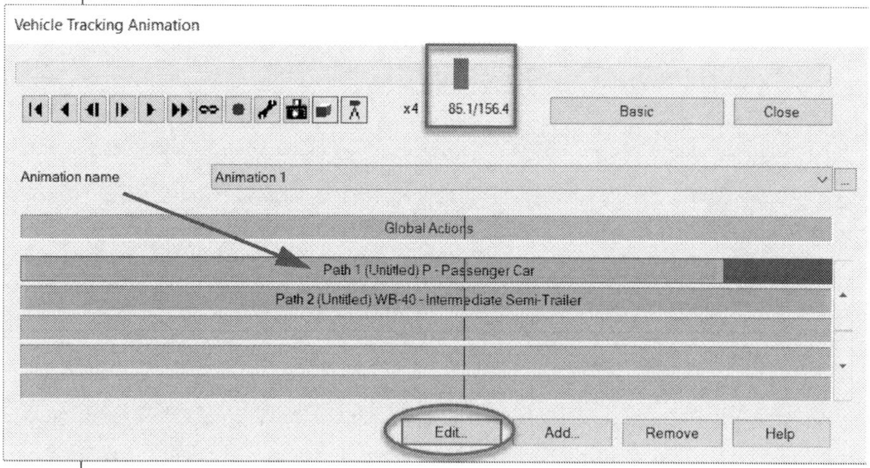

Figure 4–74

14. In the Path Animation dialog box, click **New** and set the delay to **10**, as shown in Figure 4–75. Click **OK**.

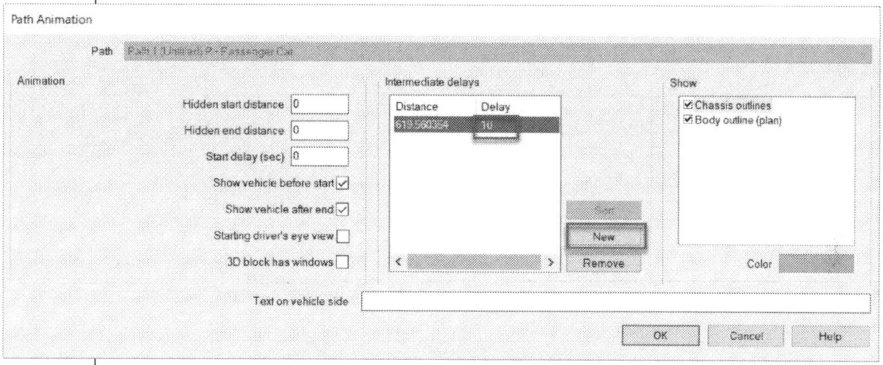

Figure 4–75

15. Move the animation cursor back to the beginning and click **Play**.

16. Note the delay that occurs while the truck approaches.

17. In the Vehicle Tracking Animation dialog box, click **Record**, as shown in Figure 4–76.

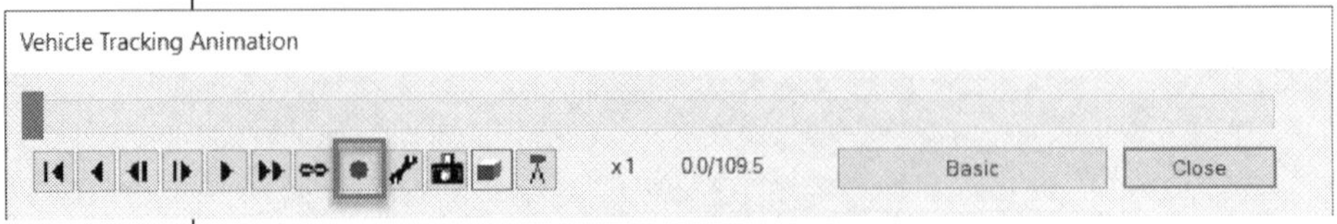

Figure 4–76

18. Browse to the *Autodesk Vehicle Tracking\Working\Settings and Analysis* folder to save the file and name it **Ascent-Place Traffic**. Leave all default settings, as shown in Figure 4–77, and click **OK**.

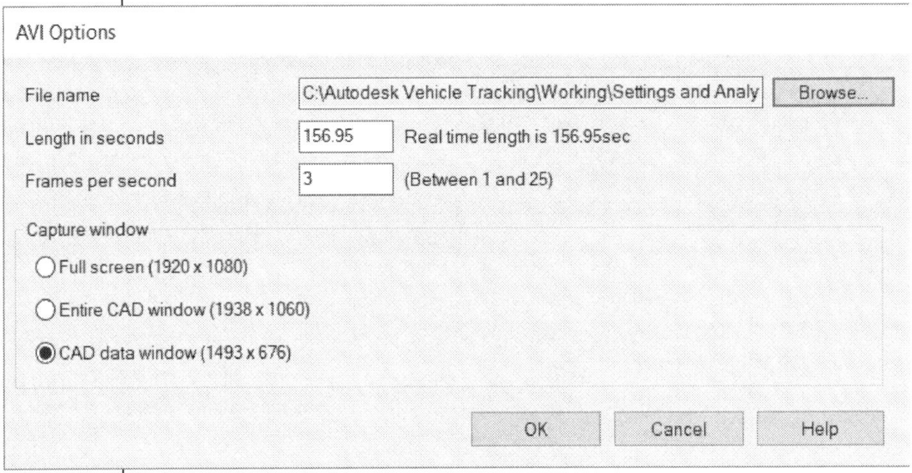

Figure 4–77

19. If the Video Compression dialog box displays, accept the default value and click **OK**.

20. Review the .AVI created.

21. Save the drawing.

Chapter Review Questions

1. In Vehicle Tracking, what are reports used for? (Select all that apply.)
    a. To list the amount of clearance vehicles have over a terrain.
    b. To display or hide different parts of Vehicle Tracking objects.
    c. To control the layers and colors of Vehicle Tracking objects.
    d. To display where errors such as oversteering occur.
2. In Vehicle Tracking, what are graphs used for?
    a. To examine if there is enough vertical clearance in a profile graph.
    b. To display where errors such as oversteering occur.
    c. To position the camera during animating vehicle paths.
    d. To help create or edit a vehicle.
3. Animations of vehicles moving along a path can be played forwards or backwards.
    a. True
    b. False
    c. Depends on the path type

Parking Lots

In this chapter, you will learn about the Parking Lot tools within Autodesk® Vehicle Tracking. Vehicle Tracking contains the features you need to optimize the layout as well as maintain a geometric standard that you can set with respect to bay width, driving aisles, and accessible spaces. Editing options are available as well, and as you make changes to the layout, you see the dynamic nature of the objects and the adherence to design standards.

Learning Objectives in This Chapter

- Navigate the Parking Standard Explorer.
- Create parking lots using various row options.
- Edit parking lots using grips and other commands.
- Add access roads to the design.

5.1 Creating Parking Lots

Parking Standard Explorer

All parking layouts are created in accordance with defined rules or standards. The Parking Standard Explorer holds a number of such standards from several countries. The **Parking Standard Explorer** command is found on the Parking Lot panel of the *Vehicle Tracking* tab (shown in Figure 5–1).

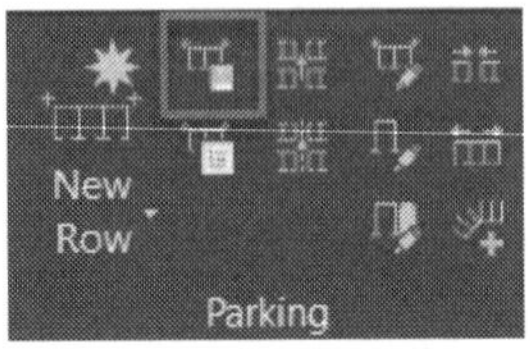

Figure 5–1

When the command is launched, the Parking Standard Explorer dialog box opens. All standards are grouped by nationality, and custom standards can be created as well. By right-clicking on a specific standard, you can view, edit a copy, or create a new standard.

All three options open the Parking Standard dialog box. This dialog box has many tabs, as shown in Figure 5–2.

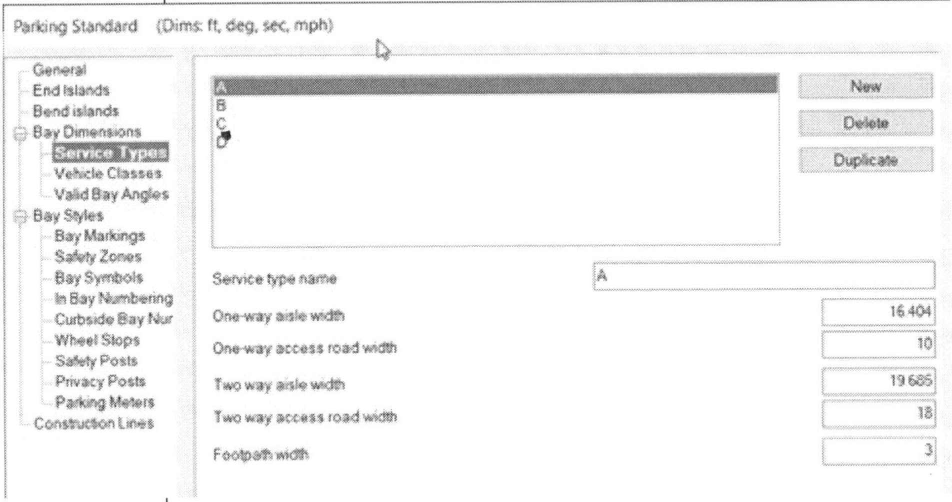

Figure 5–2

Note: You may have noticed there is not an Edit option for existing standards. To ensure that the details do not change arbitrarily, there are restrictions on who can edit them. These restrictions require that users identify themselves if they wish to access a standard to make changes. No password is needed simply to use a standard.

Once you have identified which standard will be used, set this standard as default for future use.

For custom-made parking standards, you can open the parking standard, right-click, and select **Edit**, then make changes in the Parking Standard dialog box. Note that the changes are made in real-time on the screen.

Creating Rows

There are two options for creating new parking lot rows: **New Row** and **Parallel Row**. Both are found in the New Row drop-down list on the Parking panel of the ribbon, as shown in Figure 5–3.

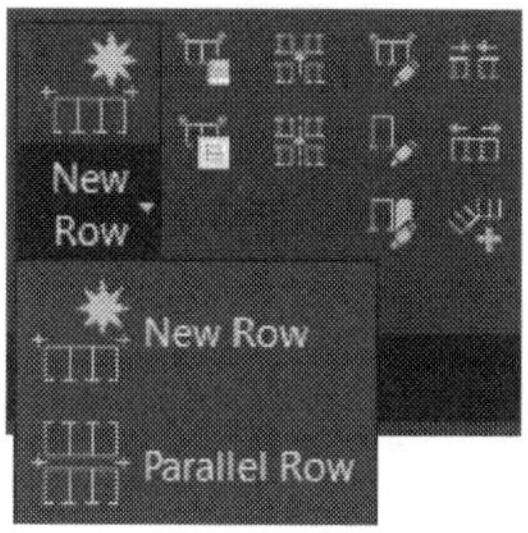

Figure 5–3

When launching either the **New Row** or **Parallel Row** command, the Parking Row Properties dialog box opens, as shown in Figure 5–4. In this dialog box, set the following:

- Type of bay being used
    - Whether the bay is **Left only**, **Right only**, or on **Both** sides
    - Type of car being used
    - Flow direction of the vehicles

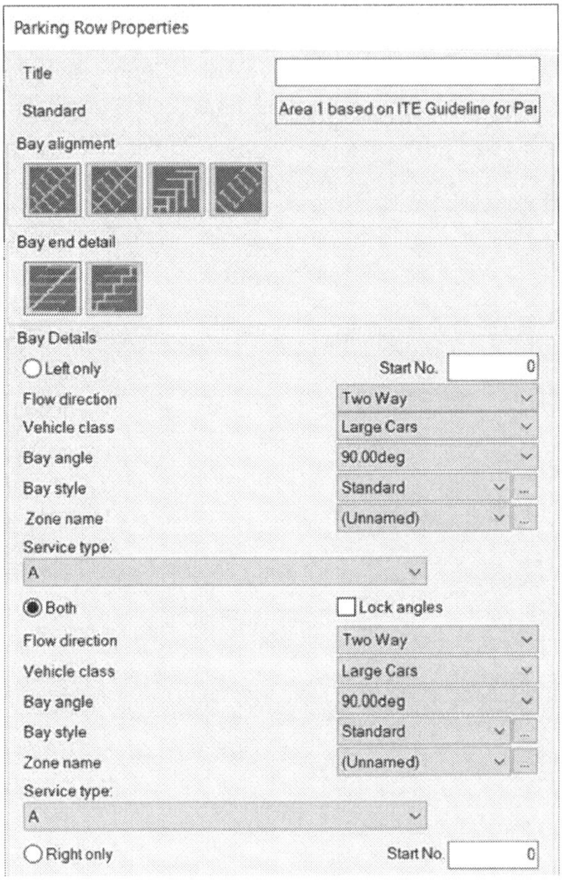

Figure 5–4

The *Islands & Footpaths* area of the Parking Row Properties dialog box (shown in Figure 5–5) determines the following:

- Whether footpaths are used
- The width of the footpaths
- Whether islands are being added

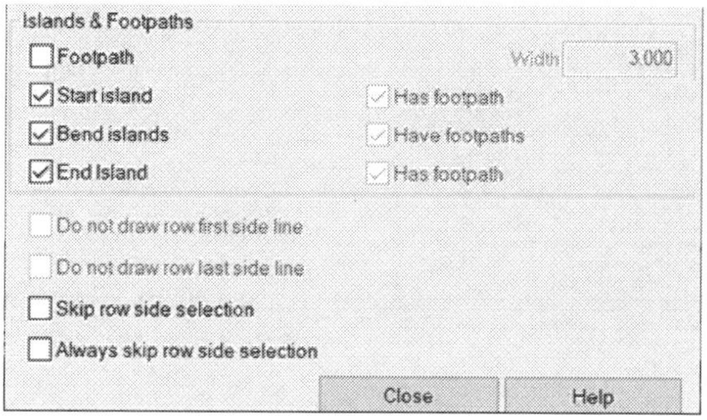

Figure 5–5

New Row

For the **New Row** command, once the settings are set, begin the layout by clicking end points of the parking lot. As you draw the parking lot (as shown in Figure 5–6), the Parking Row Properties dialog box stays open for you to add adjustments as you continue.

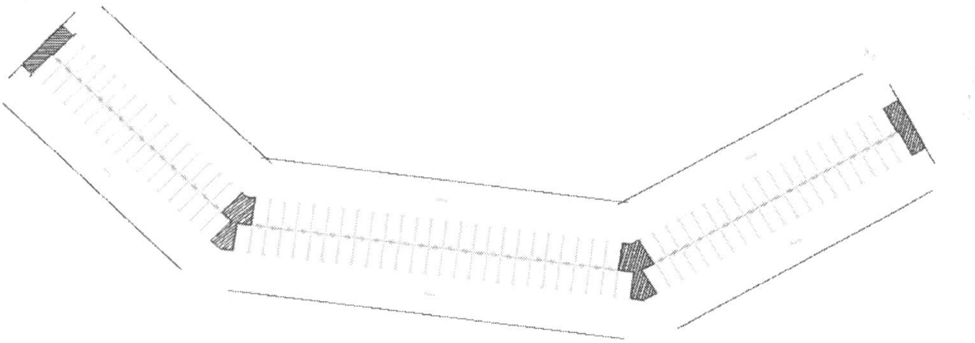

Figure 5–6

Parallel Row

If you want to add rows parallel to other objects, use the **Parallel Row** option. Launch the command and select an object in the drawing to add a parallel row to, as shown in Figure 5–7. Once the object is selected, the row will be forced to stay parallel. Click in the drawing to place the parallel row. You can select closed polylines to add parallel rows to multiple segments, as shown in Figure 5–8.

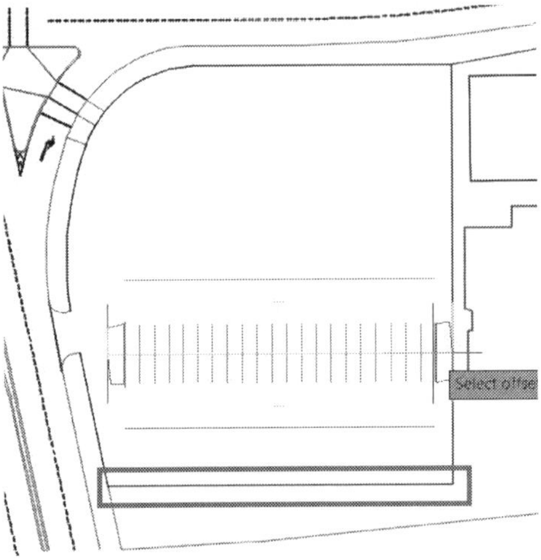

Figure 5–7

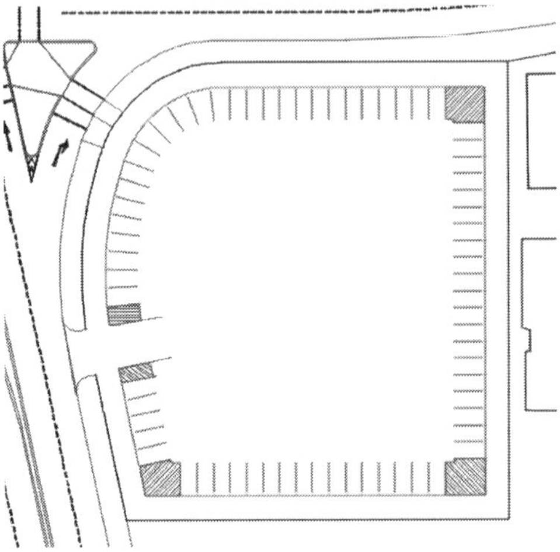

Figure 5–8

Practice 5a

Creating Parking Rows

Learning Objectives

- Examine the Parking Standards Explorer.
- Lay out a parking lot.

In this practice, you will lay out a parking area with parking rows along the perimeter and central parking rows.

1. Open **Create Parking Lot.dwg** in the *Autodesk Vehicle Tracking\Working\Parking Lots* folder.

2. In the *View* tab>Named Views panel, expand the drop-down list and select **Parking-1**.

3. On the *Vehicle Tracking* tab>Parking panel, click **Parking Standard Explorer**, as shown in Figure 5–9.

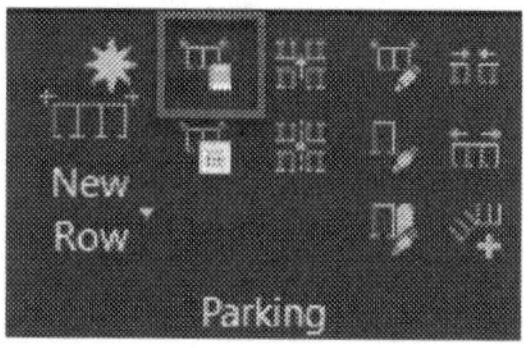

Figure 5–9

4. In the Parking Standard Explorer window that appears, click the (**+**) symbol next to *US Parking Standards*. Select the **ITE Guideline for Parking Facility Location and Design**, as shown in Figure 5–10. Right-click and select **Edit a Copy...**.

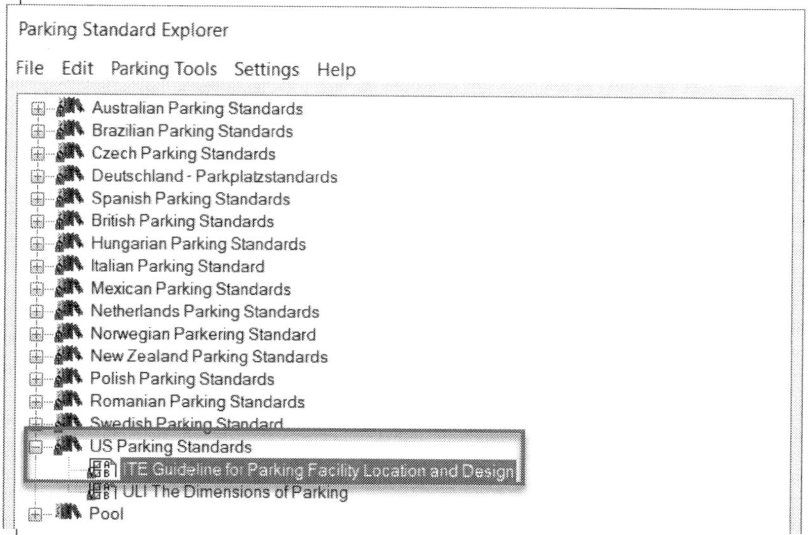

Figure 5–10

5. On the General pane of the Parking Standard dialog box, add a prefix of "ASC-" to the name of the new parking standard to distinguish it as an ASCENT parking standard.

6. If you are working on a dark or black screen in AutoCAD (known as 2D Model Space), in the Construction Lines pane, change the *Island curb boundary* color and the *Aisle clearance zone* color to **Pen 3** (Green), as shown in Figure 5–11. If you work on a light screen, change the *Flow direction arrows* to a darker color.

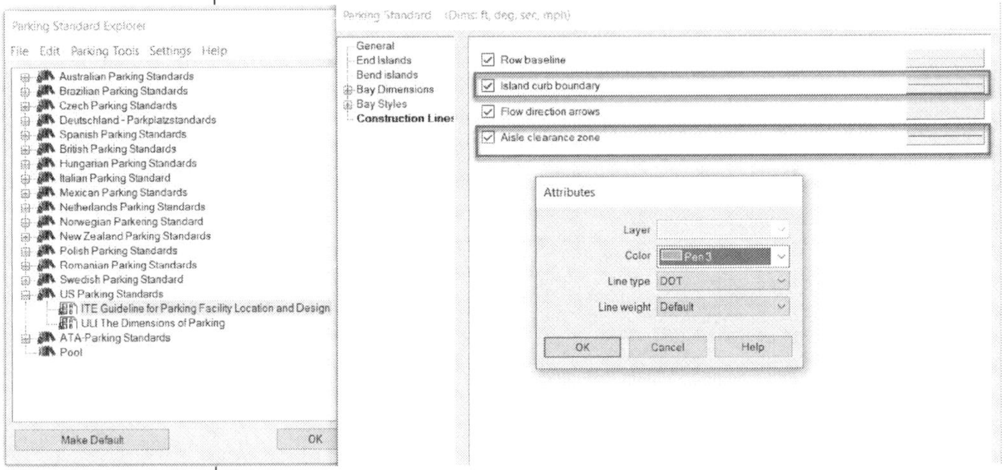

Figure 5–11

7. Click **OK** to close the Parking Standard Definition window, then click **OK** to close the Parking Standard Explorer window.

8. On the *Vehicle Tracking* tab>Parking panel, click **New Row**, as shown in Figure 5–12.

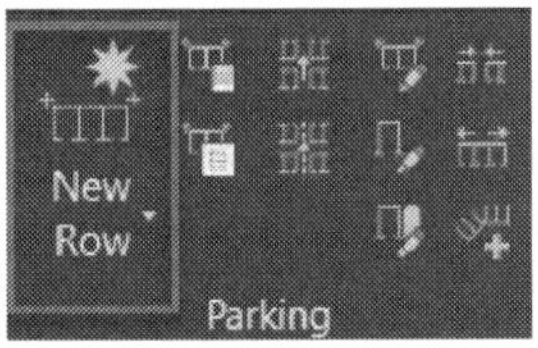

Figure 5–12

9. Select the newly created parking standard and the Parking Row Properties dialog box displays.

10. In the Parking Row Properties dialog box, verify the settings as follows (as shown in Figure 5–13):

- **Right Only** (at the bottom left corner of the dialog box)
- *Service type:* **A**
- Ensure the other settings are set as indicated (which are the defaults)

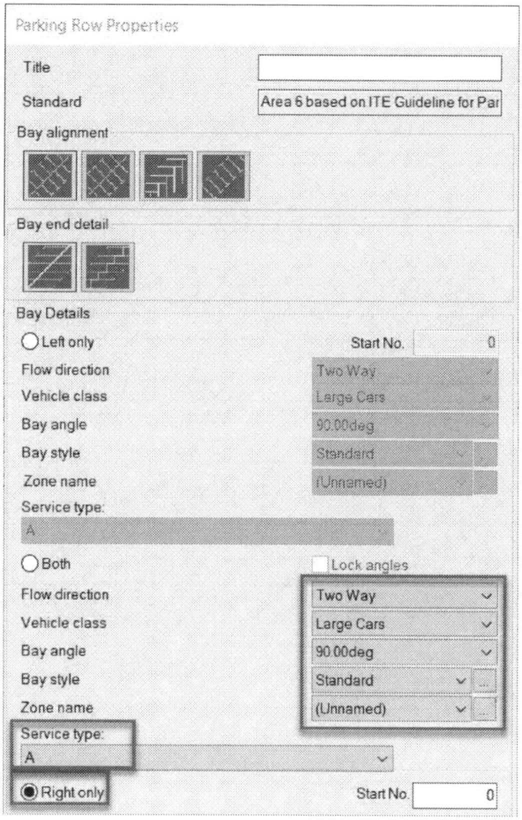

Figure 5–13

11. Turn on the **Object Snap (OSNAP)** toggle. A quick way is to press <F3>. Only the center or insertion OSNAP option is needed.

12. Using the cursor, snap to point **A** for the start point, as shown in Figure 5–14.

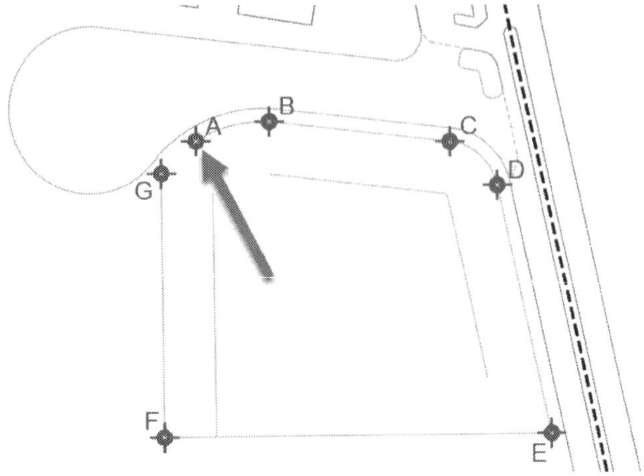

Figure 5–14

13. Continue to click points **B** through **G** (using the center OSNAP) to begin the construction of the parking lot, as shown in Figure 5–15. Press <Enter> after snapping to the target **G**.

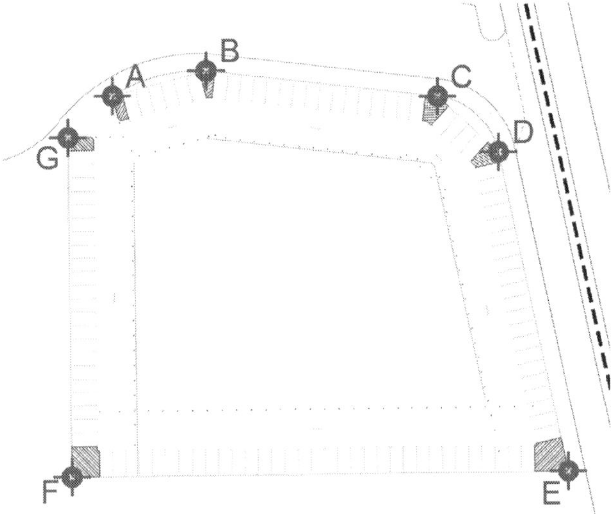

Figure 5–15

14. Press <Esc> to clear the parking lot selection.

15. Turn off the **Object Snap (OSNAP)** toggle. A quick way is to press <F3>.

16. In the Parking panel, click **Parallel Row** in the New Row drop-down list, as shown in Figure 5–16.

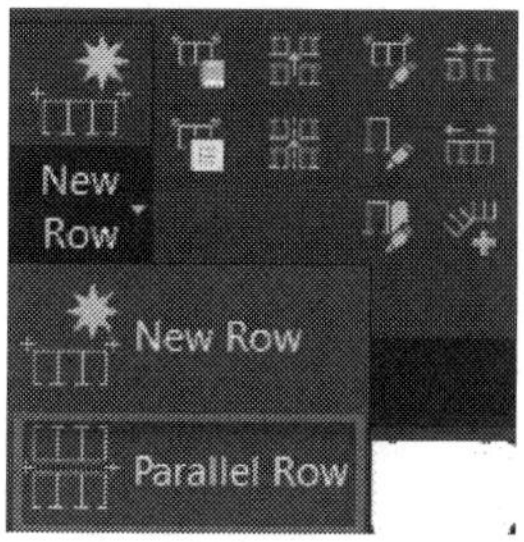

Figure 5–16

17. You may need to assign the parking standards as you did previously. Click **OK** to any dialog boxes that pop up.

18. The Parking Row Properties dialog box displays.

19. Verify that the settings are changed to **Both**, as shown in Figure 5–17. Click **Close**.

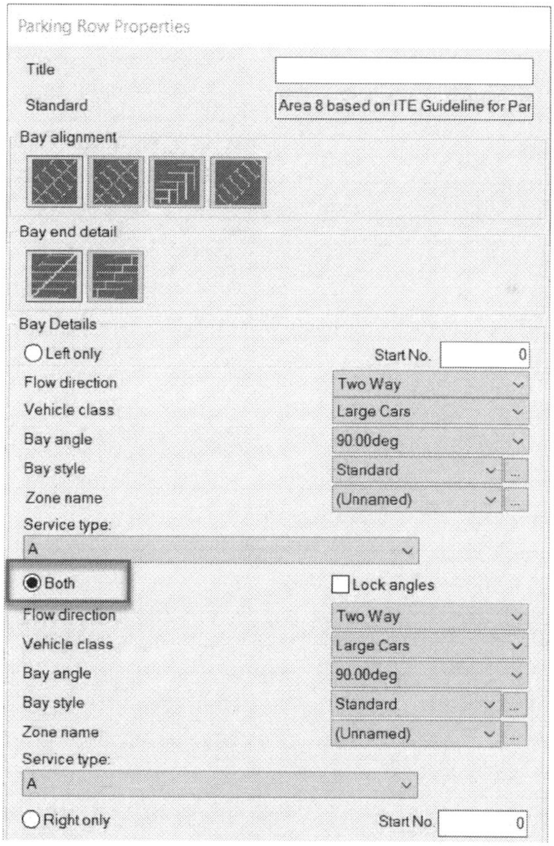

Figure 5–17

<Ctrl>+<W> is the keyboard shortcut for toggling Selection Cycling.

20. Select the line shown in Figure 5–18. You may need to use **Selection Cycling**, as the line is below the new parking lot.

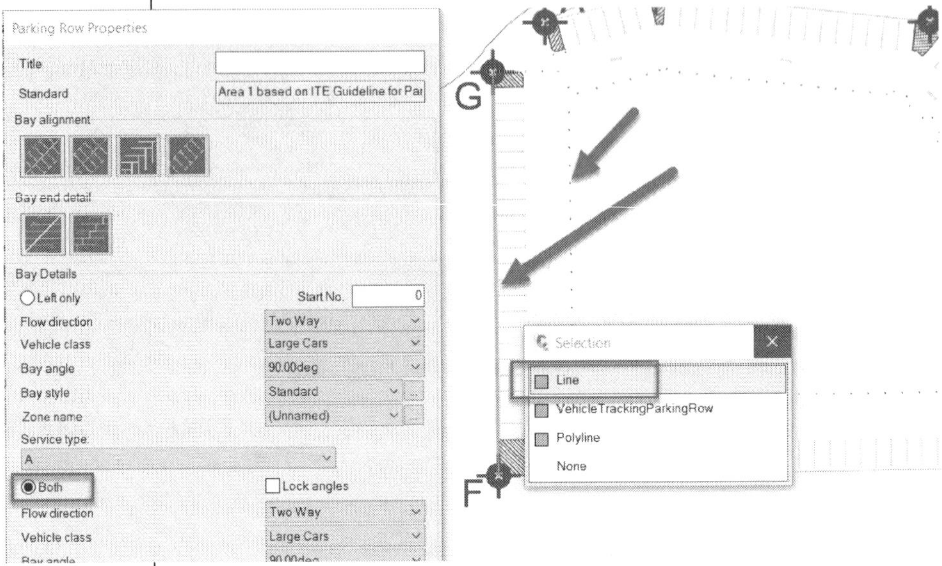

Figure 5–18

21. Move the cursor down so that the top green line of the parallel row hovers over the bottom of the green dotted line of the parking stall you had previously placed. Click to place the row.

22. When asked to select bay sides, hover over the diamond. Make sure both sides of the diamond show, as shown in Figure 5–19. Click directly on the diamond.

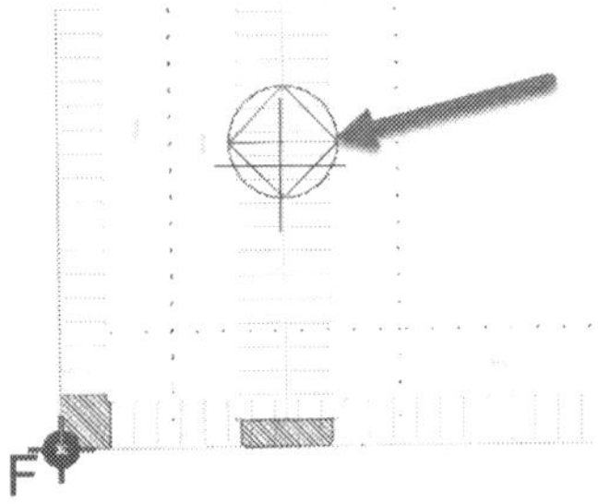

Figure 5–19

23. Press <Esc> to clear the selection.

24. Launch the **Parallel Row** command again, set the correct standard (if required), and verify that **Both** is selected. Select the recently created row.

25. Move the cursor to the right so that the bottom green line hovers over the top green dashed line of the original parking lot path. Click to place the row.

26. When asked to select bay sides, hover over the diamond. Make sure both sides of the diamond show. Click directly on the diamond.

27. The final layout should look similar to Figure 5–20.

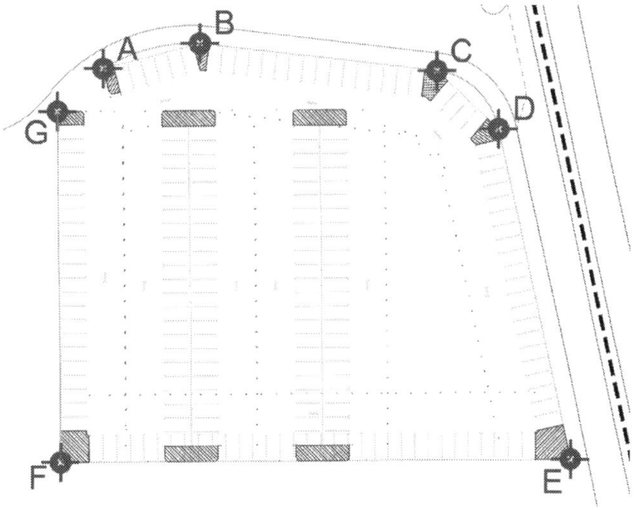

Figure 5–20

28. Save the drawing.

5.2 Working with Parking Rows

Editing Rows

There are several ways a parking row can be modified:

- Adjust the parking standards.
- Edit the parking row properties.
- Edit the parking bay properties.
- Edit the parking island properties.
- Adjust the row using grips.
- Join, extend, or add a vertex.

As mentioned before, if using a customized standard, you can open the standard and make adjustments in the dialog box. Any parking lots using that standard will update.

The **Edit Parking Row**, **Edit Parking Bay**, and **Edit Parking Island** commands are all found on the Parking panel of the ribbon, as shown in Figure 5–21. To launch the Parking Row Properties dialog box, start the command and select the parking row to update. Adjust the properties you wish to change and click to see updates.

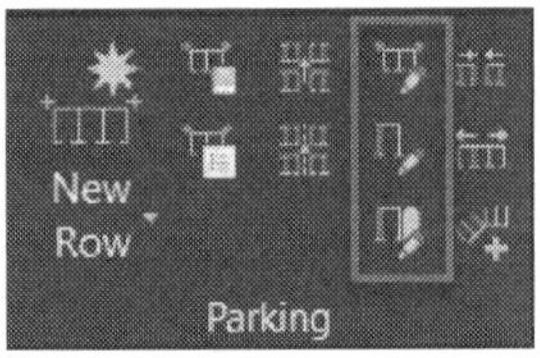

Figure 5–21

For the Parking Bay Properties dialog box, start the command, select the row to update, and then select the bay to update. Click the ellipses (**...**) button next to *Bay type* to adjust what is seen in the drawing, as shown in Figure 5–22.

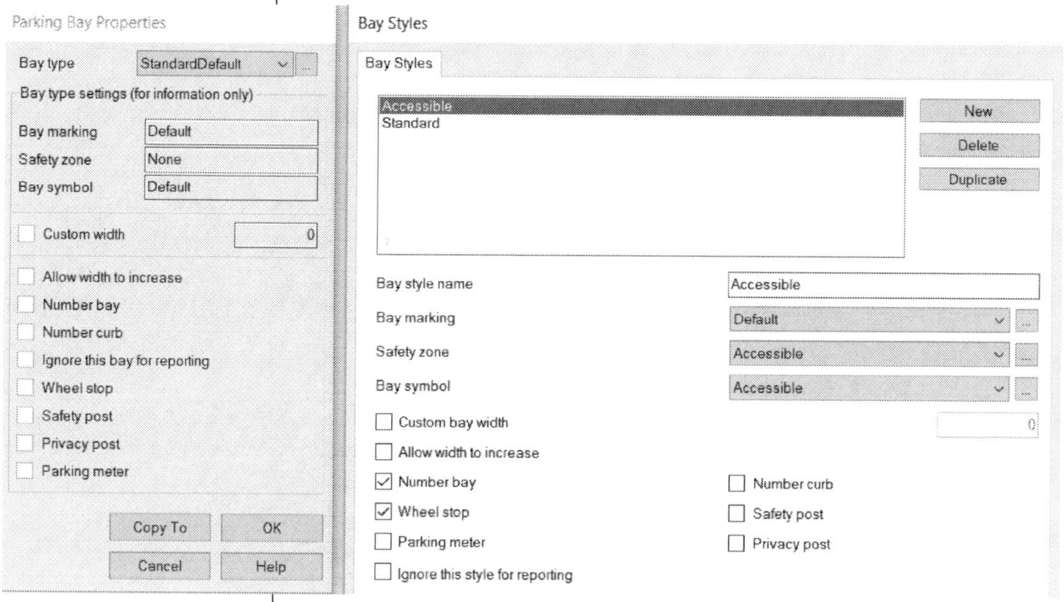

Figure 5–22

For the Parking Island Properties dialog box (shown in Figure 5–23), start the command, select the row to update, and then select the island to update. Adjust the options in the dialog box and note the changes that are made to the island.

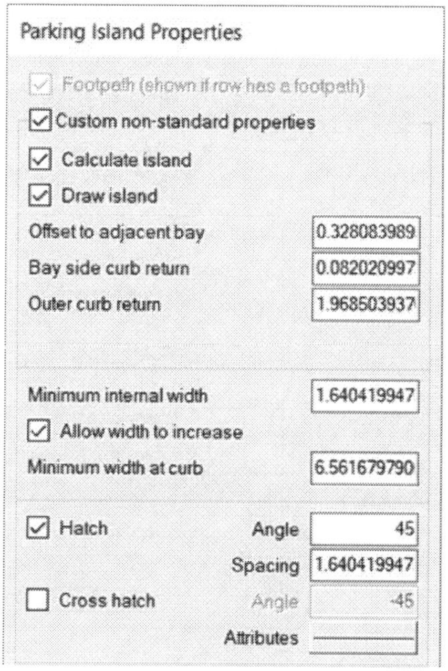

Figure 5–23

Editing with Grips

A useful way to edit parking is by using grips. Grip editing includes the options shown in Figure 5–24.

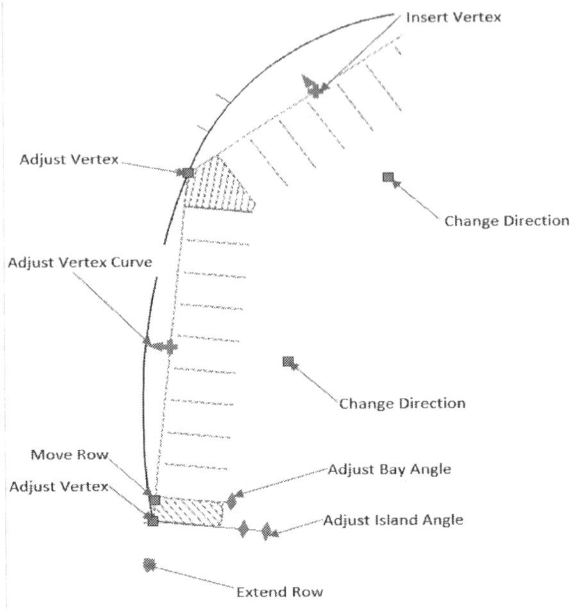

Figure 5–24

Miscellaneous Editing Commands

Miscellaneous editing options include:

- Join Parking Row
- Extend Parking Row
- Add Parking Row Vertex

Join Parking Row

The **Join Parking Row** command (shown in Figure 5–25) joins two parking lots together. Sharing end points, collinear paths, and even parking lot types does not affect the ability to join.

Figure 5–25

The joined parking lot will take on the properties of the first row selected, as shown in Figure 5–26.

Before join

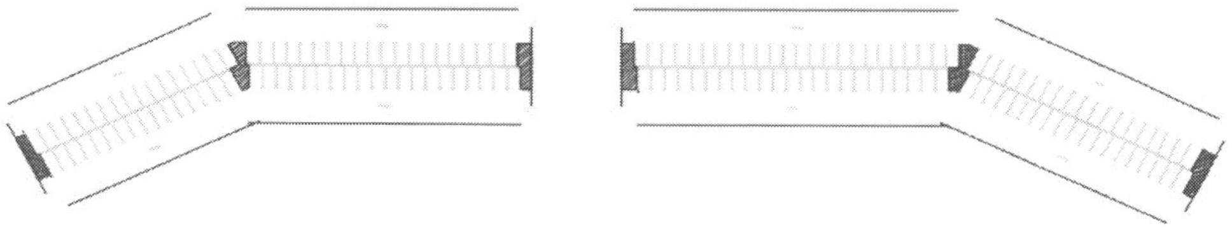

After join

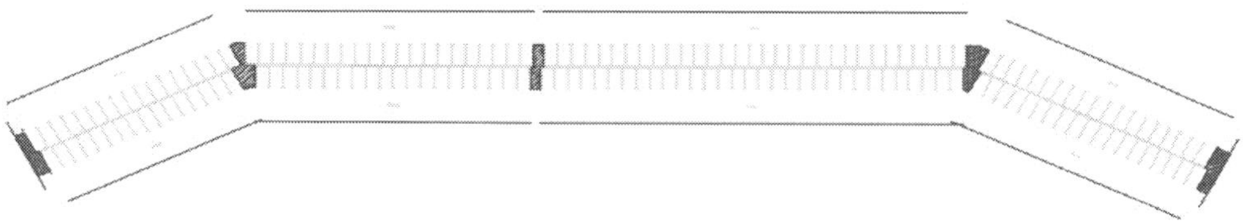

Figure 5–26

Extend Parking Row

The **Extend Parking Row** command (shown in Figure 5–27) extends the end of a selected row.

Figure 5–27

The command forces the angle to hold, as shown in Figure 5–28.

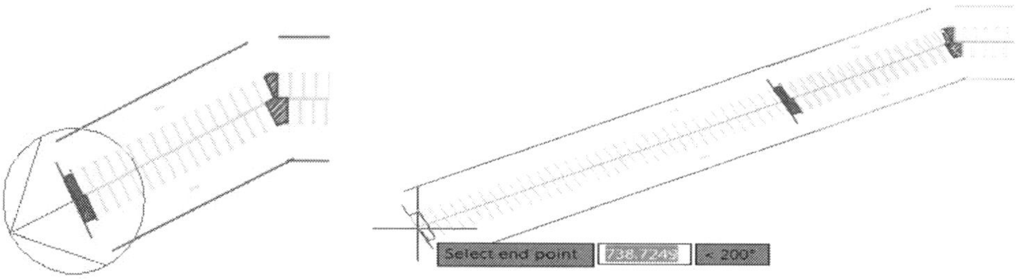

Figure 5–28

Add Parking Row Vertex

The **Add Parking Row Vertex** command (shown in Figure 5–29) adds a vertex at the end of a selected row.

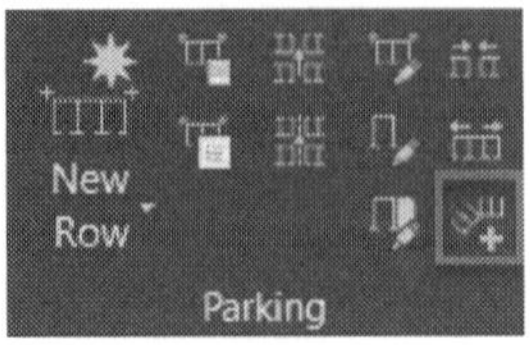

Figure 5–29

The command allows the extension of the row with an angle, as shown in Figure 5–30.

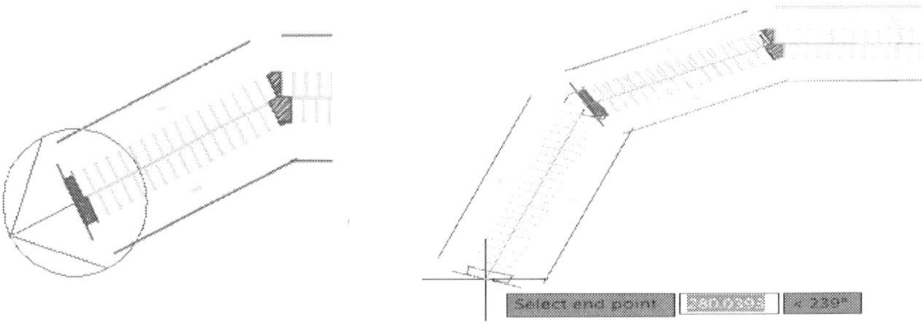

Figure 5–30

Parking Report

Parking Reports are accessible through the Parking panel of the *Vehicle Tracking* tab, as shown in Figure 5–31.

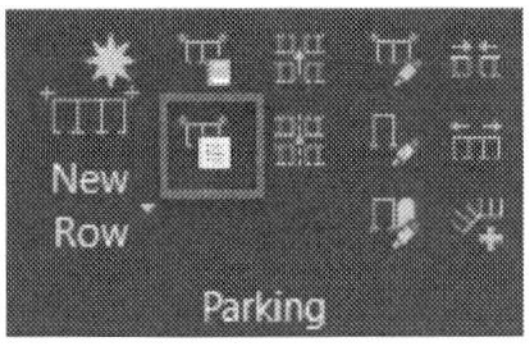

Figure 5–31

They are used to display, print, or export a report, including the following information, as shown in Figure 5–32:

- Bay type
- Vehicle class
- Service type
- Zone
- Stall count
- % of stalls in a category

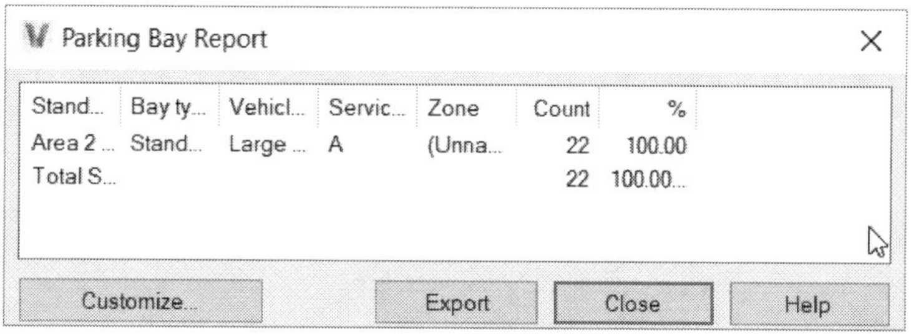

Figure 5–32

You can customize the parking report to adjust what is seen, as shown in Figure 5–33.

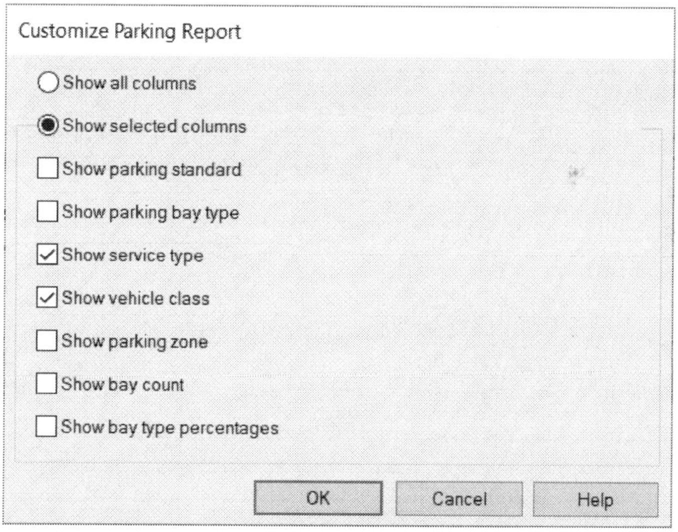

Figure 5–33

Create Access Roads

Two commands allow you to create access roads, as shown in Figure 5–34. Use the **Create Access Road** command when linework does not exist to represent the path of the road.

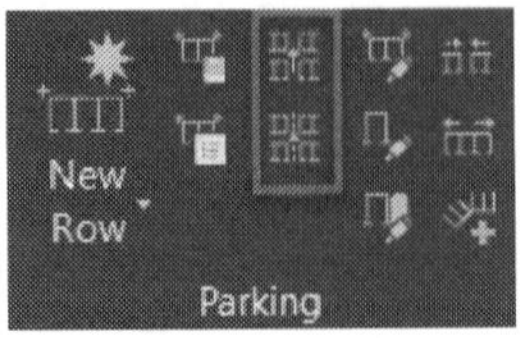

Figure 5–34

When creating the access road, use the Parking Access Road Properties dialog box to verify the width of the road passing through, as shown in Figure 5–35.

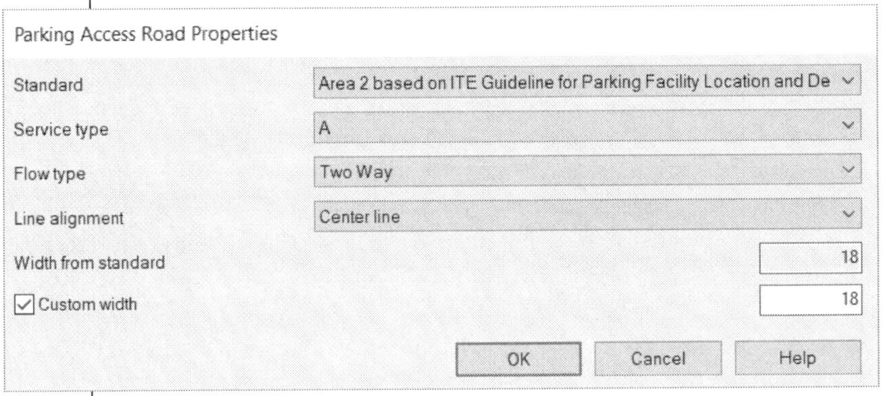

Figure 5–35

Figure 5–36 shows an access road created using the **Create Access Road** command.

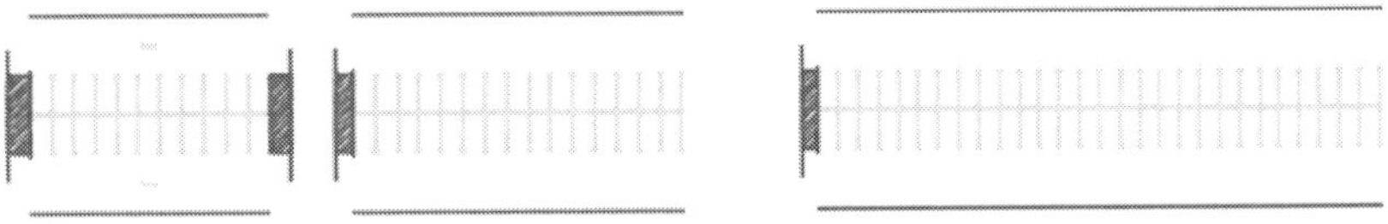

Figure 5–36

Figure 5–37 shows an access road created using the **Create Access Road From Line** command.

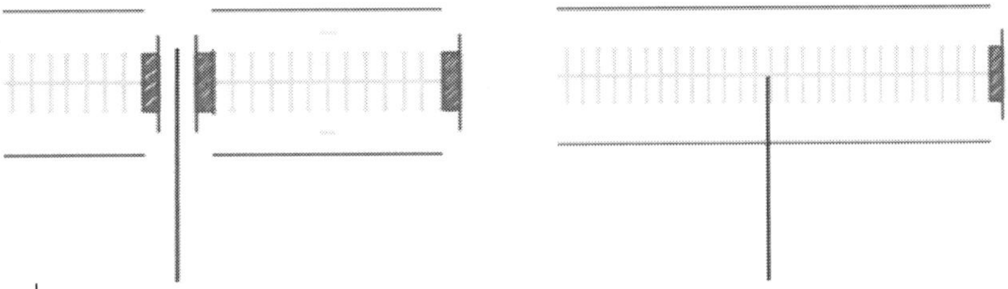

Figure 5–37

Practice 5b

Editing Parking Rows

Learning Objectives

- Modify a parking lot layout.
- Add components to the parking lot.
- Create a parking row report.

In this practice, you will edit the parking lot layout by adding walkways, adjusting the lengths of the rows, and adding an access road. You will then produce a parking row report to count how many stalls are available.

Task 1 - Edit parking rows.

1. Continue working on the current drawing or open **Edit Parking Lot.dwg** in the *Autodesk Vehicle Tracking\ Working\Parking Lots* folder.
2. In the *View* tab>Named Views panel, expand the drop-down list and select **Parking-1**.
3. You will note that there are no curves along the outer edge of the parking from **A** to **B** or **C** to **D**, as shown in Figure 5–38.

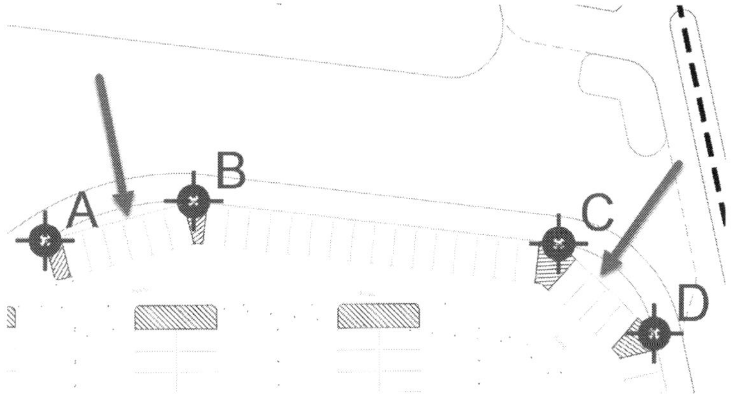

Figure 5–38

4. Select the parking object and use the triangle grip between **C** and **D** to adjust the vertex curve, as shown in Figure 5–39. Pull the grip to meet the actual edge of the parking lot. Using the midpoint object snap may help.

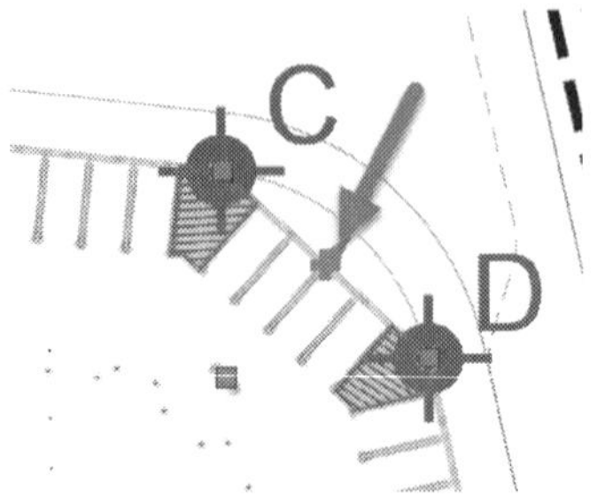

Figure 5–39

5. Repeat for the section between **A** and **B**.

6. Select the right parallel row, as shown in Figure 5–40. Use the **Move Row** grip and move the row to the right until stalls are against the solid green line and intersect with the dotted green line.
   - You cannot snap to the intersection, so you will have to "eye-ball" it. Turning on **Ortho** may help; a quick way is to press <F8>.

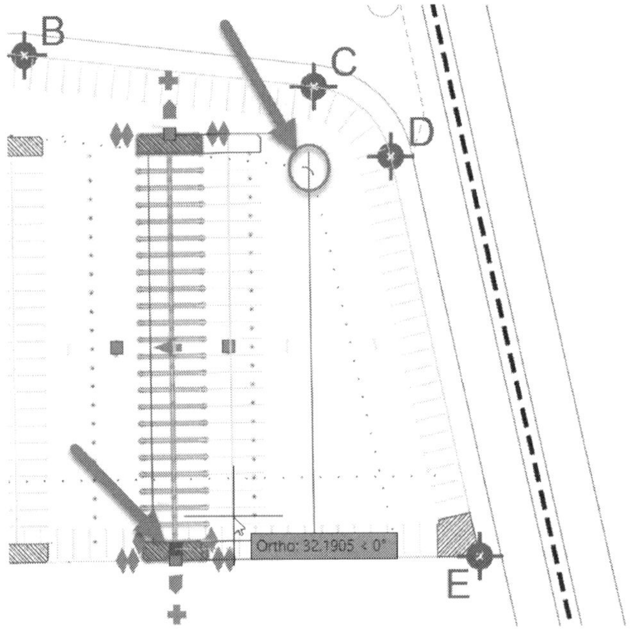

Figure 5–40

7. On the Parking panel, click **Extend Parking Row**, as shown in Figure 5–41.

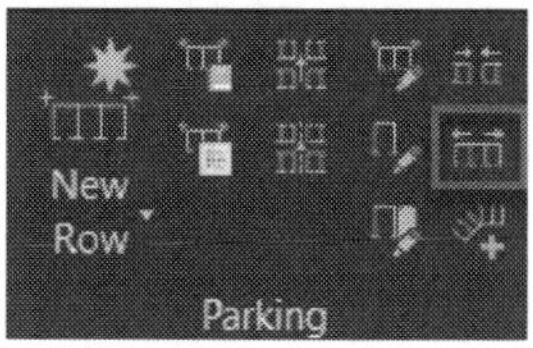

Figure 5–41

8. Select the right parallel row. Click the top side when asked which side to select. Extend the row until it intersects with the dotted green line, as shown in Figure 5–42.
   - As before, you cannot snap to the intersection, so you will have to "eye-ball" it.

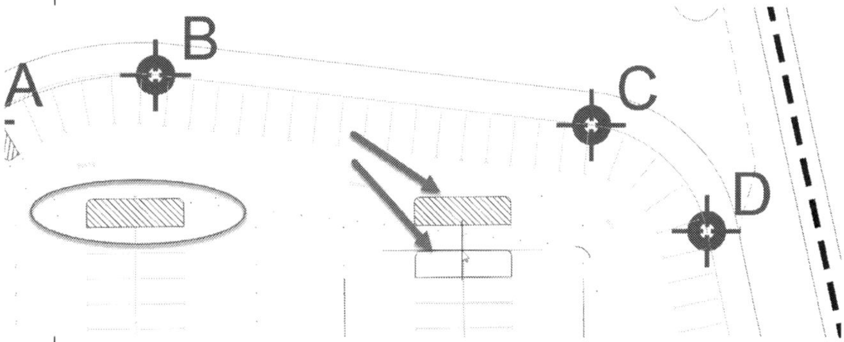

Figure 5–42

9. Repeat this process for the left parallel row. It needs to move only a fraction. The final result is shown in Figure 5–43.

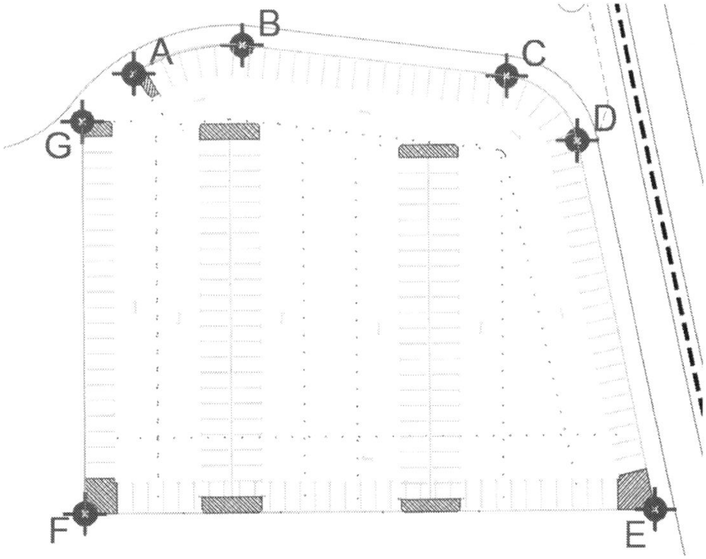

Figure 5–43

10. Zoom in to the top right parallel row. Select the row. Use the **Adjust Island Angle Both Sides** grips to adjust the angle of the islands to match as close as possible with the green dotted line, as shown on the left in Figure 5–44. Once the bay is aligned, use the **Extend** grip to adjust the row so it extends once again to the green dotted line, as shown on the right in Figure 5–44.

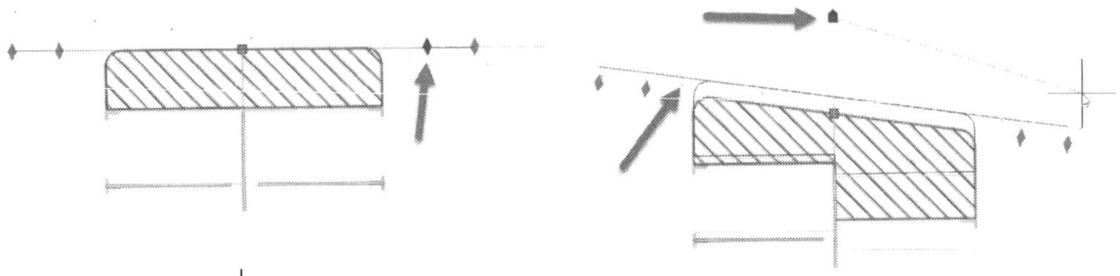

Figure 5–44

11. Repeat this process for the left row. You will need to use the **Adjust Island Angle This Side** grip (on both sides) for this island, as shown in Figure 5–45.

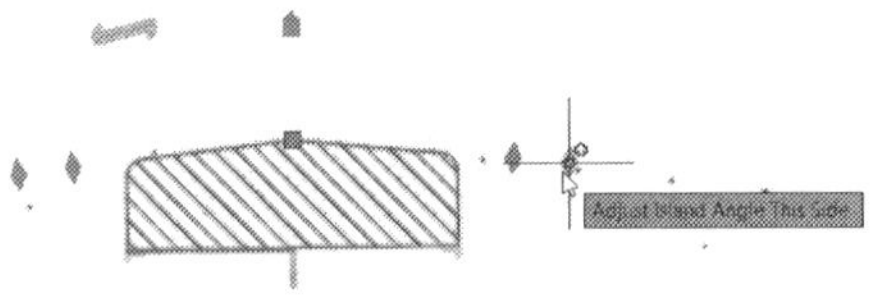

Figure 5–45

12. The final result is shown in Figure 5–46.

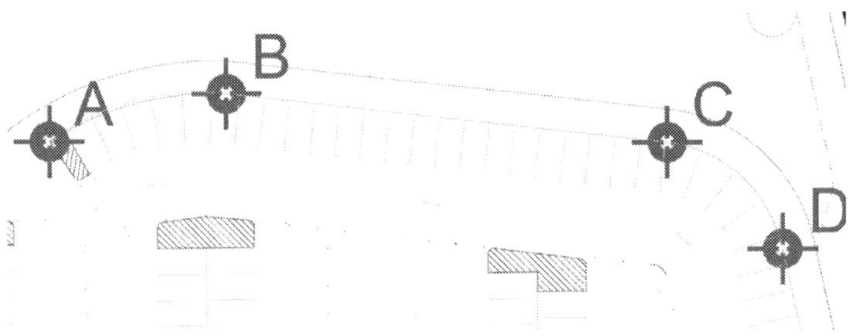

Figure 5–46

13. Launch the **Extend Parking Row** command. Select the left parallel row.

14. Pull the cursor to the left to trim the parking row to the green dotted line.

15. Repeat with the right parallel row.

16. The final result is shown in Figure 5–47. Save the file.

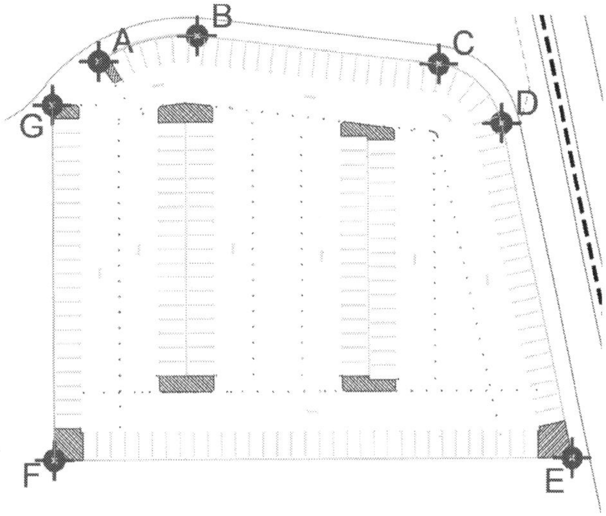

Figure 5–47

Task 2 - Working with parking row properties.

1. Stay in the same file.
2. On the Parking panel, click **Edit Parking Row**, as shown in Figure 5–48.

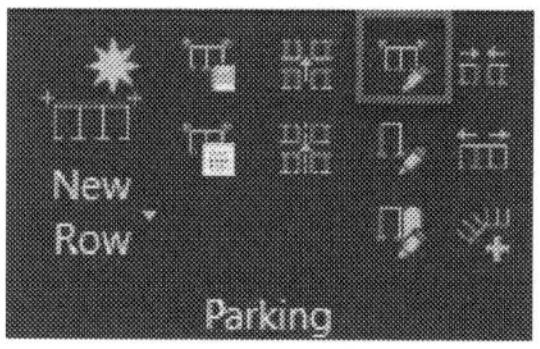

Figure 5–48

3. Select the parallel row between **D** and **E**.

4. Change the *Bay alignment* as shown in Figure 5–49 and click **OK**.

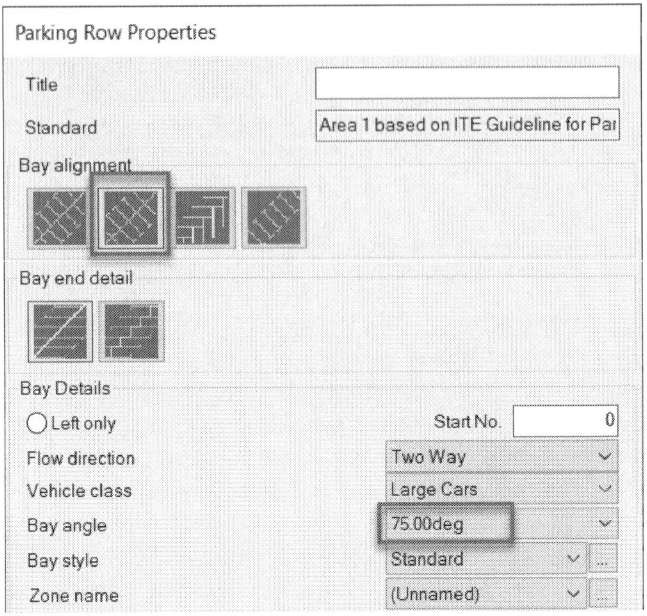

Figure 5–49

5. Repeat for the left row of the right island rows. Set the *Bay angle* to **75.00deg Contra-Flow**. The result is shown in Figure 5–50.

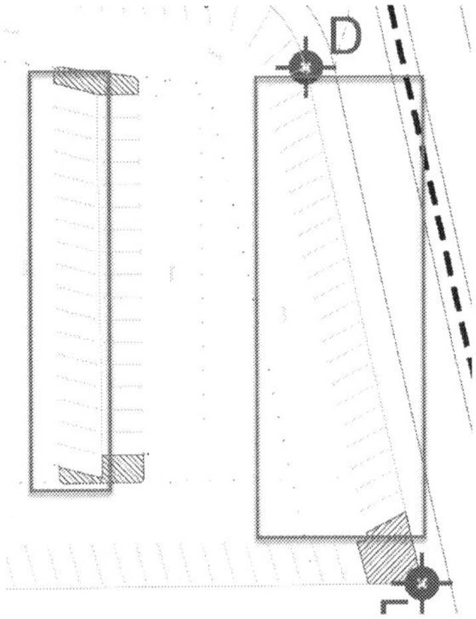

Figure 5–50

6. Press <Esc> to clear all selections.

7. Launch the **Edit Parking Row** command.

8. Select the left island rows.

9. Select **Footpath** and click the **Apply** button, as shown in Figure 5–51.

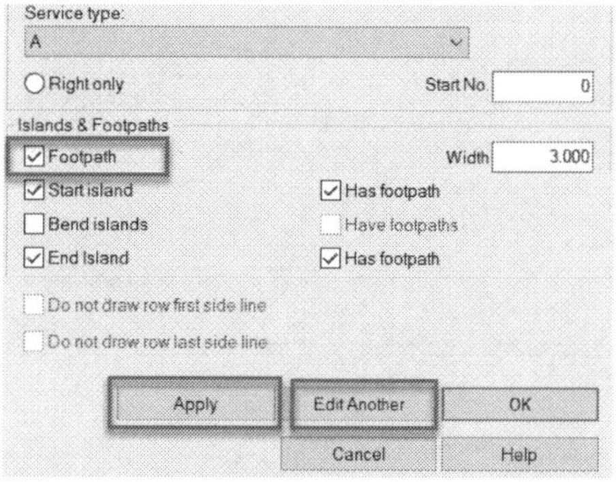

Figure 5–51

10. Click the **Edit Another** button (as shown above in Figure 5–51) and select the right island rows. Add a footpath to this island as well.

11. Click **OK** to dismiss the dialog box, then save the file.

Task 3 - Add an access road.

1. Stay in the same file.

2. On the Parking panel, click **Create Access Road**, as shown in Figure 5–52.

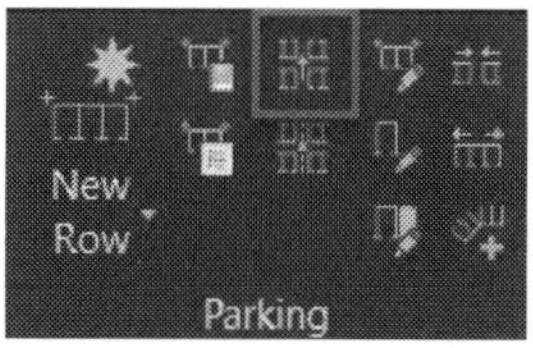

Figure 5–52

3. Draw a line between **D** and **E**, as shown in Figure 5–53. Leave the Parking Access Road Properties dialog box settings as the defaults and click **OK**.

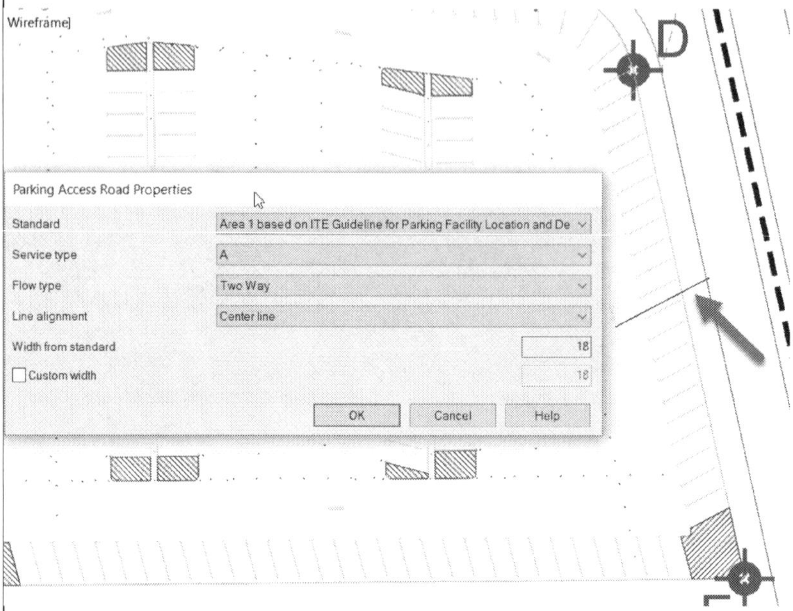

Figure 5–53

4. The access road is shown in Figure 5–54.

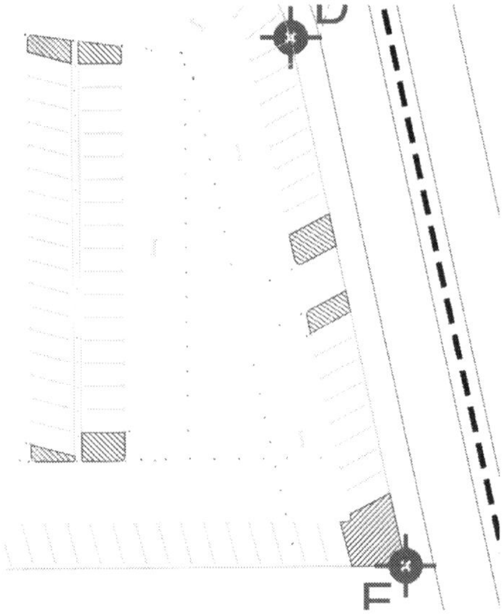

Figure 5–54

5. On the Parking panel, click **Edit Parking Bay**, as shown in Figure 5–55.

Figure 5–55

6. Select the row near the target **G**, as shown in Figure 5–56.

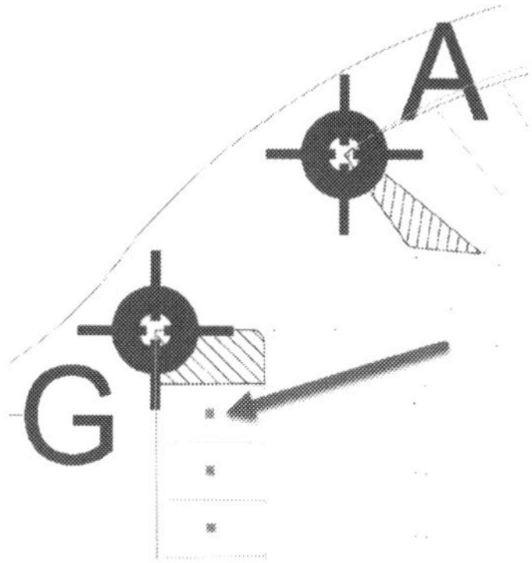

Figure 5–56

7. Hover over the first square. It should turn red. Click on the red square.

8. In the Parking Bay Properties dialog box, change the *Bay type* to **Accessible**, as shown in Figure 5–57. Click **OK**.

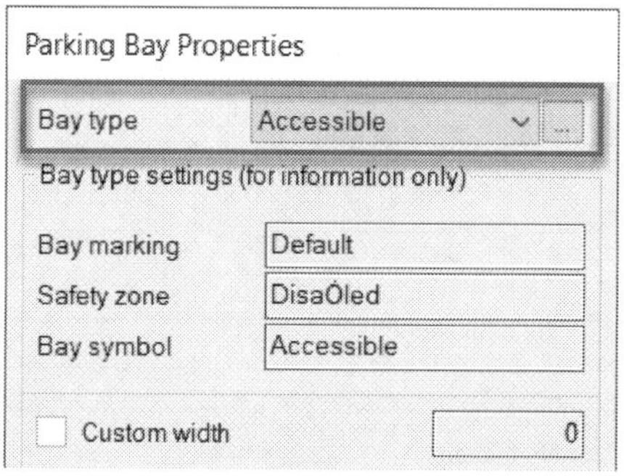

Figure 5–57

9. Repeat this process two more times to add a total of three accessible spots, as shown in Figure 5–58. Press <Esc> a couple of times to clear all selections.

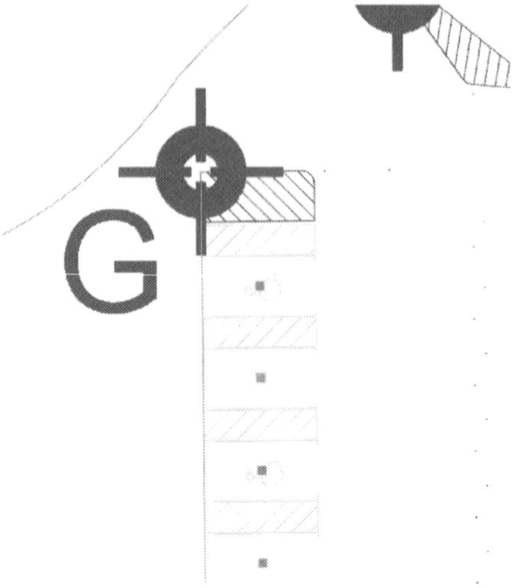

Figure 5–58

10. Verify the drawing is complete, as shown in Figure 5–59.

Figure 5–59

11. On the Parking panel, click **Parking Bay Report**, as shown in Figure 5–60.

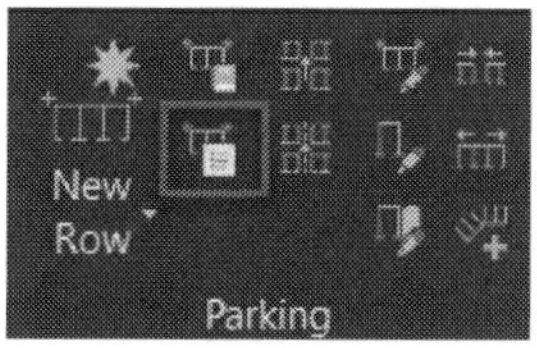

Figure 5–60

If you are using AutoCAD for this exercise (not Autodesk Civil 3D), the report may only show the total number of stalls rather than the stall breakdown shown in Figure 5–61.

12. Review the report, as shown in Figure 5–61.

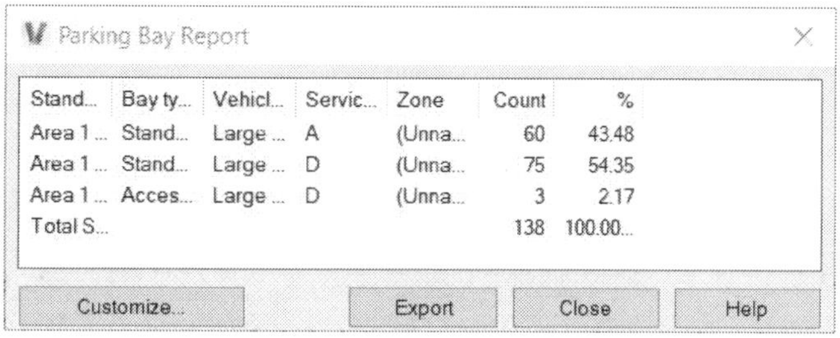

Figure 5–61

13. (Optional) For additional practice, in the *View* tab>Named Views panel, expand the drop-down list and select **Parking-2.** Here are some hints:

- Use the **New Row** command.
- In the Parking Row Properties dialog box, do the following:
    - Select **Right Only**.
    - Set the *Bay angle* to ***75.00deg Contra-Flow***
    - Uncheck **Start**, **Bend**, and **End Islands**.
- The first point you pick needs to be the upper end point, and the second point you pick needs to be the lower end point, since you selected **Right Only** in the Parking Row Properties dialog box.
- Use the triangular grip to turn the segment into an arc.
- Use the extend grips to fill in the space with stalls, where required.

Figure 5–62 shows the final result.

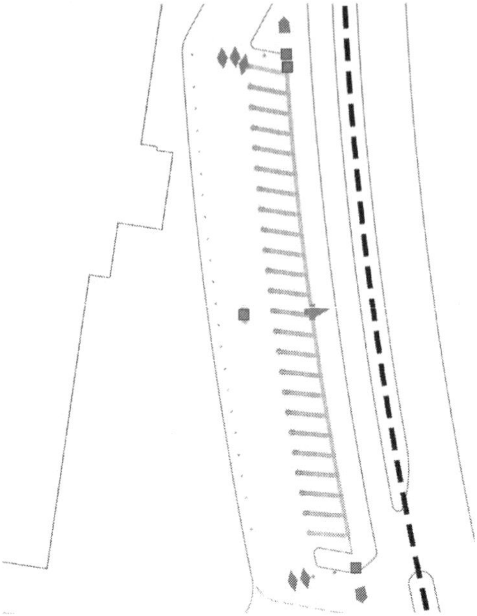

Figure 5–62

14. (Optional) For additional practice, in the *View* tab>Named Views panel, expand the drop-down list and select **Parking-3**. You can use **Parallel Row** for this area.

15. Save the drawing.

Chapter Review Questions

1. Can existing parking standards be modified?
   a. Yes
   b. No
   c. Only by authorized people in your organization
2. What is the most efficient way to tally up parking spaces in the proposed layout?
   a. Count them and enter into a spreadsheet.
   b. Use AutoCAD's QuickSelect command.
   c. Produce a parking bay report.
   d. Select all parking bays and invoke the AutoCAD Properties command.
3. How do you add accessible parking stalls?
   a. Modify a parking standard.
   b. Add an AutoCAD block as a symbol to the stall.
   c. Change the parking stall style.
   d. In the Parking Bay Properties dialog box, change the *Bay type*.

Chapter 6

Roundabouts

In this chapter, you will learn about the Roundabout tools within Autodesk® Vehicle Tracking. Vehicle Tracking has powerful features to simplify preliminary layout of roundabout geometry.

Editing options are also available, and as you make changes to the layout, you will see the dynamic nature of the objects as well as the adherence to design standards. Using the geometrically constrained roundabout object makes it viable to explore multiple design solutions.

Learning Objectives in This Chapter

- Navigate the Roundabout Standard Explorer.
- Create roundabouts with and without corridor functionality.
- Edit roundabouts using grips and other commands.
- Create corridors from roundabouts.

6.1 Roundabout Tools

Roundabout Standard Explorer

All roundabouts are created in accordance with defined rules or standards. The Roundabout Standard Explorer holds a number of these standards from several countries. The **Roundabout Standard Explorer** is found on the Roundabouts panel of the ribbon (as shown in Figure 6–1).

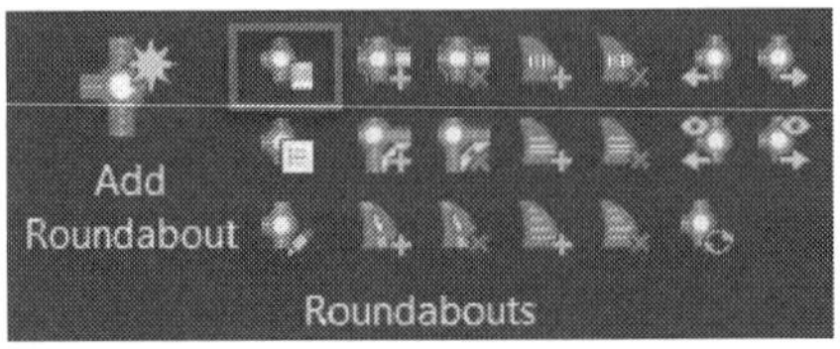

Figure 6–1

When the command is launched, the Roundabout Standard Explorer window opens, as shown in Figure 6–2. All standards are grouped by nationality, and custom standards can be created as well.

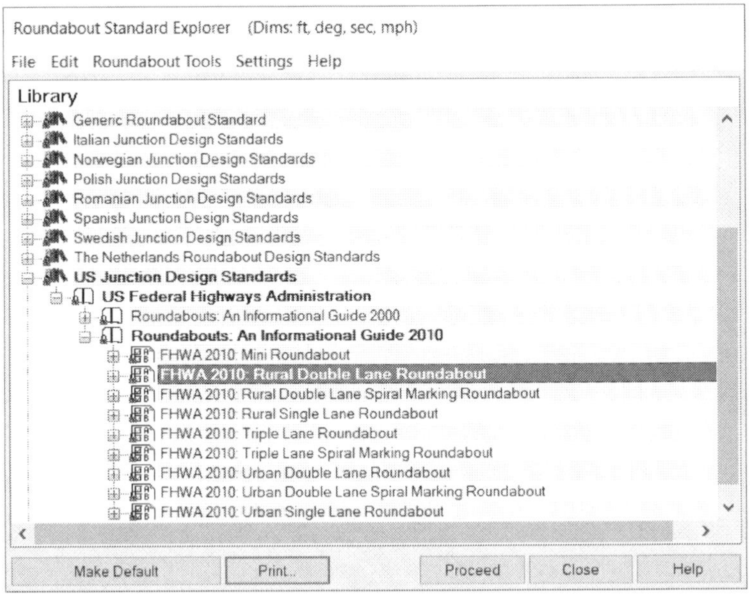

Figure 6–2

By right-clicking on a specific standard, you can view, edit a copy, or create a new standard.

All three options open the Roundabout Standard Editor dialog box. This editor has many sections that can be modified. Different aspects of the geometry will also highlight to help the user identify the areas to change.

Note: The standards provided "out of the box" are locked to prevent accidental (or intentional) changes.

Included sections in the editor are as follows (as shown in Figure 6–3):

- General
- Roundel Geometry
- Arm Geometry
- Fastest Path Analysis
- Swept Path Analysis
- Visibility Analysis
- Signage
- Road Markings

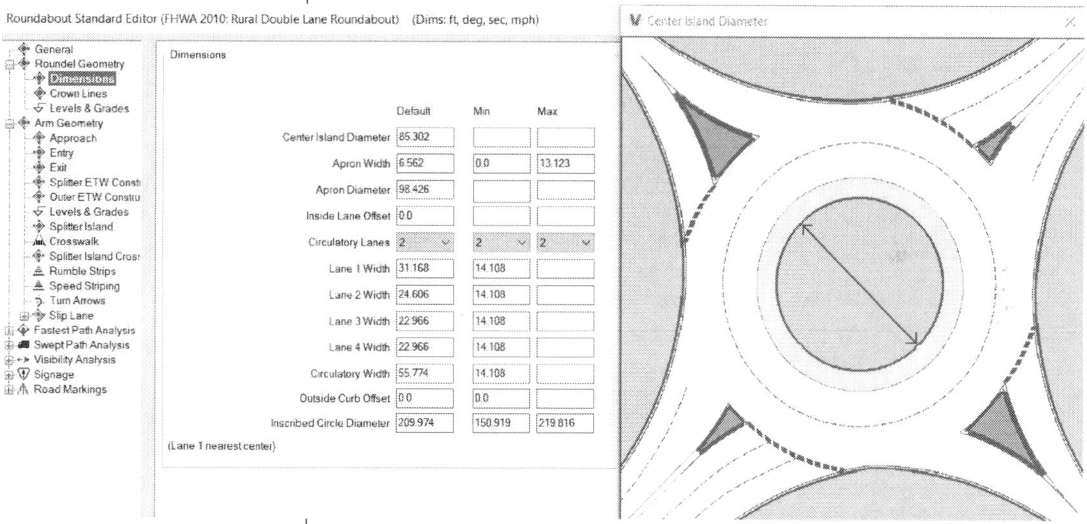

Figure 6–3

The diagram shown in Figure 6–3 above is displayed by clicking the **Diagram** button at the bottom of the Roundabout Standard Editor dialog box.

The diagram is useful for identifying the many parameters of the roundabout. Simply click on a value within the editor and the parameter will highlight with a red line in the diagram.

Creating Roundabouts

The **Add Roundabout** command is found on the Roundabouts panel of the ribbon, as shown in Figure 6–4.

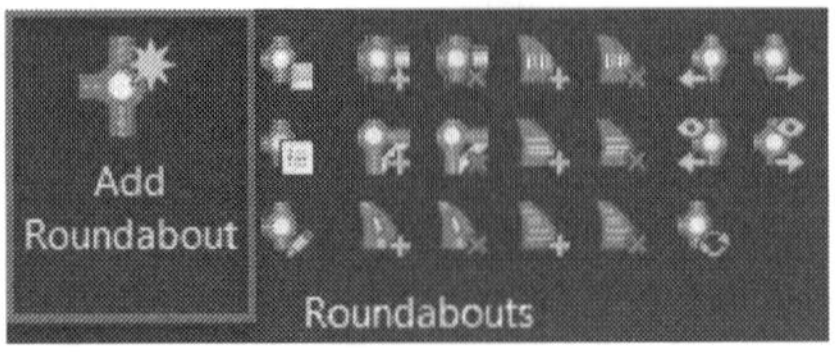

Figure 6–4

Before you create your roundabout, there are several settings you need to review first. When Vehicle Tracking is run in Autodesk Civil 3D, extra functionality is available that allows you to go construct a 3D corridor model. These settings are found in Drawing Settings, which is found on the Settings panel of the ribbon. If default settings have not been set, this dialog box will display when the **Add Roundabout** command is launched.

The options for Civil 3D object creation include:

- Civil 3D existing and final surfaces (as shown in Figure 6–5)
- Alignments and profiles (as shown in Figure 6–6)
- Including horizontal alignments along each nearside and offside definition line, the ICD, the apron, the island, and the circulatory area crown line
- A 3D corridor model

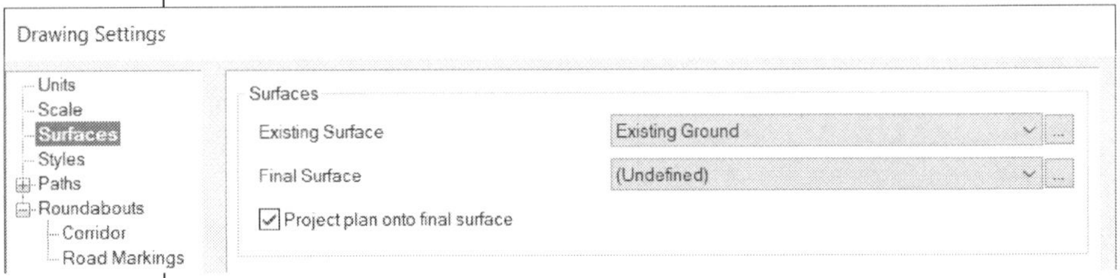

Figure 6–5

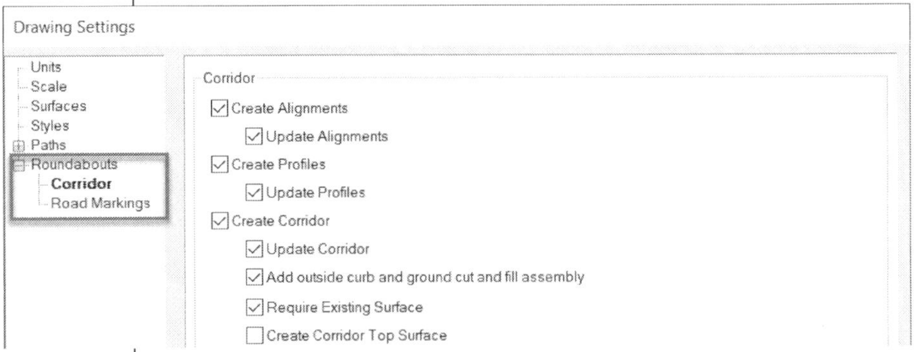

Figure 6–6

Once you have your settings and standards in place, launch the **Add Roundabout** command. The New Roundabout Details dialog box will appear, as shown in Figure 6–7. Set all the appropriate settings.

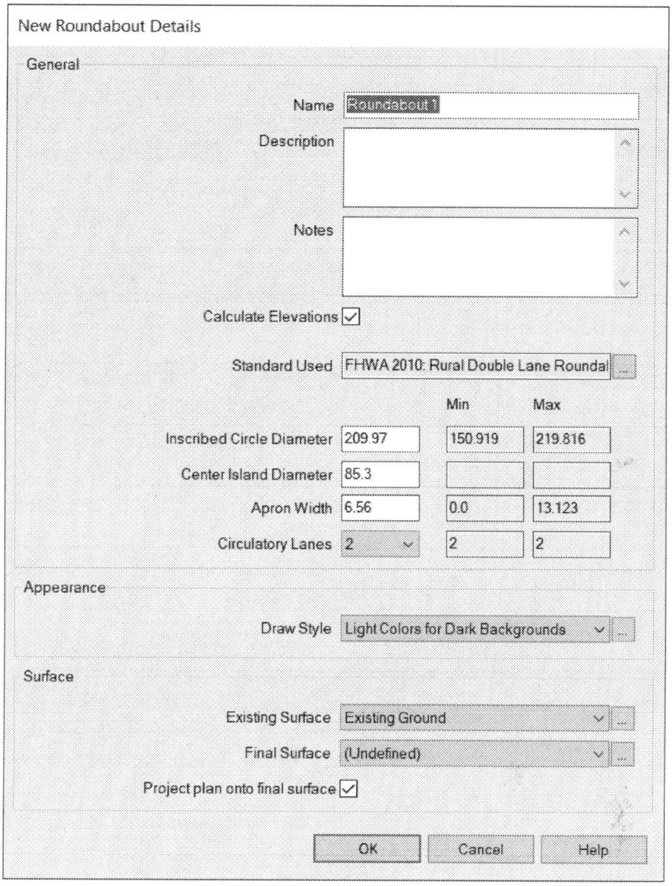

Figure 6–7

Place the center point of the roundabout in the drawing, then add the arms (or approaches) of the roundabout by clicking AutoCAD or Civil 3D linework.

When adding each approach, the New Arm dialog box will appear, as shown in Figure 6–8. Enter a unique name for each new arm created.

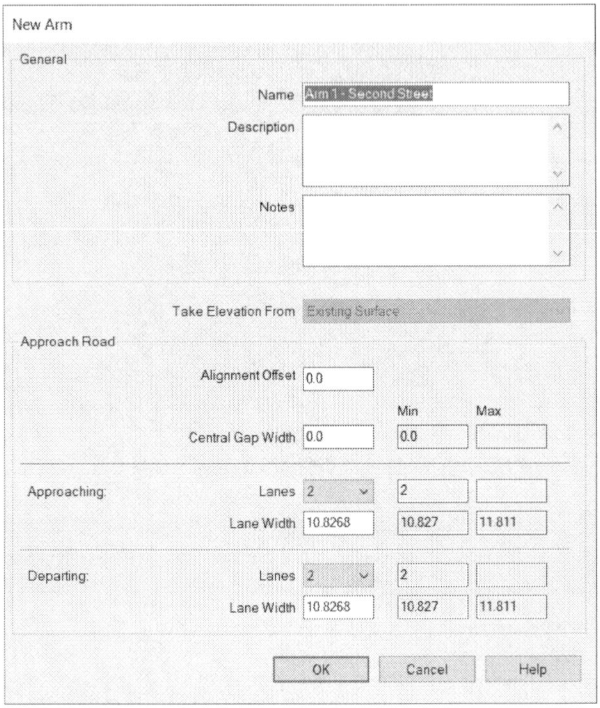

Figure 6–8

Each new approach creates the full geometry necessary for the roundabout. As the roundabout is created, either a 2D vehicle roundabout or a full 3D corridor model is created, depending on the drawing settings, as shown in Figure 6–9. The corridor model settings are able to be turned on at any time during the creation or editing process.

With corridor model settings turned off ***With corridor model settings turned on***

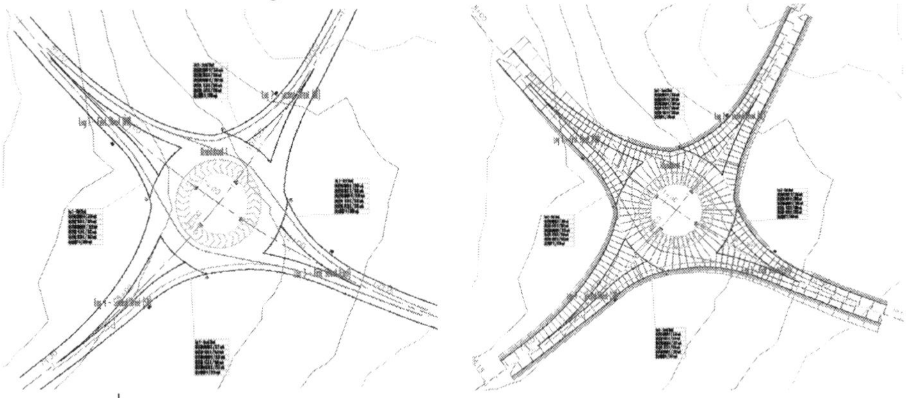

Figure 6–9

Real-time feedback is also added when the roundabout is created. A table is provided for each arm of the roundabout, providing fastest path and performance data. All tables stay up to date as the roundabout is being created and edited.

If using the corridor model creation while creating the roundabout, the corridor properties will populate with all of the appropriate baselines and regions, as shown in Figure 6–10.

Note: It is recommended that you name the roundabout when you first launch the command, so that the alignments are automatically created with the correct names. Autodesk Vehicle Tracking does not rename alignments if you change the roundabout name after creation.

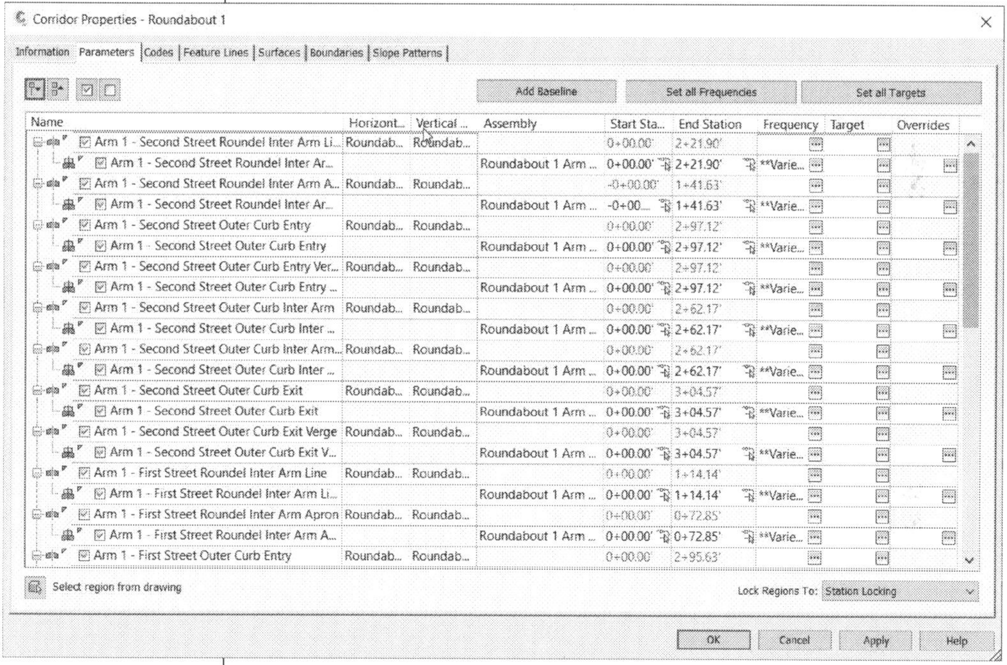

Figure 6–10

The Vehicle Tracking roundabout is dynamically linked to the objects it was created with and the objects created from it.

- When the roundabout geometry is changed, the associated alignments, profiles, and corridor are automatically rebuilt.
- If the roundabout was created using existing Civil 3D alignments, the roundabout will update automatically as those alignments are adjusted.

Heads Up Display

As you create the roundabout, little boxes appear for each approach arm, as shown in Figure 6–11. This is called a Heads Up Display (HUD). HUDs show the critical design values related to each approach arm. These include radii and speeds calculated by Vehicle Tracking.

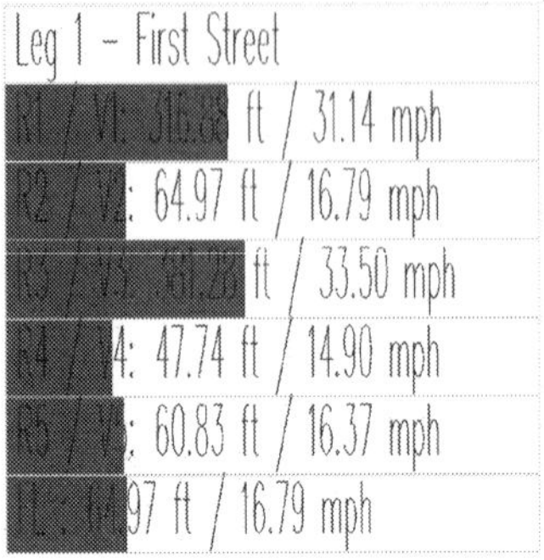

Figure 6–11

The data is color coded:

- Green: Values are within the limits specified in the standards.
- Amber: Values are getting close to the limiting value.
- Red: Values are outside of the limits.

The HUDs are dynamic tables. If you adjust the roundabout, the values will update. You will also notice color changes as limits are approached.

6.2 Editing Roundabouts

There are several ways a roundabout can be modified:

- Adjust the roundabout standards
- Edit the roundabout properties
- Adjust roundabouts using grips
- Add/remove roundabout structures
- Add/remove roundabout markings

As mentioned before, if using a customized standard, you can open the standard and make adjustments in the dialog box, and any roundabouts using that standard will update.

There is also an **Edit Roundabout** command found on the Roundabouts panel of the ribbon. When the command is launched, the Roundabout Properties dialog box opens, as shown in Figure 6–12. Adjust the properties you wish to change and click to see updates. A diagram also displays to help you understand what is being adjusted when modifying the many aspects of the roundabout.

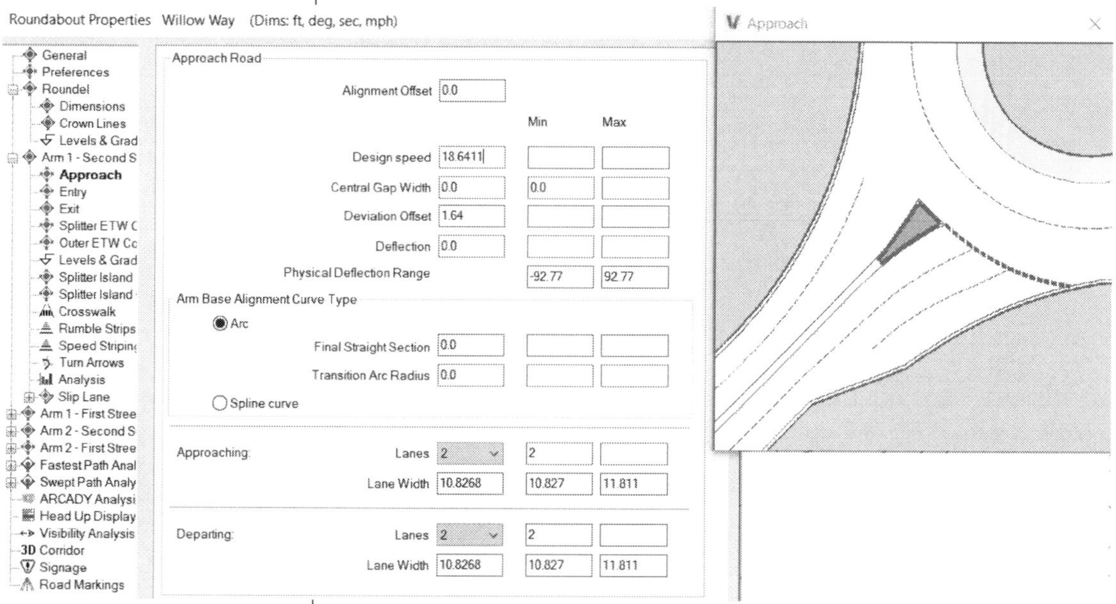

Figure 6–12

Analysis Options

There are several analysis options in the Roundabout Properties.

- **Fastest Path Analysis:** Also known as the fastest line speed. This is used to determine the maximum realistic speed of a vehicle on the most direct line. The calculations are automatically calculated for you by the Vehicle Tracking software, as shown in Figure 6–13. The fastest path line is displayed within the roundabout.

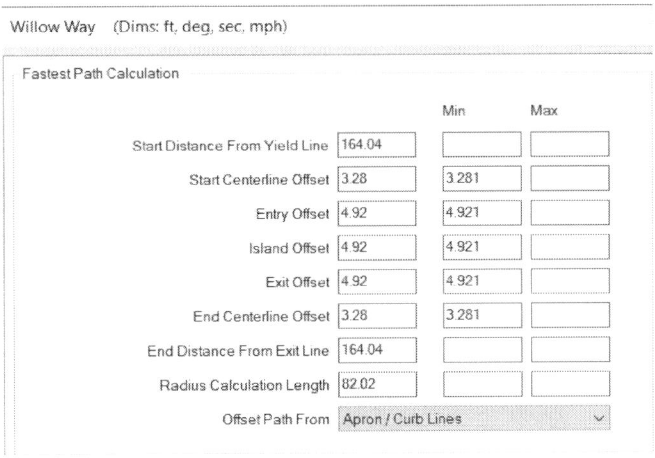

Figure 6–13

- **Swept Path Analysis:** This allows you to manage the use of design vehicles you specify for the project. Add, edit, or delete vehicles at any time.

The ARCADY analysis tools are not covered in this guide.

- **ARCADY Analysis:** ARCADY is used for predicting capacities, queues, delays (both queuing and geometric), and accident risk at roundabouts. There is an ARCADY/ Vehicle Tracking two-way link to let users view ARCADY results directly in Vehicle Tracking. The link is dynamic and changes happen in real-time. Full copies of Vehicle Tracking and ARCADY 8 (or above) are needed.

- **Visibility Analysis:** This is another analysis automatically calculated by the Vehicle Tracking software. Control which sightlines are displayed with the roundabout properties, as shown in Figure 6–14. *Stopping Sight Distance* and *Intersection Sight Distance* are available for each approach arm.

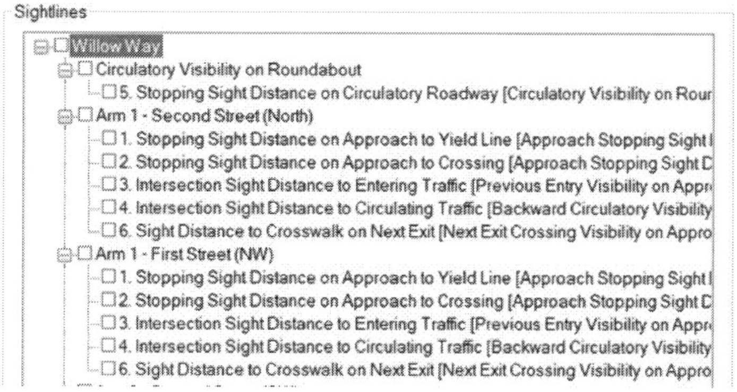

Figure 6–14

Editing with Grips

There are many ways to edit roundabouts using grips (shown in Figure 6–15). Easily adjust center, island, and splitter radius values, cross slopes, apron widths, and yield lines, add additional lanes, move the entire roundabout, and more.

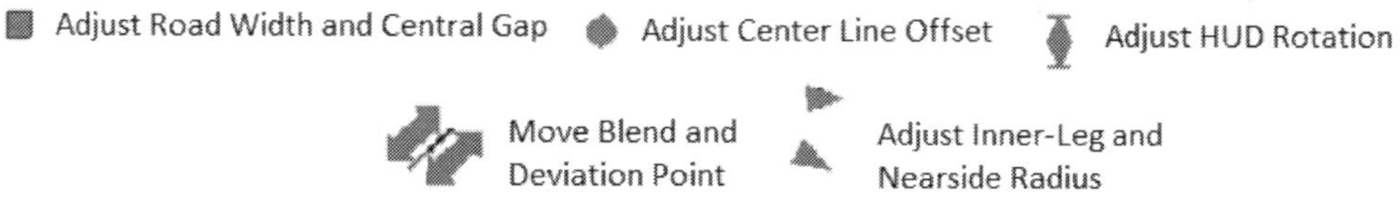

Figure 6–15

Constraints are a benefit of using grips to edit the roundabout over manually editing values in the Roundabout Properties dialog box.

If you hold <Ctrl> when moving a grip, other elements are constrained to move at the same time.

Below is a diagram of the effects of moving each grip with and without holding <Ctrl>. The grips are shown in Figure 6–16.

Grip	Effect without <Ctrl>	Effect with <Ctrl>
Inscribed Circle Grip	Outermost circulatory lane width changes.	Lane widths remain constant and central island and apron change size.
Centre Island Grip	Outermost circulatory lane width changes.	Lane widths remain constant and apron and inscribed circle change size.
Apron Width Grip	Outermost circulatory lane width changes.	Lane widths remain constant and inscribed circle changes size.

Lane Grips	Outermost circulatory lane width changes.	All lane widths outside remain constant and inscribed circle changes size.
Road Width Grip	Road width on only one side of centerline changes.	Road widths on both sides of central divide change.
Centre Gap Width Grip	Lane widths change as center gap width changes.	Lane widths remain constant as gap width changes.

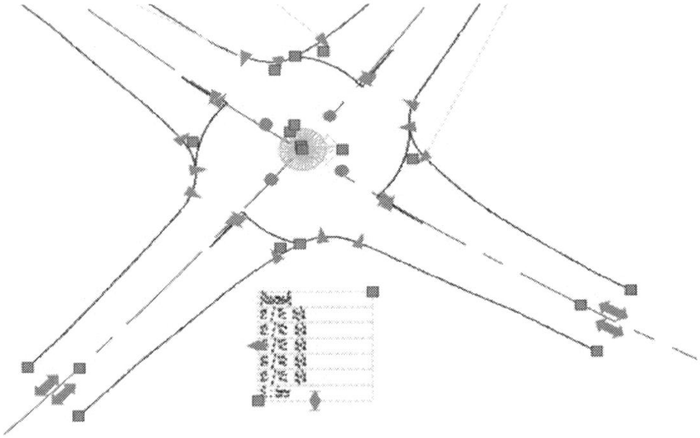

Figure 6–16

In some cases, moving a grip or changing a value in the Roundabout Properties dialog box may cause a warning triangle to be displayed, as shown in Figure 6–17. These occur when a value goes outside the limits provided in the standard. A short description of the problem is displayed next to the warning symbol.

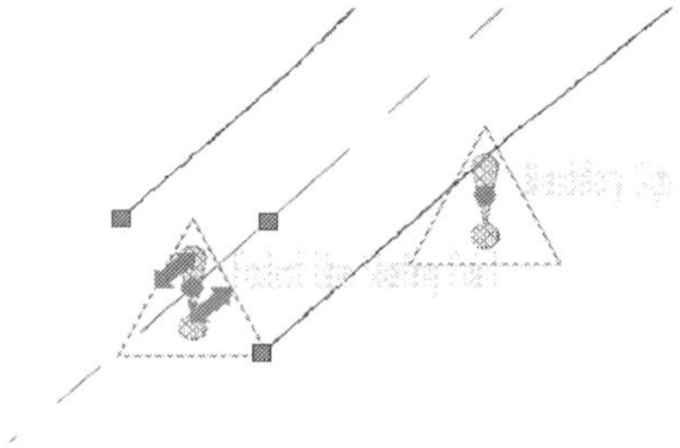

Figure 6–17

These values update dynamically, making grip editing of your roundabout precise.

Note: If you do not see the warning triangles, it is because they are switched off in the style editor, as shown in Figure 6–18.

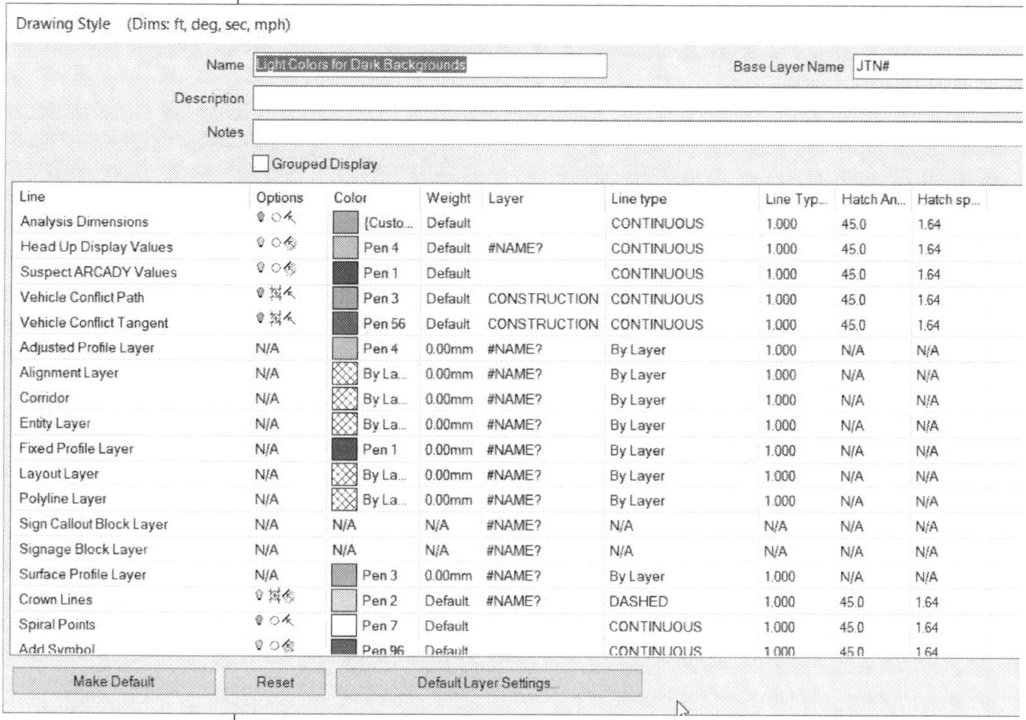

Figure 6–18

Roundabout Structures

There are two roundabout structures that can be added to the roundabout after it has been created: approaches and splitter islands.

Add/Remove Approach

The **Add Approach** and **Remove Approach** commands are found on the Roundabouts panel of the ribbon (as shown in Figure 6–19). These commands add and remove approaches in the roundabout selected.

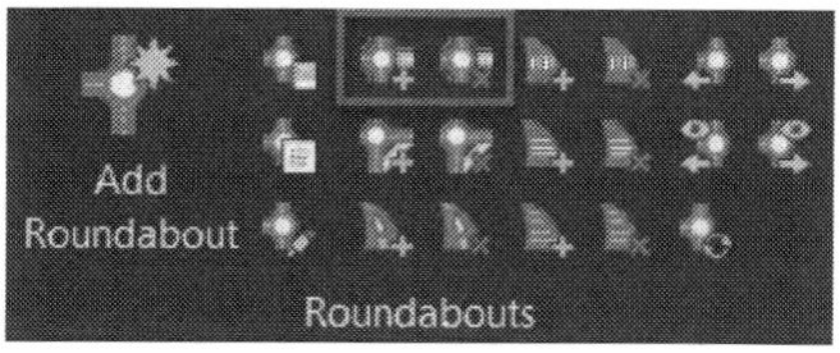

Figure 6–19

To add a new road, launch the **Add Approach** command, select the roundabout, and click the linework representing the new approach arm. Fill in the appropriate information in the New Arm dialog box. A new approach arm is added to the roundabout. The command stays active and multiple roads can be added until you press <Enter>.

To remove a road, simply launch the **Remove Approach** command and place the cursor over the approach arm you want to remove. A red X will appear to verify the approach arm you are removing, as shown in Figure 6–20. Click on the X and the approach arm is removed.

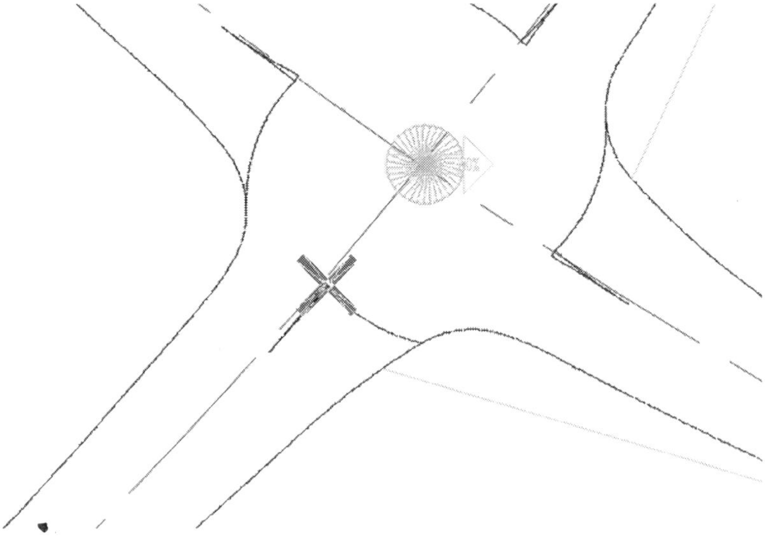

Figure 6–20

Add/Remove Splitter Island

The **Add Splitter Island** and **Remove Splitter Island** commands are found on the Roundabouts panel of the ribbon (as shown in Figure 6–21). These commands add and remove splitter islands to the roundabout selected.

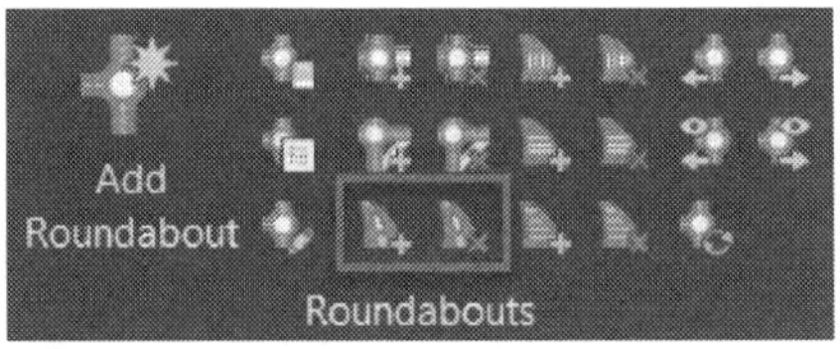

Figure 6–21

To add a splitter island, launch the **Add Splitter Island** command and select the roundabout. A green X will appear over the approach arm where you want the splitter island to go, as shown in Figure 6–22. Click the approach arm to place the splitter island. The command stays active and multiple splitter islands can be added until you press <Enter>.

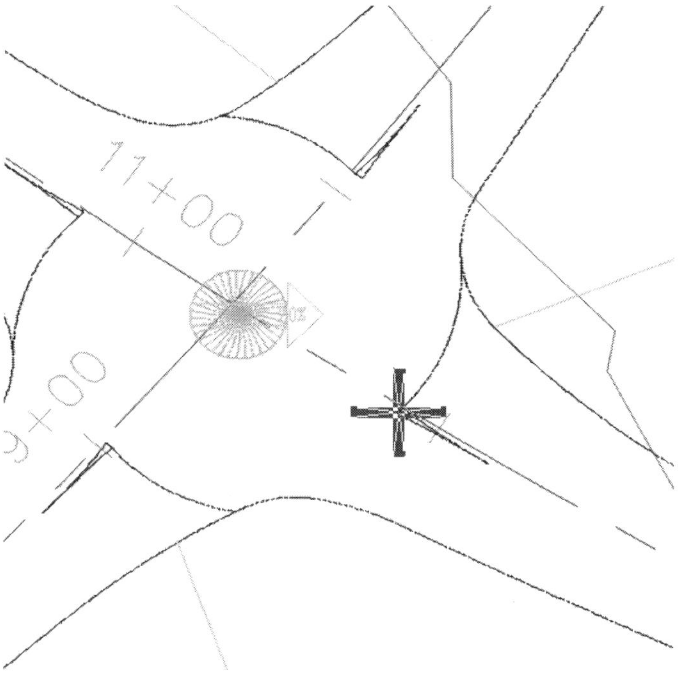

Figure 6–22

To remove a splitter island, launch the **Remove Splitter Island** command and place the cursor over the splitter island you want to remove. A red X will appear to verify the splitter island you are removing. Click on the X and the island is removed.

Roundabout Markings

There are three roundabout markings that can be added to the roundabout after it has been created: crosswalks, rumble strips, and speed striping.

Add/Remove Crosswalks

The **Add Crosswalk** and **Remove Crosswalk** commands are found on the Roundabouts panel of the ribbon (as shown in Figure 6–23). These commands add and remove crosswalk markings in the roundabout selected.

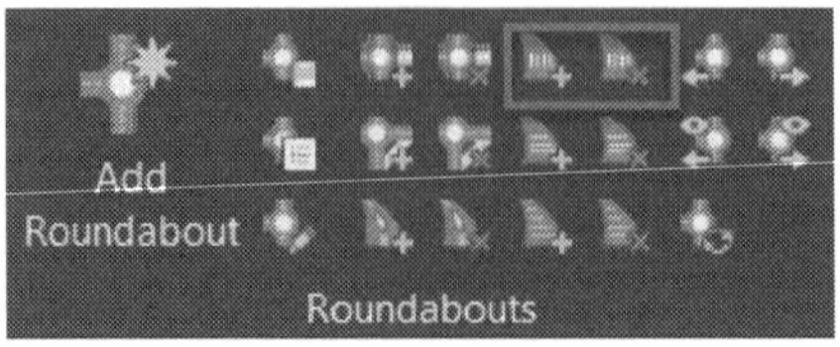

Figure 6–23

To add a new crosswalk marking, launch the **Add Crosswalk** command, select the roundabout, and click the location the markings will be placed on the approach arm, as shown in Figure 6–24. The command stays active and multiple crosswalks can be added until you press <Enter>.

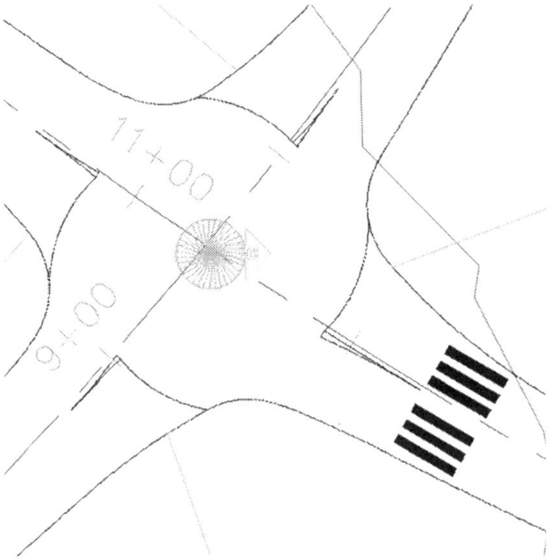

Figure 6–24

Grips are available for extending the crosswalk, offsetting the crosswalk, and adjusting the crossing angle and location.

To remove a crosswalk, launch the **Remove Crosswalk** command and place the cursor over the crosswalk you want to remove. A red X will appear to verify the crosswalk you are removing. Click on the X to remove the crosswalk.

Add/Remove Rumble Strips

The **Add Rumble Strips** and **Remove Rumble Strips** commands are found on the Roundabouts panel of the ribbon (as shown in Figure 6–25). These commands add and remove rumble strip markings in the roundabout selected.

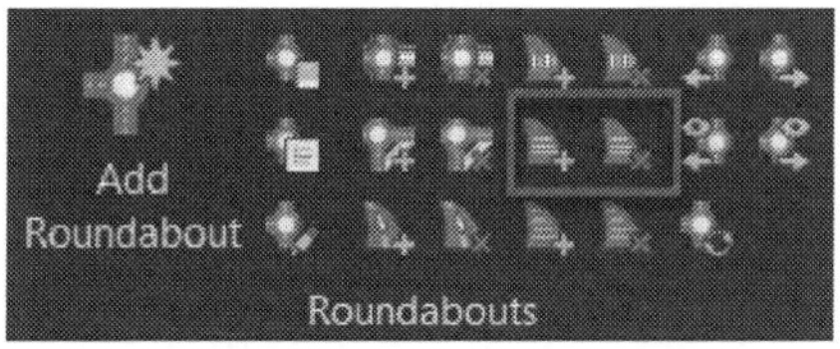

Figure 6–25

To add a new rumble strip marking, launch the **Add Rumble Strip** command, select the roundabout, and click the location the markings will be placed on the approach arm, as shown in Figure 6–26. The command stays active and multiple rumble strips can be added until you press <Enter>.

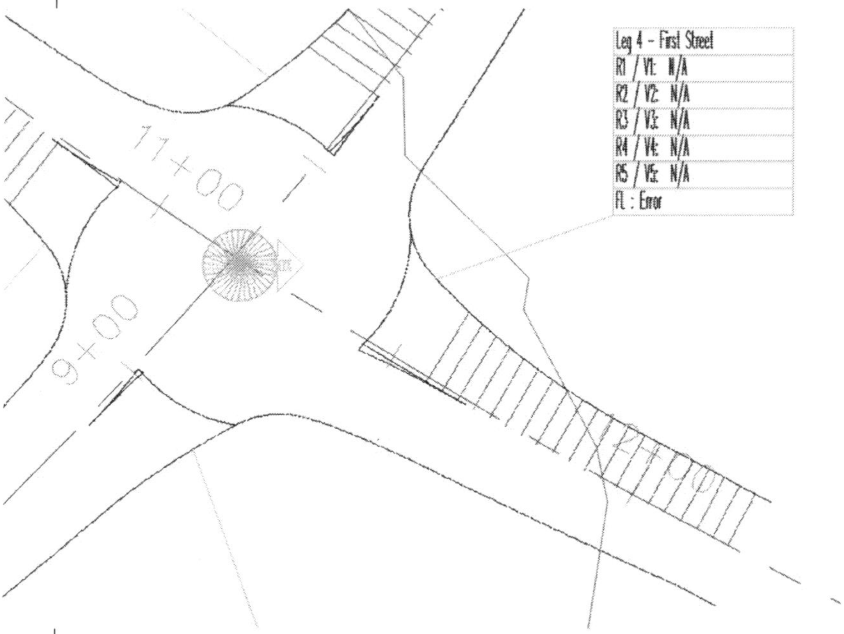

Figure 6–26

Grips are available for adjusting the inner and outer spacing, inner and outer offset, and angle of the rumble strips.

To remove a rumble strip, launch the **Remove Rumble Strip** command and place the cursor over the rumble strip you want to remove. A red X will appear to verify the rumble strip you are removing. Click on the X to remove the rumble strip.

Add/Remove Speed Striping

The **Add Speed Striping** and **Remove Speed Striping** commands are found on the Roundabouts panel of the ribbon (as shown in Figure 6–27). These commands add and remove speed striping markings in the roundabout selected.

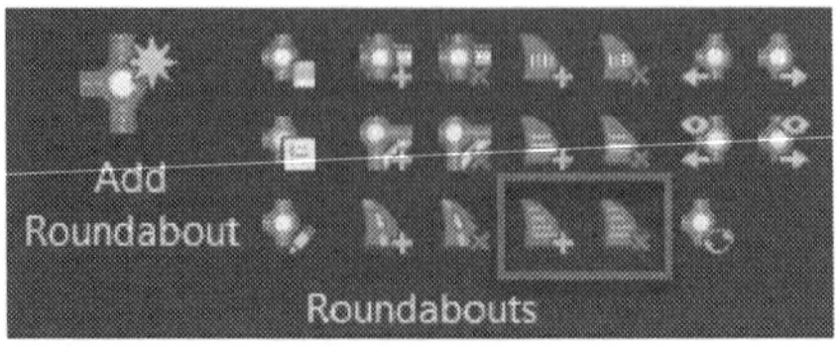

Figure 6–27

To add a new speed striping marking, launch the **Add Speed Striping** command, select the roundabout, and click the location the markings will be placed on the approach arm, as shown in Figure 6–28. The command stays active and multiple speed striping markings can be added until you press <Enter>.

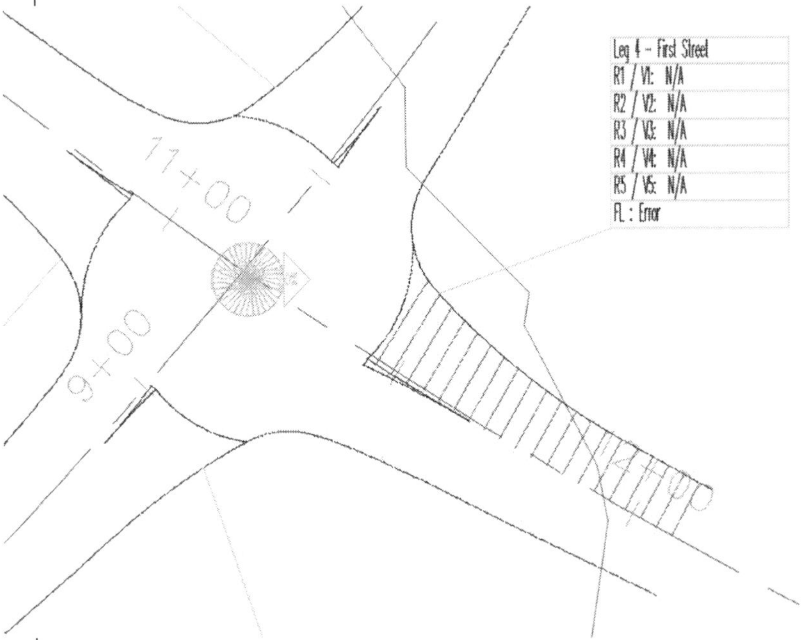

Figure 6–28

Grips are available for adjusting the inner and outer spacing, inner and outer offset, and angle of the speed striping.

To remove the speed striping, launch the **Remove Speed Striping** command and place the cursor over the speed striping you want to remove. A red X will appear to verify the speed striping you are removing. Click on the X to remove the speed striping.

You will notice that the rumble strips and speed striping look very similar. You can control the look of the added markings on the Styles page of the Drawing Settings dialog box, as shown in Figure 6–29. Drawing Settings can be accessed from the Settings panel of the ribbon.

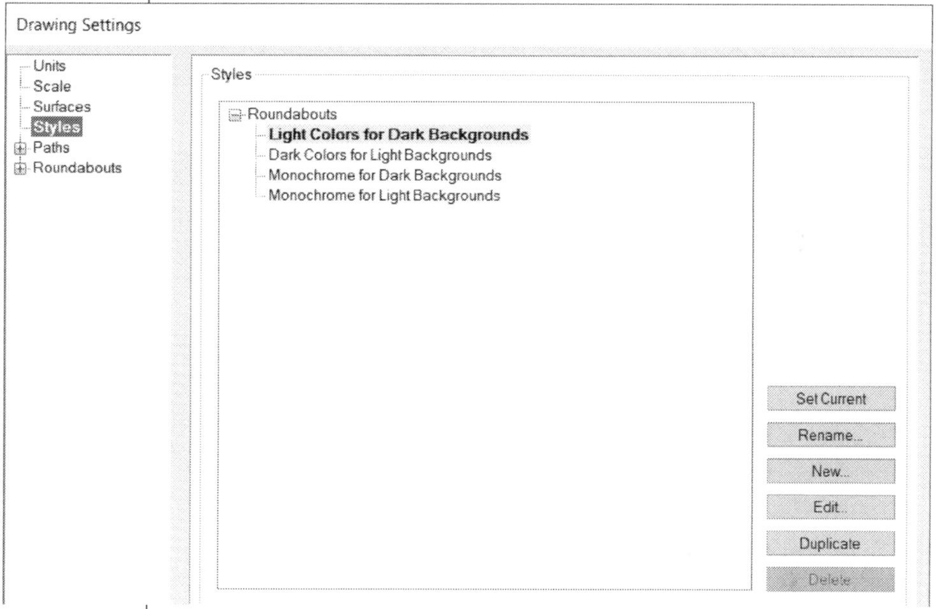

Figure 6–29

The *Draw Style* can also be accessed through the Roundabout Properties dialog box, in the *Appearance* section of the General page, as shown in Figure 6–30.

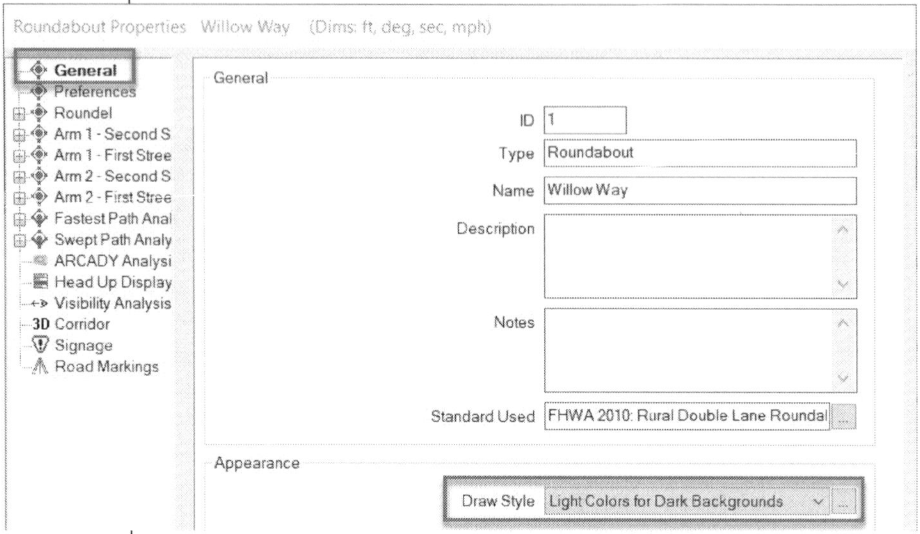

Figure 6–30

Figure 6–31 shows the drawings styles for crosswalks, rumble strips, and speed striping. Also note that the Drawing Style dialog box contains many other aspects of the roundabout.

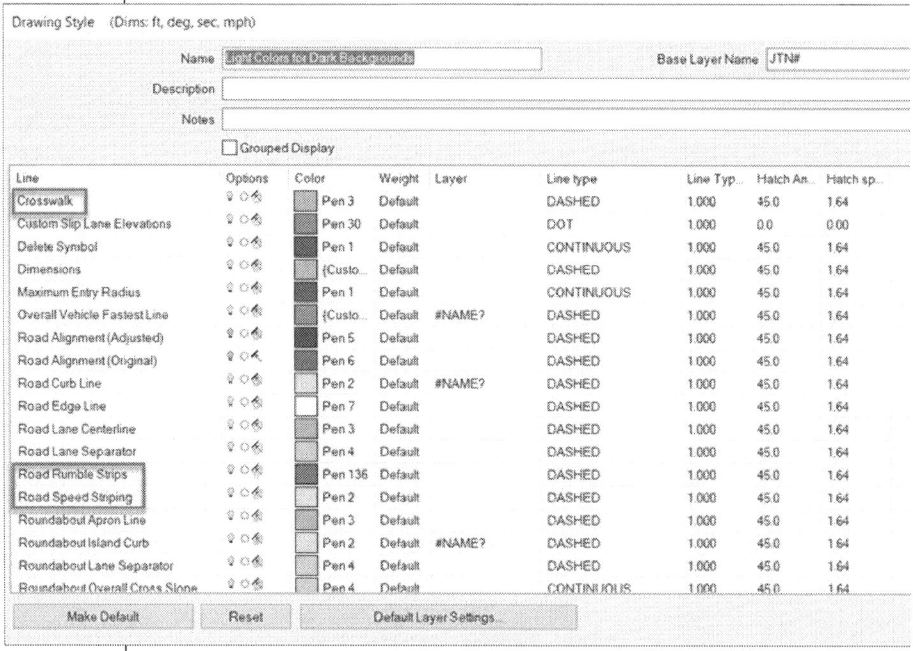

Figure 6–31

Roundabout Report

The roundabout report is an updated display of the fastest path speed, as well as entry radius and ARCADY data. The **Roundabout Report** command is found on the Roundabouts panel in the ribbon (as shown in Figure 6–32). You can display, print, and export the roundabout report.

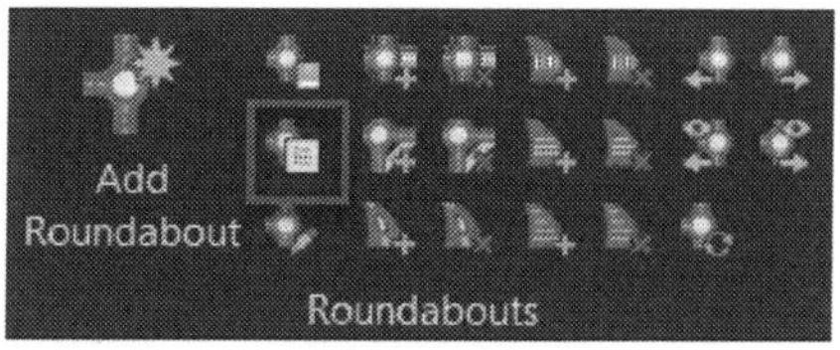

Figure 6–32

You can easily customize the Roundabout Report to adjust which columns are seen (as shown in Figure 6–33):

- Roundabout count
- Arm count
- Seq: internal values – user does not usually need this information
- LOS: ARCADY data
- RFC: ARCADY data
- Queue: ARCADY data
- Delay: ARCADY data
- Max Speed: fastest path speed

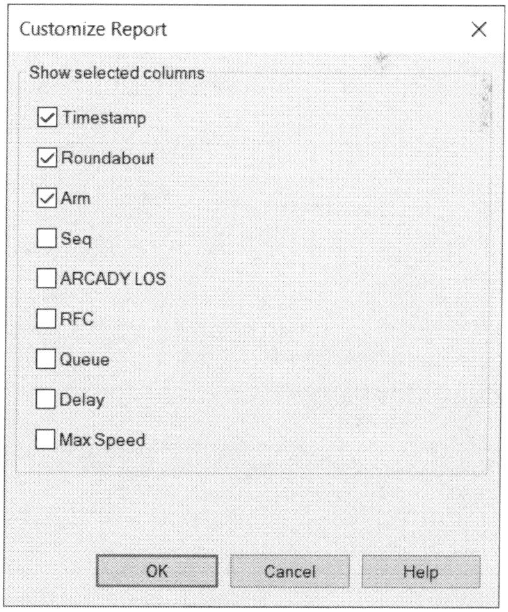

Figure 6–33

Practice 6a Roundabout with Corridor

Note: Civil 3D is required for this practice. If you do not have access to Civil 3D, skip this practice.

Learning Objectives

- Create a 3D roundabout.
- Turn off the Civil 3D corridor aspects of the roundabout for easy viewing.

In this practice, you will create a 3D roundabout using Civil 3D alignments and surfaces. Then, upon studying the roundabout and its specifications, you will simplify the drawing by turning off the Civil 3D corridor.

1. Open **Create Roundabout with Corridor.dwg** in the *Autodesk Vehicle Tracking\Working\Roundabouts* folder

2. On the *View* tab>Named Views panel, set the current view to **Roundabout**, as shown in Figure 6–34.

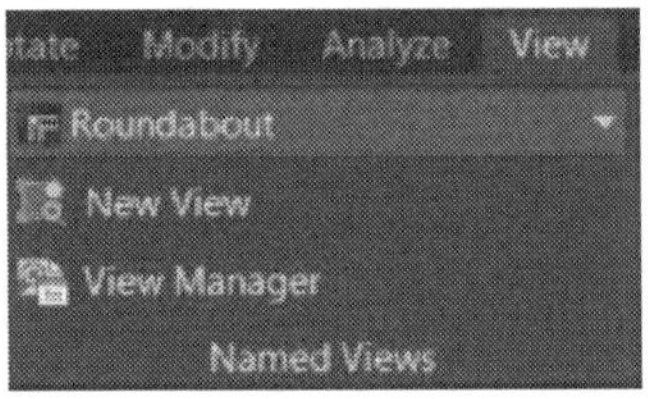

Figure 6–34

3. You will note that corridors have been built along the intersection of Ascent Boulevard and Jeffries Ranch Road, as shown in Figure 6–35. You will use Vehicle Tracking tools to place the roundabout with a corridor.

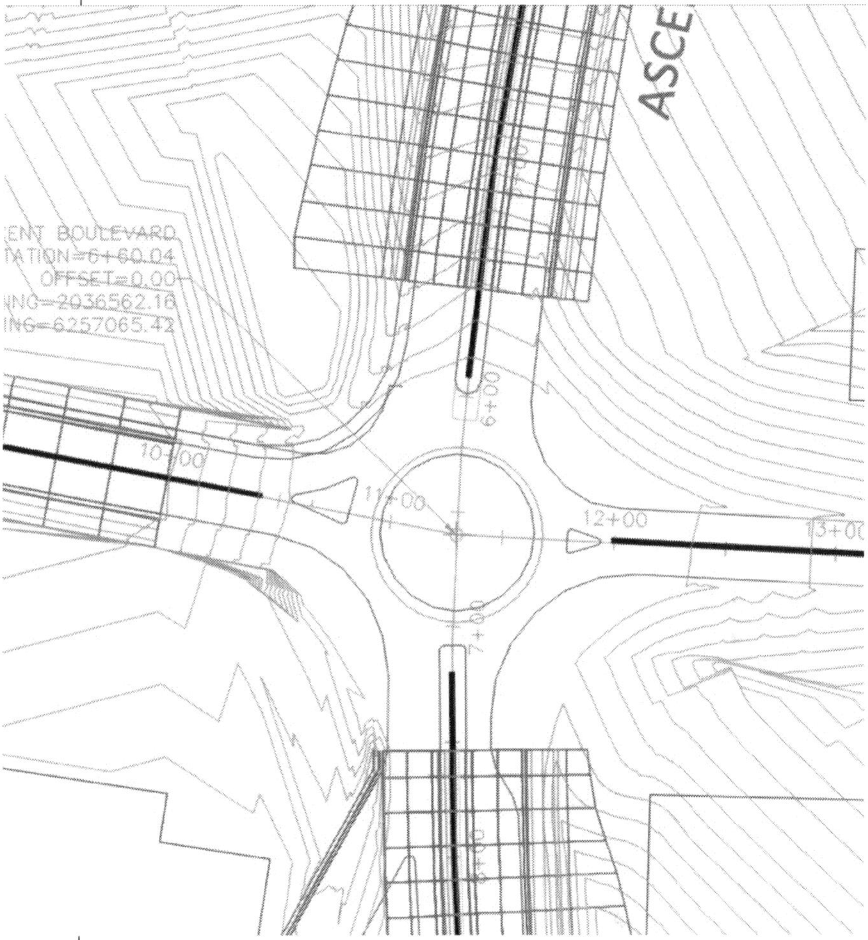

Figure 6–35

4. On the *Vehicle Tracking* tab>Settings panel, select **Drawing Settings** from the drop-down list, as shown in Figure 6–36.

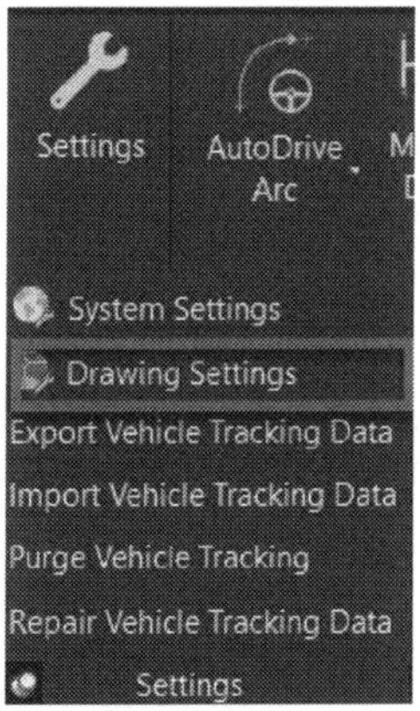

Figure 6–36

5. In the Drawing Settings dialog box, under *Roundabouts*, select **Corridor**.
6. Verify that **Create Alignments** is checked (as shown in Figure 6–37), which will enable all other options. Click **OK**.

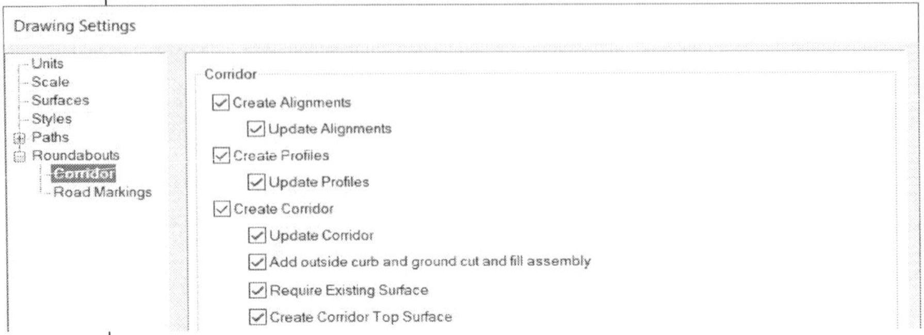

Figure 6–37

7. On the *Vehicle Tracking* tab>Roundabouts panel, click **Add Roundabout**, as shown in Figure 6–38.

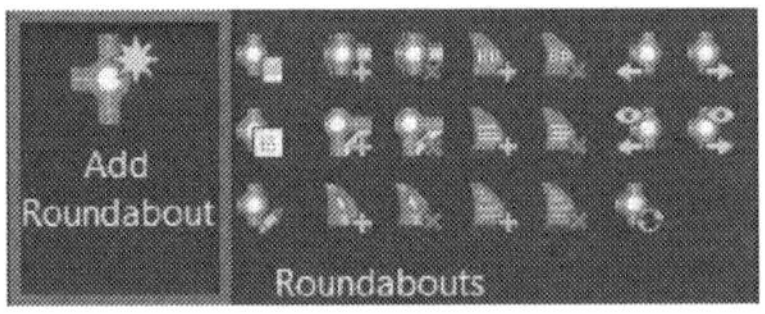

Figure 6–38

8. A dialog box may pop up asking you to assign the roundabout standard you want to use. If this does not appear, it will prompt you later. However, if it does occur, set the roundabout to **FHWA 2010: Urban Single Lane Roundabout** (under *US Junction Design Standards>US Federal Highways Administration>Roundabouts: An Informational Guide 2010*), as shown in Figure 6–39.

Figure 6–39

9. Click **Proceed** and select **Yes** to set these settings as the default.

10. In the New Roundabout Details dialog box, do the following (as shown in Figure 6–40):

   - Set the *Name* to **Jeffries-Ascent Blvd Roundabout**.
   - Select **Calculate Elevations**.
   - If you did not set the standard in Step 9, set the *Standard Used* within this dialog box by clicking on the ellipsis (**...**) and selecting **Roundabout to FHWA 2010: Urban Single Lane Roundabout**.
   - Set the *Circulatory Lanes* to **1**.
   - Set the *Existing Surface* to **Existing-Site**.
   - Click **OK**.

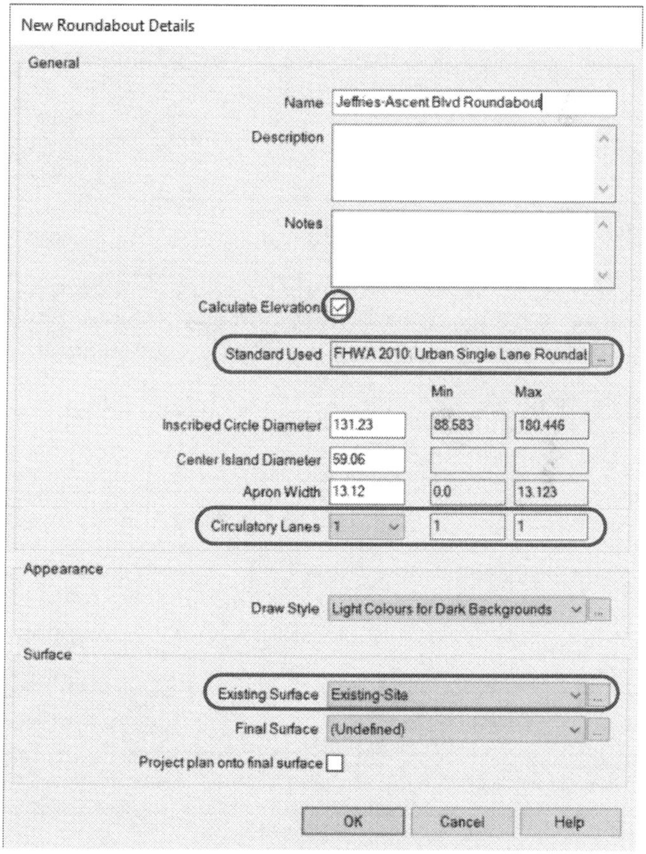

Figure 6–40

11. When asked to select the location of the center of the new roundabout, click the intersection shown in Figure 6–41. Use the **Endpoint** Object Snap to snap to the end of the intersection label arrow to help select the correct location.

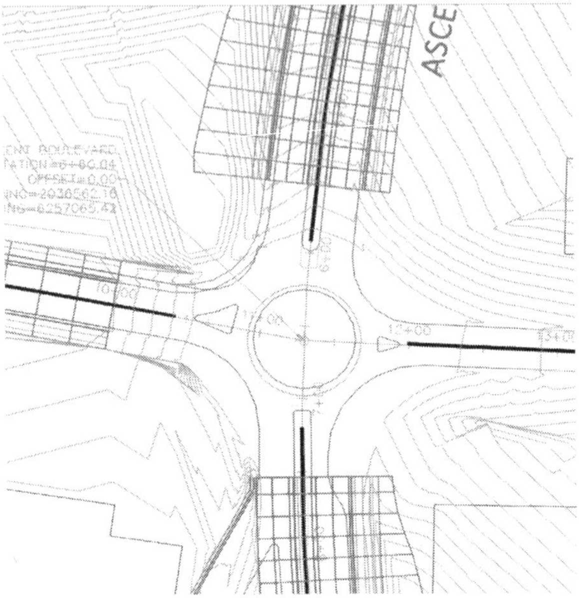

Figure 6–41

12. When asked to select the line for the approach, select the east side of the Jeffries alignment.

    Note: The alignment may be hard to select under the other entities in the drawing. Use **Selection Cycling** or click on the alignment closer to the intersection point.

<Ctrl>+<W> is the keyboard shortcut for toggling Selection Cycling.

13. In the New Arm dialog box, set the following (as shown in Figure 6–42):

    - *Approaching: Lane Width*: **15.5**
    - *Departing: Lane Width*: **15.5**

    Leave the other options as their defaults.

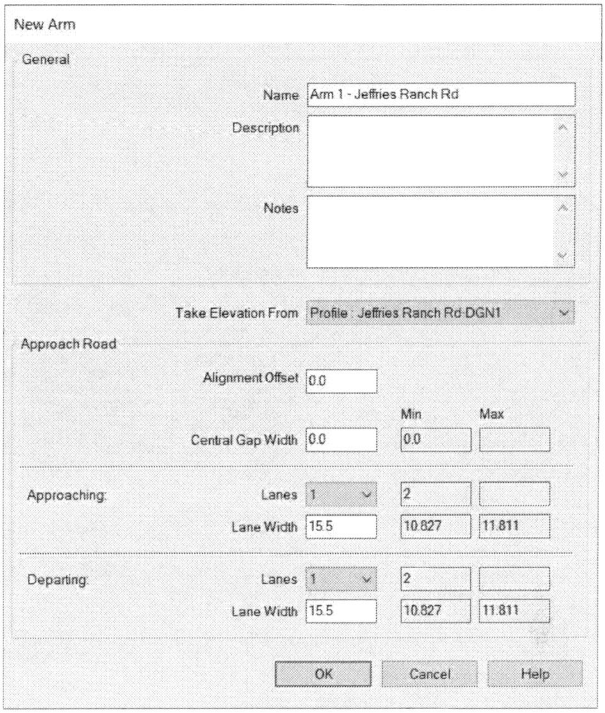

Figure 6–42

14. Click **OK**.

15. Continue to select the other approaches by selecting the north side of the Ascent Boulevard alignment, the west side of the Jeffries alignment, and the south side of the Ascent Boulevard alignment. Change all *Lane Width* values to **15.5**.

16. When you are finished selecting all four approaches, press <Enter>.

17. The roundabout and corridor will be created, as shown in Figure 6–43.

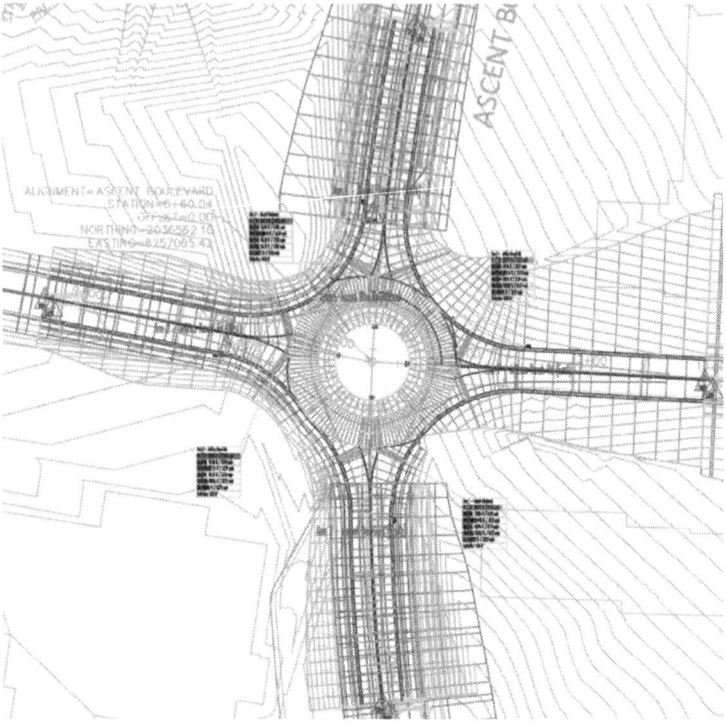

Figure 6–43

18. Save the drawing.

19. Select the Vehicle Tracking roundabout.

    Note: If you select the corridor, the *Corridor* contextual tab opens. If you select a feature of the Vehicle Tracking roundabout, the *Roundabout* contextual tab opens. Try selecting the HUD displays to ensure you pick the roundabout object and not the corridor. (The HUD displays are the small tables at each quadrant of the roundabout seen in Figure 6–43.)

20. On the *Roundabout* contextual tab>Modify panel, select **Roundabout Properties**, as shown in Figure 6–44.

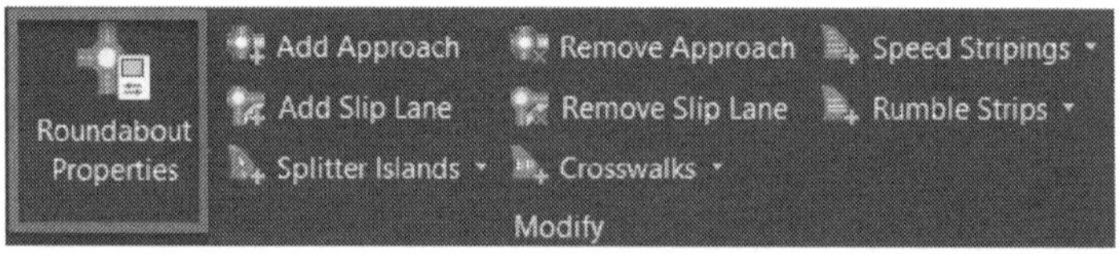

Figure 6–44

21. In the Roundabout Properties dialog box, select **3D Corridor** on the left-hand side, as shown in Figure 6–45.

22. Uncheck **Create Alignments** and click **Rebuild Now**, as shown in Figure 6–45.

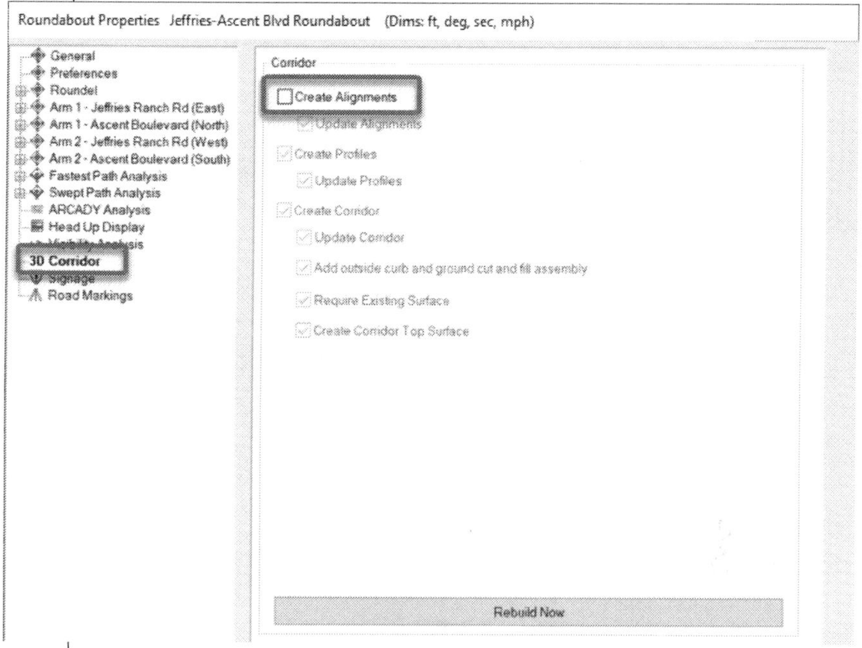

Figure 6–45

23. Click **Close**. This will remove the creation of the corridor to review the Vehicle Tracking model better, as shown in Figure 6–46.

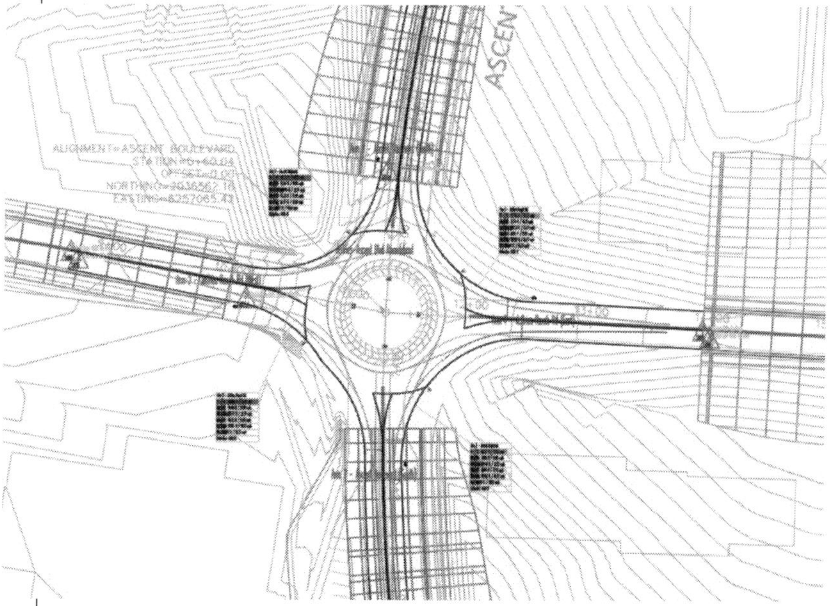

Figure 6–46

Practice 6b Roundabout without Corridor

Learning Objectives

- Create a 2D roundabout in regular AutoCAD.
- Test the roundabout design with swept path analysis.

In this practice, you will create a roundabout without any Civil 3D objects, instead using AutoCAD objects to represent the center lines of the roads.

If you do not use Civil 3D software with Vehicle Tracking, you will want to verify that some settings are turned off before using the **Roundabout** command. You may also prefer to not create a corridor initially when reviewing a roundabout for vehicle path options.

1. Open **Roundabout without Corridor.dwg** in the *Autodesk Vehicle Tracking\Working\Roundabouts* folder.

2. Zoom to the west side of the Jeffries Ranch Road intersection, as shown in Figure 6–47.

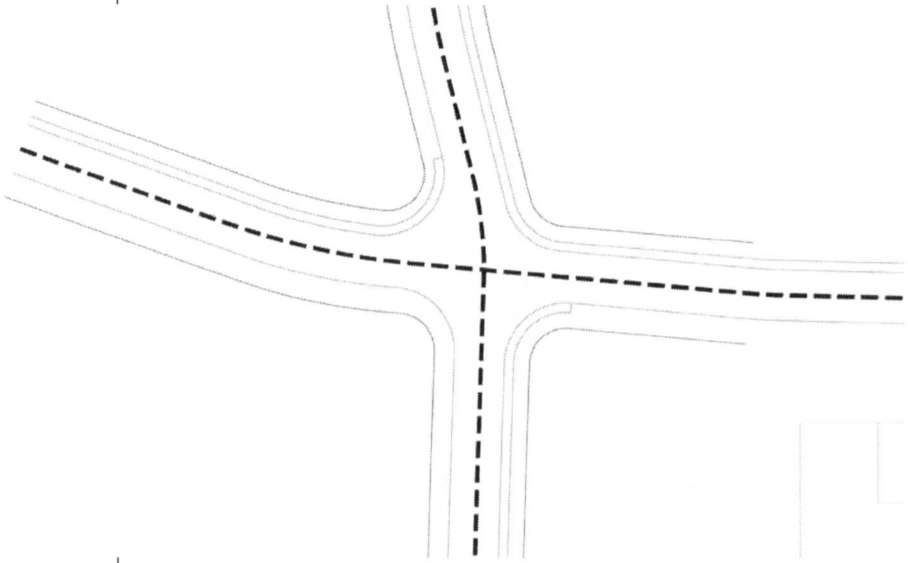

Figure 6–47

3. On the *Vehicle Tracking* tab>Settings panel, select **Drawing Settings** from the drop-down list, as shown in Figure 6–48.

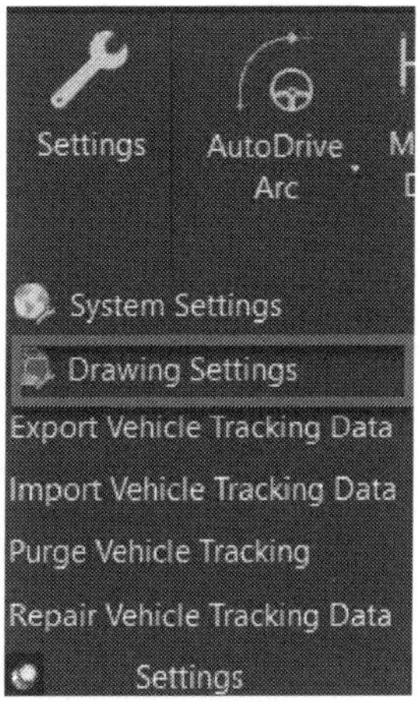

Figure 6–48

4. In the Drawing Settings dialog box, under *Roundabouts,* select **Corridor**.

5. Verify that **Create Alignments** is unchecked, as shown in Figure 6–49. This will fade all the other options.

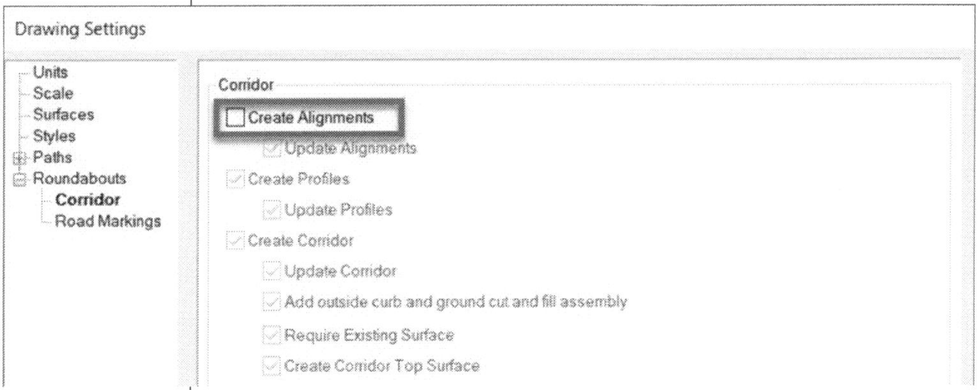

Figure 6–49

6. Click **OK**.

7. On the *Vehicle Tracking* tab>Roundabouts panel, click **Add Roundabout**, as shown in Figure 6–50.

Figure 6–50

8. In the New Roundabout Details dialog box, do the following, as shown in Figure 6–51:

    - Set the *Name* to **Jeffries-Del Mar Roundabout**.
    - Uncheck **Calculate Elevations**.
    - Set the *Circulatory Lanes* to **1**.
    - For *Standard Used*, click the ellipse (**...**) button to adjust the standard to **FHWA 2010: Urban Single Lane Roundabout** (under *US Junction Design Standards>US Federal Highways Administration>Roundabouts: An Informational Guide 2010*), as shown in Figure 6–52.
    - Click **OK**.

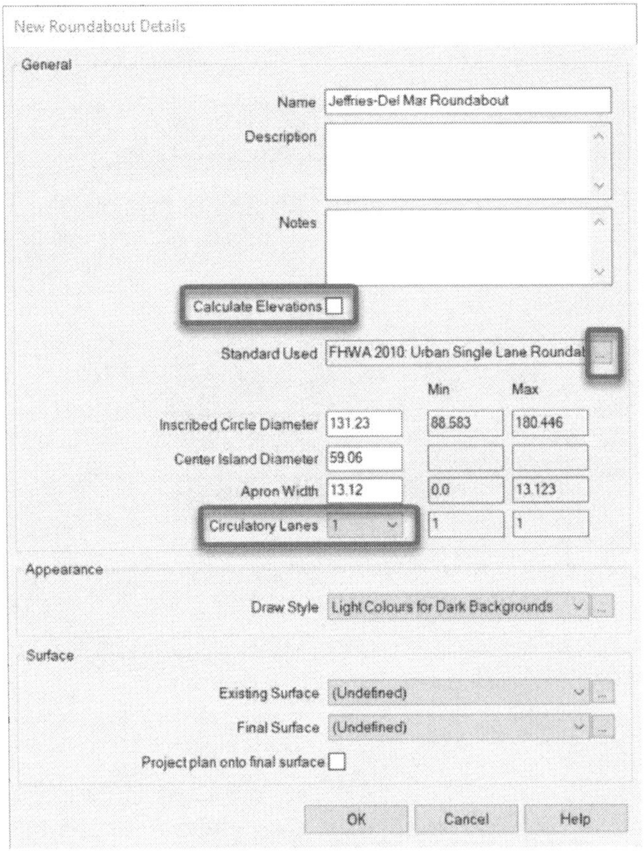

Figure 6–51

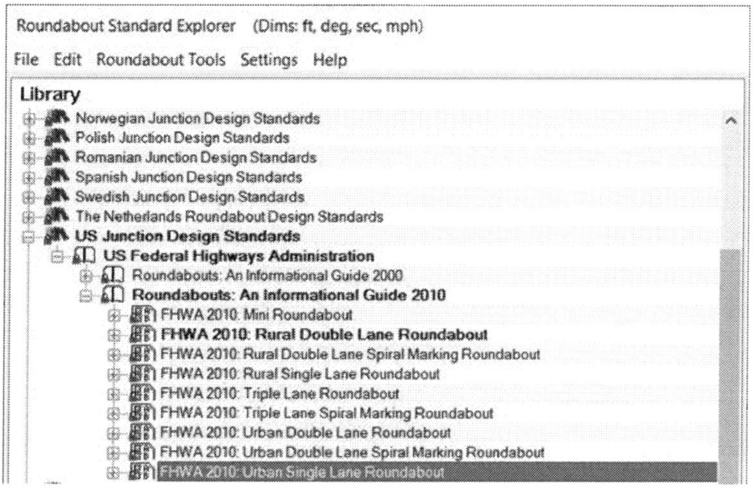

Figure 6–52

9. When asked to select the location of the center of the new roundabout at the western end of Jeffries Ranch Rd, click the intersection shown in Figure 6–53. Use the **Intersection** object snap.

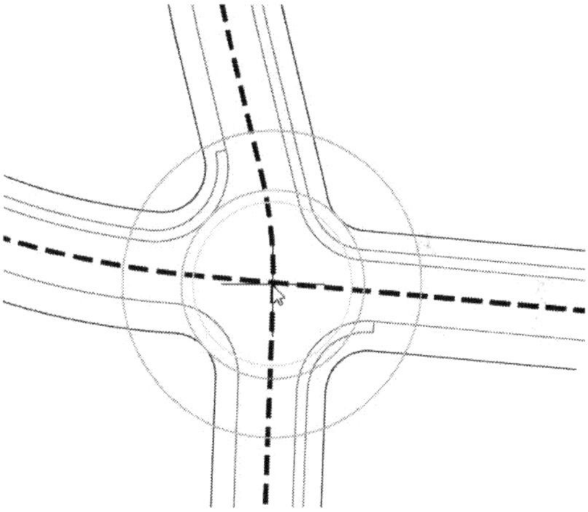

Figure 6–53

10. When asked to select the line for the approach, select the east polyline.

11. In the New Arm dialog box, set the following (as shown in Figure 6–54):

    - *Name*: **Jeffries East**
    - *Approaching: Lane Width*: **15.5**
    - *Departing: Lane Width*: **15.5**

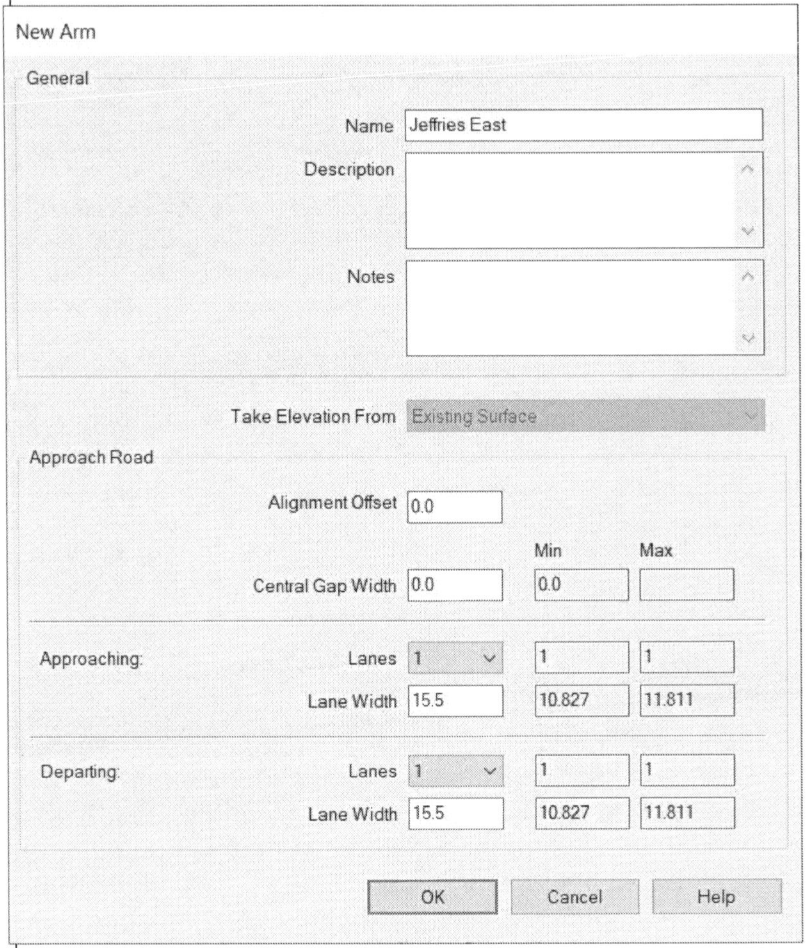

Figure 6–54

12. Click **OK**.

13. Continue to select the polylines shown in Figure 6–55, assigning the names **Ranch View North**, **Jeffries West**, and **Del Mar South** with the same **15.5** lane widths.

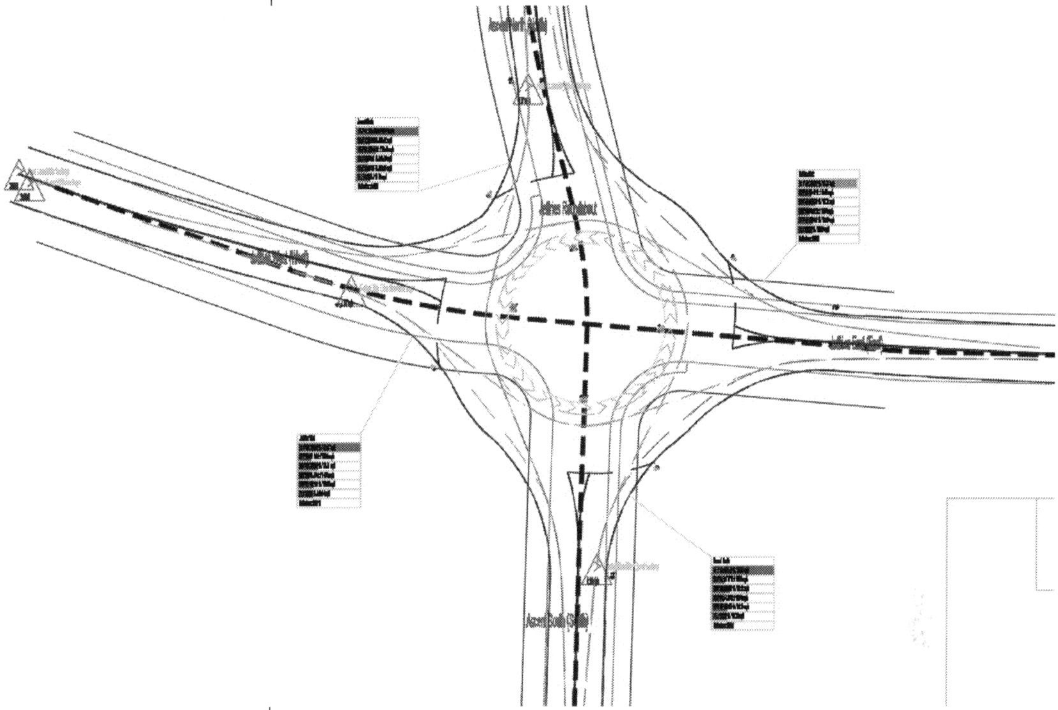

Figure 6–55

14. On the *Vehicle Tracking* tab>Swept Paths panel, select **AutoDrive Arc**, as shown in Figure 6–56.

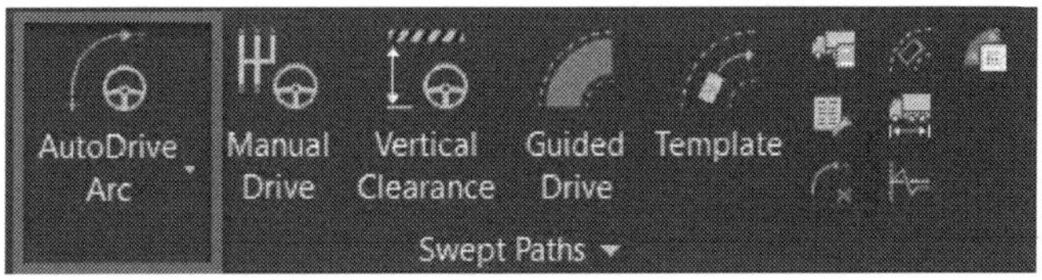

Figure 6–56

15. Move the cursor over the Ranch View North approach. You will see the cursor catch within the lane. Click to place the vehicle, as shown on the left in Figure 6–57.

16. Move the cursor to the east approach – do not move the cursor too far to the right. The cursor will catch again and automatically create a path around the roundabout, as shown on the right in Figure 6–57. Click to add to the path. Continue to click and add points to the path.

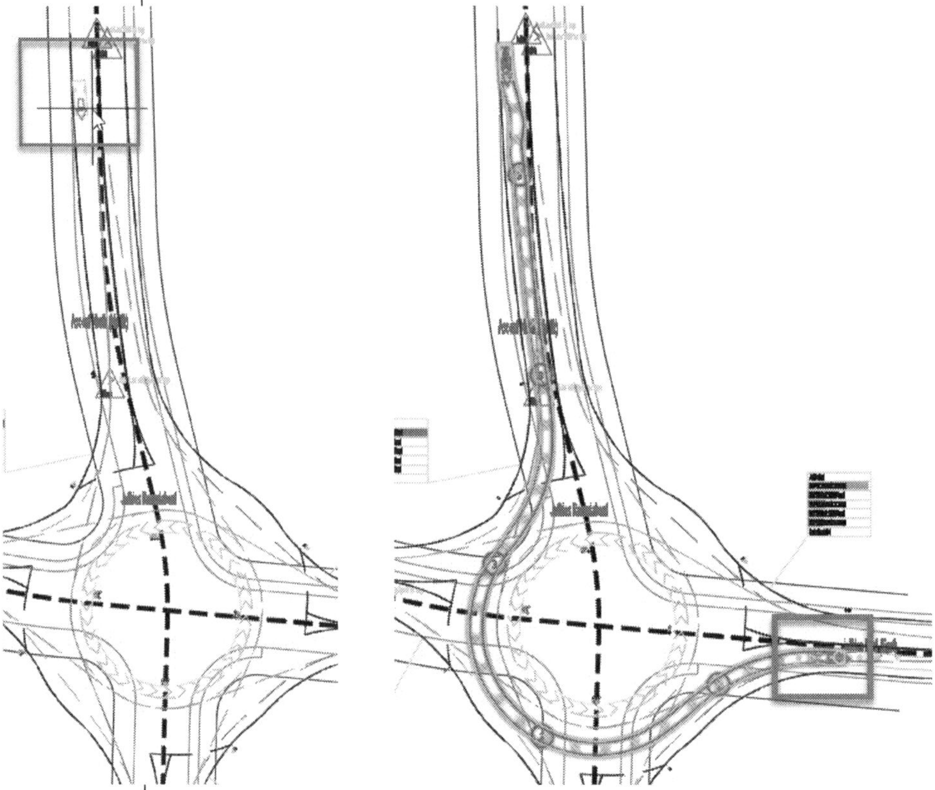

Figure 6–57

17. (Optional) Continue to add details to your roundabout using islands, crosswalks, rumble strips, etc.

6.3 Final Result

Vehicle Tracking works directly with your Civil 3D entities. As you have seen, alignments, profiles, and corridors can be created automatically as the roundabout is being created. Continue with this data to create the corridor surface and finished ground of the site, as shown in Figure 6–58.

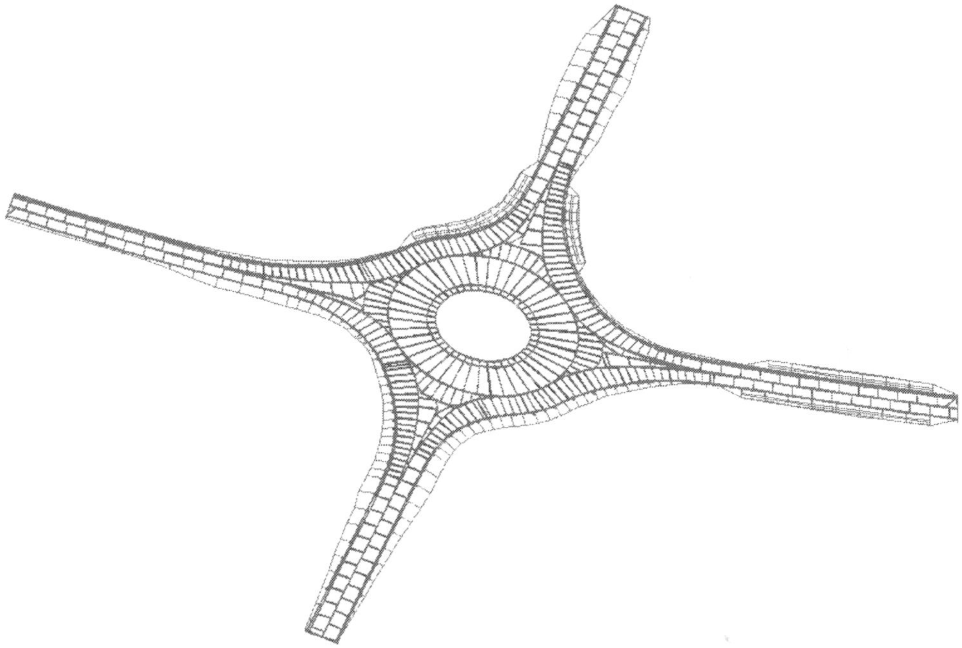

Figure 6–58

In a more complete Civil 3D workflow, use Civil 3D and Vehicle Tracking for:

- Creating the 2D geometric layout
- Analyzing the capacity
- Vehicle path analysis
- 3D model creation
- Checking your slopes and volumes using Civil 3D tools
- Checking for drainage

These steps are beyond the scope of this guide.

Chapter Review Questions

1. Civil 3D alignments and surfaces are required to create roundabouts.
    a. True
    b. False
2. A Civil 3D corridor and a roundabout are the same thing.
    a. True
    b. False
3. Can path analysis be done directly in the roundabout?
    a. Yes, Vehicle Tracking will find the lanes and perform the analysis.
    b. It must be done using the standard Swept Path Analysis tools.
    c. No, roundabouts are incompatible with path analysis.

Made in United States
Orlando, FL
04 November 2026

90200943R00107